FLEEING THE HOUSE OF H(

Women Who Have Left Abusive Partners

Based on in-depth interviews with thirty-nine women, *Fleeing the House of Horrors* is a study of survivors of abusive domestic situations. Through a mainly feminist orientation, Aysan Sev'er analyses the many definitions and prevailing theories of violence against women. She incorporates an extensive review of the literature, while covering a number of topics, including feminist, non-feminist, and social-psychological theories of abuse. She then proceeds to relate, often in the form of first-person accounts, the intimate stories of women who survived.

These interviews, which were conducted outside of institutional settings, candidly reveal the women's strengths and weaknesses and their strategies for survival – some successful, some eventually destructive. The women's stories allow Sev'er to analyse the role of social support systems and to develop a new model for post-violence adjustment. Powerful, revealing, and ultimately affirming, Sev'er's study provides a new perspective on the issue of violence against women, and new hope for abused women.

AYSAN SEV'ER is Associate Professor in the Department of Sociology at the University of Toronto.

Fleeing the House of Horrors: Women Who Have Left Abusive Partners

AYSAN SEV'ER

UNIVERSITY OF TORONTO PRESS
Toronto Buffalo London

© University of Toronto Press Incorporated 2002
Toronto Buffalo London
Printed in Canada

ISBN 0-8020-3726-7 (cloth)
ISBN 0-8020-8521-0 (paper)

Printed on acid-free paper

National Library of Canada Cataloguing in Publication

Sev'er, Aysan, 1945–
  Fleeing the house of horrors : women who have left abusive
  partners / Aysan Sev'er.

  Includes bibliographical references and index.
  ISBN 0-8020-3726-7 (bound).   ISBN 0-8020-8521-0 (pbk.)

  1. Abused wives – Interviews.   2. Abused women – Interviews.
  3. Wife abuse.   4. Conjugal violence.   I. Title.

  HV6626.S43 2002   362.82'92   C2002-901358-5

This book has been published with the help of a grant from the Humanities
and Social Sciences Federation of Canada, using funds provided by the
Social Sciences and Humanities Research Council of Canada.

University of Toronto Press acknowledges the financial assistance to its
publishing program of the Canada Council for the Arts and the Ontario
Arts Council.

University of Toronto Press acknowledges the financial support for its
publishing activities of the Government of Canada through the Book
Publishing Industry Development Program (BPIDP).

This book is dedicated to my beloved niece
Didem Fatoş Ülserim

Contents

Acknowledgments

As women academics who venture beyond studying the mundane forms of social reality, we occasionally encounter research problems that change our beliefs, thoughts, and the course of scholarship. This study most certainly has been one of those occasions in my career that challenged and altered me as a person, as a woman, and as a sociologist. I am very indebted to the thirty-nine women who shared the most intimate, painful, and vulnerable aspects of their lives with me. I am deeply honoured to have been entrusted with the important work of telling their tales of horror and despair as well as for the opportunity to reflect their strength, resolve, and survival. I hope that in every word, sentence, and chapter, I have been true to the complexity of these women's lives rather than inadvertently overlooking their individuality or reducing them to numbers. I hope that when I reiterated their words or summoned my own conceptual knowledge in the area, I did not at the same time dilute the dignity of their struggles.

Although I personally conducted all the interviews, a few carefully selected women students helped me through some difficult aspects of this research project. Myrna Dawson and Sandhya Ram deserve many thanks for their insights, support, and both theoretical and methodological input in the initial stages of this work. I benefited from the insights of the dedicated personnel at the Scarborough Women's Centre, especially the gentle but effective social activism of its executive director, Lynda Kosowan. I also thank my colleagues Vappu Tyyskä and Nancy Howell for their endless patience in listening to the puzzling aspects of my findings. Deirdre Byrne's long-term commitment to this project and wizardry in editorial help needs a special mention. Deirdre has been simply extraordinary in cleansing my writing of the bumpy artefacts of my first-generation immigrant English. I also thank David Hillock for his unwavering support throughout my difficult work and his tolerance of my less than joyful company during the aftermath of the interviews. His supportive role during the most crucial period of my study never faltered.

Last but not least, I am very grateful for the help I received from a major funding institution. Without the generous support of the Social Sciences and Humanities Research Council of Canada (SSHRC-410-96-0411), this in-depth work on violence against women would not have been possible. Despite the well-known academic pressures towards conducting positivistic science, it is a great comfort to know that institutions such as the SSHRC still make it possible for feminist social scientists like myself to connect with individual lives and to learn from individual struggles.

FLEEING THE HOUSE OF HORRORS

Introduction

On 6 September 2000, police pulled over a motorcycle driven by 31-year-old James Vernon Randall for a routine traffic check. In a box securely fastened to the back of his motorcycle, they found the decomposed head of Jennifer Zumach, Randall's common-law wife. Zumach had disappeared shortly after giving birth to a son from Randall and had last been seen on 15 January 1999. Randall was the one who had reported her missing almost two years before the discovery of her severed head (*Toronto Star*, 9 September 2000: A3). Police are now re-investigating the 1992 suicide of Randall's first wife, Karen Randall. Although Karen had left a handwritten suicide note, people who knew her always felt that there was something incomprehensible about her alleged suicide (*Toronto Star*, 12 September 2000: A4).

In Miami, Florida, a 100-year-old husband was charged for pouring gasoline on his female companion and threatening to set her on fire (*Toronto Star*, 24 May 2001: A16). Joseph Theodore Willemsen, a 53-year-old father, ordered two of his young daughters out of the room, and then shot and killed their mother, Laurie Lynn Vollmershausen. Laurie was 35 years old. Police had no record of previous domestic disputes between Joseph and Laurie (*Toronto Star*, 18 July 2000: A14). Only about a week before Laurie died, another family tragedy shook the Canadian media. Vilem Luft Jr stabbed his wife more than thirty times and then shot and killed four of his children who ranged from 3 months to 7 years in age. After the mayhem, Vilem killed himself (*Toronto Star*, 7 July 2000: A1, A20). On another summer day in 2000, Gillian Hadley ran out of her house, completely naked, carrying her 1-year-old baby in her arms. She was shouting and desperately looking for a neighbour to whom she could hand over her baby for safekeeping. The man pursuing her was her estranged husband. As a last altruistic act, Gillian managed to hand her baby to a neighbour, who was horrified by the events taking place before his eyes. Just after this act of motherly love, Gillian was shot to death by her estranged husband (*Toronto Star*, 21 June 2000: A1). A public inquest into Gillian's murder revealed that Ralph had planned the fatal attack to the last detail. He had brought with him a satchel filled with a knife, tools, lighter fluid, duct tape, surgical gloves, and a dog collar attached by a metal loop to a wedding band (*Toronto Star*, 23 October 2001: B1). He had also audiotaped a chilling message about the murder–suicide declaring that the only way he could get Gillian back was to kill her (*Toronto Star*, 24 October 2001: A1).

A 6-year-old boy saw his father throw a litre of sulphuric acid at his mother's face. He watched her face melt down right in front of his eyes. The 27-year-old woman was grossly disfigured and in critical condition with severe toxic burns to 80 per cent of her body (*Toronto Star*, 24 July 2000: B1). A couple of months before this barbaric incident took place, another woman was poisoned to death by her husband. To add insult to injury, her murder took place on Mother's Day (*Toronto Star*, 16 July 2000: A5). On a three-day rampage, John Bauer slaughtered his wife, his children, and one of his relatives before killing himself. At the end of the carnage, there were seven dead (*Toronto Star*, 22 September 2001: A27).

Many people, including laypersons, lawmakers and law enforcers, politicians, and some academics, want to interpret these horrifying incidents as the acts of sick and crazy men. For many, more horrifying than the incidents themselves is acknowledging that, in fact, the great majority of these men were neither sick nor crazy. They were husbands or lovers with whom the murdered and/or mutilated women lived, loved, and had children. These men had friends, neighbours, work associates, and children who had nice things to say about them. Yet they were capable of committing the most horrendous crimes against their female partners, sometimes extending their violence even to their own children.

The incidents sketched above, as shocking as they may be, represent just the tip of the iceberg. There are many other men who behave in mostly normal ways in various dimensions of their lives, but who also inflict long and extreme suffering and pain on their intimate female partners. Some women die at the hands of these abusive men. A significant proportion endure the pain and humiliation throughout their lives. Some women manage to leave. However, as the research I will review shows that the odds are against them doing so successfully. This book is about thirty-nine women survivors of abuse who found a way to leave their abusive partners without losing their lives. I will attempt to share their years of suffering as well as their enormous efforts to escape their tormentors and establish a different kind of life for themselves and for their dependent children.

When I wrote my first book, on divorce (Sev'er, 1992), the very first thing I acknowledged was my own personal biases about divorce. At the time, I tried to honestly disclose my understanding of the social issues surrounding divorce by underscoring my status as a feminist sociologist, a divorced woman, and a single parent. Writing this book on leaving abusive partners requires a similar declaration of located-ness. Of course, I am still a feminist sociologist who is deeply concerned about issues relating to battered women. I am still divorced, but am now the mother of a completely independent adult. I still seek solutions to women's problems within theoretical orientations that challenge the entrenched male hegemony in society. However, my experiences about family violence are all second-hand. Indeed, my first exposure to the poison of family violence in a woman's life occurred when I was already in my early thirties. It occurred at a time when the sociologist in me was still uneducated, and the feminist in me unawakened. I had no cognitive categories, concepts, or theories available to help me understand the shocking incident that I witnessed. Maybe that is why the experience had had such an enduring impact. I was not raised to think about violence, especially violence within the family, as an unavoidable part of living. Despite the patriarchal nature of my cultural background, my family was loving and non-violent. My marriage was also peaceful even though my former husband and I had irreconcilable differences. Therefore, for most of my life, I erroneously assumed that families, by nature, were non-violent.

The incident that truly jolted my beliefs and perceptions took place in the early 1970s. I had been married for almost a decade, was a mother with one child, and was leading an extremely sheltered life in every imaginable way. The boredom of my uneventful existence led me to seek a volunteer position as a translator for the Ministry of Community and Social Services in a southern Ontario town. As a new landed immigrant myself, I thought that I could help other recent arrivals whose proficiency with English was perhaps not as good as mine.

The first request for my services came months after I had put in my name as a volunteer. I had all but forgotten about having volunteered in the first place. The call was about an emergency. I was requested to attend a meeting with police, social workers, and a new immigrant woman of my own ethnic origin (Turkish) whom I will call 'Rosie.' The officer who gave me a ride to the police station told me that Rosie was seeking shelter from her abusive husband. I had no other preparation for the situation I was about to face. (Rosie has been more fully discussed in Sev'er 1997a, 1997b, 1998.)

Rosie was a very small woman, probably about 25 years old, yet strangely old-looking. She described and explained in detail all the tortures she had endured. Her voice was sometimes barely audible; at other times, she spoke in a shrill cry that hurt my ears. Rosie had come to Canada as a bride selected by the parents of her husband, a Turkish immigrant. Her own parents were eager to close the marriage deal. They thought that the prospective son-in-law could provide their daughter with a much better life than their poor rural existence offered. Rosie herself was thrilled by the prospect of becoming the princess in a fairy tale union. The fairy tale, however, lasted only a few months.

Rosie urged me to translate her predicament to the male police officer and the female social worker, who appeared to be attentive yet distant. Rosie claimed that she was routinely beaten and frequently deprived of food. As evidence of her beatings, she showed us marks ranging in severity from barely visible to variations of raw pink and purple. She also had barely healed scars around her mouth and her eyes. I was mesmerized by the scar around one side of her mouth which curved slightly upwards, giving her an eerie, permanent smile. The scar around the other side of her mouth curved down, more accurately reflecting the pain in her eyes. It was as if someone had grabbed her mouth and ripped it open.

Rosie's whole body was living proof of her second claim, of having been starved. It was not as if her husband could not afford food. On the contrary, he earned good wages in the auto industry. Rosie said that her husband was a very jealous man, although they had only recently married. He went into a rage if Rosie went out without him, even if it was for a walk around the block. When she did something on her own, without his permission, she was punished. Her husband frequently locked the door from outside. Sometimes, he did not come back for several days.

Rosie had no pretty dresses. In fact, her husband did not buy her anything and he did not leave her any money. He was jealous. This jealousy reached dangerous levels when Rosie found out that she was pregnant. When she told her husband, he kicked her right in the stomach, shouting obscenities and accusing her of infidelity. A few days after the kick, Rosie miscarried and was unable to stand up straight for a week. She was bleeding continuously and was in excruciating pain. A couple of weeks went by before her husband allowed her to see a doctor. The doctor immediately referred her to a hospital. Rosie claimed she underwent an operation that left her barren. Understandably, this was a severe blow for a woman from a patriarchal culture that reveres the reproductive capabilities of women and equates their personal worth with their capacity for motherhood.

Listening to Rosie's story was very difficult for me. I remember feeling aghast at the sight of Rosie's leathery complexion, dried-up body, and scarred mouth when the social worker wanted me to ask her why she stayed with him for as long as she did. I remember the incredible change in Rosie's eyes, the softening of the frenzied sharpness in the tone of her speech when she said, 'He loves me, he brings me roses!'

After this emotional encounter, I was driven back to my home by one of the social workers. I felt drained and in a haze. But most of all, I remember my own (former) husband's inquiry about where I had been and why I had been gone for so long. Although his cold inquiry made me recoil at the time, I now realize that he must have known where I had been. The child-care worker the police brought over to look after our infant daughter while I was acting as a translator must have briefed my husband upon his arrival. Although I was not aware of this at the time, I now believe that my former husband's inquiry about my whereabouts was actually a control tactic, not a benign inquiry for information.

After hearing about my experience, my husband sternly concluded that I should not 'stick my nose into other families' business.' I would react differently if anyone told me such a thing now, but at the time, his cold judgment about my involvement with Rosie made me shiver. I felt ashamed about interfering with another family's business. I felt ashamed about being away from my home for such an intrusive mission, although my daughter had been provided with excellent alternative care. The violence in Rosie's life had spilled into my own life to make me feel confused, guilty, and out of place. Without any knowledge about intimate violence against women at my disposal, I felt only guilt and shame for having gazed into another family's 'private' affairs. It is only much later that I was able to deconstruct my husband's behaviour as a part of the 'conspiracy of silence,' a theme I will often invoke in this book. I now equate being silent about witnessing violence with being a passive participant in that violence. My efforts, culminating in this book, have been focused on breaking the silence about violence against women by intimate partners. Through this book, I will serve as a channel for the thirty-nine survivors to do the same.

Months after my first encounter with Rosie, I heard through the ethnic grapevine that she had been placed in the only existing shelter in town. It is not uncommon for men to attack women who are seeking refuge in shelters, as I now know; for example, in Quebec, Michel Bernier kicked his way into a shelter and shot and killed his wife (*Toronto Star*, 11 June 1999: A3). Sure enough, I also heard that Rosie's husband had attempted to forcibly remove her from her shelter. According to the rumours, he had broken the baby finger of a shelter worker in a physical scuffle. Most distressing of all, Rosie went back to him, dropping all the charges. In the early 1970s, victims themselves were expected to lay charges against their abusers, which meant that they could drop those charges out of fear, love, or shame. Like many other women, Rosie returned to more beatings, further starvation, and perhaps, to a few more of the roses that she associated with being loved.

Although I understood none of these complex processes at the time, even then I knew that something was seriously wrong. Sometimes, I associated the problem with members of my own ethnic community and blamed them. At other times, I personalized the event and blamed myself. It hurt most, however, when I heard that Rosie had recanted her story, requesting a different translator for dropping her charges. She claimed that she had never been abused but had just fallen down the steps. She said the error must have been in the first translation – the one I had provided! For years, I resented Rosie for that lie. At the time, I could not understand the all-encompassing darkness that must have enveloped her life – even though I had seen her scars with my own eyes. Looking back, I am quite sure that her fear of her husband and her isolation in a strange country forced her to alter the truth. She may have been trying either to save face or to save her life by lying about the abuse. In any case, I never forgot that encounter, and I never forgot Rosie's torn smile and the suffering in her eyes.

Since the early 1970s, family violence has been one area of focus in my thoughts, learning, writing, and teaching. After that first encounter, I also heard about many other incidents: all devastating and unique but all strangely similar in the pain and anguish they produced.

In the early 1980s, I interviewed divorced women who had custody of their children. Although violence was not one of the topics I inquired about in that study, almost half of my interviewees took it upon themselves to tell me about how their husbands had physically, verbally, and sometimes sexually hurt them. They did not use the term 'abuse.' They did not call it violence. Instead, they used words like pushed, slapped, or punched. Some had been burned with cigarettes. My interviewees also told me that both the level and the frequency of the abuse escalated once they threatened to leave or shortly after they had left (also see Sev'er and Pirie 1991a, 1991b, and Sev'er 1992). I found a general sense of relief in some of my divorced respondents, who considered themselves lucky to have been given a new lease on life. Their relief was surprising, given that most of them were disadvantaged compared with their standard of living during their married lives (see Sev'er and Pirie, 1991a and 1991b).

Over the years, I have gained additional insights about intimate violence through some of my own students. Each time I have given a lecture about what Straus, Gelles, and Steinmetz (1980, 1986) call the 'dark side of the family,' a few students would seek me out to discuss their aunts, cousins, or nieces, or to talk about themselves as victims of abuse. They would use terms such as 'situation' or 'problem,' but would never call their own predicament 'assault,' 'abuse,' or 'violence.' I started to stockpile pamphlets from women's centres, emergency hot lines, and shelter information in my office for these occasions. Each time a student came to see me, there was a request to close my office door, which is usually kept open. Often there were tears and almost always a difficult struggle to part with the dark secret. Through sharing their stories, my students unknowingly encouraged me to be a committed foot soldier in the war against intimate violence against women. Many years earlier, Rosie had done the same.

Over time, each story I heard stirred complex feelings in me; ranging from sorrow, pity, and disbelief to admiration, respect, anger, and even horror. However, there are two cases that disturbed me most. In the early 1990s, a bright, hard-working Sri Lankan student from a feminist course I was teaching was forced into an arranged marriage by her parents. She tried to resist. Her resistance increased the parental and cultural pressures on her to the extent that she was forced to quit her studies and was sent back to Sri Lanka for the completion and consummation of her arranged marriage. Soon after her emotional departure, I heard from another student that she had attempted to kill herself in the first month of her marriage. I never heard from her or about her again, but her story still hurts me. The second case, which equally bothered me, relates to two East Indian sisters who were married to two brothers through an arranged marriage. The husbands were much older than the young women and were extremely jealous and controlling. The sisters lived in an extended family compound with their husbands, in-laws, and the wives and children of other brothers. Both women were routinely maltreated by all male members of the household and routinely beaten by their husbands. The only freedom they had was to take a course at the university. Even then, one of the brothers drove them to school and another picked them up. They told me that there was no way to get out of these relationships, because their own family had threatened to disown them if they ever tried. Like in the drama of the two sisters, abuse and control are themes that are disclosed by the thirty-nine survivors in this book.

These and other life experiences I have heard about have made me particularly attuned to the complex effects of ethnocultural and religious factors in family violence, although violence cuts across all classes, races, and religions. Most theories that try to explain violence against women do grave injustice to the topic by overlooking the cultural, patriarchal, and ethnoreligious systems that buttress such violence. I am going to try to address such complex patterns by avoiding an artificial simplification about how personal, social, cultural, economic, legal, and political systems come to bear upon the continuation of violence. This book will synthesize many years of my work to combine sociology, feminism, and social activism to recognize, understand, and suggest changes for the disease of male-partner violence.

The thirty-nine interviews I personally carried out were done with the utmost respect for and sensitivity to the participants' feelings. However, as far as my own analysis of the topic is concerned, I must warn my readers that my stance is not neutral. I see little place for a rigidly constrained intellectual interest on violence against women, despite the teachings of 'objectivity' and/or 'depersonalization' that the fathers of sociology have called for. Instead, in line with the feminist teachings (Eichler and Lapointe, 1985), I find that the plight of these women affects me personally, although I hardly know them and I certainly have never experienced their pain. I hope to be able to share with you some of the heart-wrenching feelings I myself experienced when they told their stories to me without falling into the trap of presenting myself as the 'objective/rational/in-control/distant' researcher. During the interviews, I admit that I was often deeply affected by my respondents' pain. Of course, I will try to wear my sociologist's cloak when I review the literature, summarize the existing theories, and expand on or criticize their assumptions and assertions. I will, however, let my feminist activism take over when I relate some of the stories I have heard about the struggles of women against their abusers and against their accusers, who often include their friends and family. Most importantly, I will try to highlight their diminished sense of self by using their own meanings and preserving their own words. I will try to find patterns in their accomplishments, while I also try to emphasize negative social or personal patterns that continue to entrap these women. Whenever possible, I will let the women speak for themselves so that you, the reader, can hear their stories in their own voices. After all, this book aims to make sense of the all-too-common problem of male violence against female intimates; it is about thirty-nine women who have found the strength to transcend this violence. Who can have more legitimacy in describing the violence than those who have escaped from 'the house of horrors'?

In Chapter 1, I review the literature about the different definitions of abuse and the dilemmas embedded in different conceptualizations of it. In Chapter 2, I review the incidence of violence against women. Although the works I cite are predominantly from Canada and the United States, I occasionally use findings from other countries to highlight the global nature of violence against women. Chapter 3 reviews and discusses the strengths and weaknesses of existing theories in the area, while Chapter 4 introduces the methods of this study. In Chapter 5, I discuss examples of different forms of violence that the participants in this study have endured. The focus of Chapter 6 is violence against children. Chapter 7 is dedicated to the strategies the thirty-nine survivors of abuse developed to facilitate their own as well as their children's safety and survival. Some of these strategies have created additional problems for these women in the long run. It goes without saying that part of the survival strategies involves social support systems. Thus, in Chapter 8, social networks and social support systems of the respondents are discussed. As I am going to demonstrate, some social networks have played very positive roles during the women's escape from violence. Other social networks have been unhelpful or outright destructive. Chapter 9 deals with a very controversial and divisive issue: women's own violence. I do not have the illusion of bringing a resolution to all the controversy that surrounds women's own violence and how this topic has been approached by feminists, pro-feminists, and anti-feminists. Nevertheless, in this chapter, I will openly and honestly try to make sense of my observations and of what my respondents told me about their own actions. In Chapter 10, I will try to bring some synthesis to the complexities that surround intimate violence and propose a new model for post-violence adjustment.

With these words, I welcome you to a challenging and thought-provoking journey towards understanding the lives of women who have escaped their abusive partners. These women do not represent the entire spectrum of abused women. However, it is my sincere belief that there is much to be gained from their experiences, insights, strength, and resolve. It is also my belief that there is much we can learn from their human weaknesses, indecisiveness, and failures. I will make no attempt to reify these survivors, just as I will make no attempt to hide their genuine suffering. After all, they are women, they are mothers, mates and friends, daughters and sisters like the rest of us. Yet they are women who have lost a portion of their lives to violence. They are also women who are on the winding road to reclaiming their lives.

Chapter One

Definitions of and Dilemmas about Intimate Partner Abuse of Women

The women's movement of the 1970s rightfully made the abuse of women by intimate partners an area of intense study and awareness. It is not surprising that most of these efforts involved defining the problem, measuring its magnitude, figuring out its causes, sheltering its victims, and trying to find ways to eliminate its occurrence. This chapter addresses what can be considered the first step of such efforts: determining definitions of partner abuse. It also highlights the strengths and weaknesses of different conceptualizations and the overall dilemmas in trying to address the complexity of violence against women.

Definitions

Legal Definitions

The Canadian Criminal Code does not directly define violence against women as a unique category of crime. Instead, violence against women is subsumed under section 244, which defines 'assault,' and sections 245 and 246, which define assault with a weapon, aggravated assault, sexual assault, and aggravated sexual assault. The Criminal Code definitions of assault require 'intent' to harm (*mens rea*, or the mental component of the crime, which literally translates as 'guilty mind'). The code only punishes 'acts' (*actus reus*, which literally translates as the actual occurrence of a criminal act; see Mannle and Hirschel, 1988), not thoughts. With very few exceptions (e.g., treason), planning or intending to hurt someone without translating one's thoughts into action does not constitute an offence. Likewise, accidentally hurting someone without the intention to do so falls outside the definition of assault. Thus, the commission of an assault is contingent upon both intent and injury. Another point that needs to be stressed is that the Criminal Code definition of any kind of assault, including sexual assault, is gender-blind. In the eyes of the law, whether committed by men or women and whether committed against men or women, the injurious acts are conceptualized in an identical way. Moreover, the Criminal Code definition does not make any reference to the type of relationship, if any, between the perpetrator and his or her victim.

Two other sections of the Canadian Criminal Code deal with 'intimidation' (section 381) and the more recent 'stalking' legislation passed in August 1993 (criminal harassment, section 264). In both of these cases, the burden of proof to show 'intent' to harm lies with the target of intimidation. However, the 'physical component' of the criminal act could be harassing phone calls, stalking, or verbal or written threats and not necessarily an actual assault on the victim. Just like the sections on assault, the intimidation and stalking sections are also legislated as gender-blind. Moreover, there is no attempt to identify the relationship between the offenders and their victims, although these types of controlling tactics are disproportionately used by men to threaten or repeatedly harass their current or former partners, spouses, and girlfriends (Sev'er, 1998).

Social Definitions

For the purposes of social analyses, numerous issues arise from the aforementioned legal definitions. One obvious issue is that the Criminal Code definitions of 'assault' are inadequate in responding to the social and psychological turmoil that women suffer at the hands of their intimate partners. Addressing the latter issue requires a few additional definitions and points to the need to genderize these concepts.

Dictionary definitions of 'violence' include: rough force in action, rough or harmful action or treatment, harm or injury, or unlawful use of force. In a way, dictionary definitions of violence closely parallel the Criminal Code definition of assault by emphasizing the physical nature of the act. Moreover, dictionary definitions of violence are also gender-blind and omit the relationship between the perpetrator and the victim. Unlike the Criminal Code definitions, however, dictionary definitions do not refer to the 'intent' of the violator. For example, a very young child can act violently towards another young child, yet his or her violent act will not constitute a criminal offence. Legally, young children are not considered able to plan (intend) such an act or to understand the ramifications of their acts.

Another term we have to explore is 'abuse.' Dictionary definitions of 'abuse' include: use wrongly or make bad use of, treat badly, bad practice or custom, and scold severely or use harsh or insulting language. Like the previously discussed terms, abuse is also gender-blind. However, it captures two dimensions that assault and violence leave untouched. First, albeit indirectly, the definition of abuse implies going beyond or violating the customary expectations about relations, thus underscoring some type of relationship between the people involved. Second, the definition of abuse goes beyond physical types of violation and subsumes other forms of degradation such as insulting language and put-downs.

Feminist Definitions

In the feminist literature, numerous conceptualizations have been tried, each with its own strengths and weaknesses. For example, 'battering' is a term that some feminists use to identify the very specific type of violence that men inflict on women. According to MacLeod (1980: 7), battering captures the repeated nature of violence towards intimate partners and insinuates the traditions, laws, and attitudes that directly or indirectly condone such violence.

Whether one uses the term 'violence' to focus on mostly the physical dimensions of hurt or uses the term 'abuse,' which better covers controlling behaviours and psychological transgressions, there is a need to make these terms gender-specific. Although there are a few social scholars who prefer undifferentiated terms like 'family violence' or 'domestic violence' (see Gelles and Loseke, 1993), feminist and profeminist theorists and researchers insist on identifying and emphasizing that in violence between intimates, perpetrators are mostly men, while the vast majority of their targets are women (see DeKeseredy and MacLeod, 1997; Kelly, 1997; Sev'er, 1998; Yllö, 1993).

In the 1980s, the frequent use of the term 'wife abuse' was an attempt to highlight the intimacy of the relationship as well as the direction of the abuse (towards the wife). Others preferred the term 'wife battering' to highlight both the serious and the repeated nature of the abuse (see MacLeod, 1980). Still others found the term 'wife' objectionable, because violence occurs between dating as well as common-law partners, and frequently continues after the dissolution of dating, common-law, or marital relationships (Kelly, 1997; Kurz, 1998; Sev'er, 1996, 1998). Moreover, attempts to genderize violence or abuse with the term 'wife' were claimed to be dismissive of violence among same-sex partners (Renzetti, 1992).

As this summary makes clear, none of these conceptualizations is perfect. Each has its own set of proponents and critics, and the debate on conceptualizations is not closed. More recent literature, however, seems to favour the term 'partner' or 'intimate partner' to avoid legalistic and heterosexist biases. Those who specifically study men's violence prefer 'violence against female intimate partners' (see Sev'er, 1997a, 1997b, 1999) or 'woman abuse' (DeKeseredy and MacLeod, 1997). Of course, the problem with the former is that it is a too-long description rather than a term. The problem with the latter is that it does not specify the level of intimacy between the abuser and the abused.

Naming the Targets of Abuse

Additional debates surround what to call women who have suffered abuse and violence. After the women's movement of the 1970s, the preferred term was 'victim.' The shelter movement of the 1970s in most of the western world was the logical outcome of this early conceptualization of women as victims (Dobash and Dobash, 1992). Of course, women are victimized by their abusive partners, but are they just victims? Despite the countless gains from the maturation of feminist efforts, the word 'victim' remains at the core of one of the heated debates about women's own agency. There is a gnawing fear that the earlier efforts of the shelter movement may have inadvertently and ironically reduced women to passive social actors while the woman/victim and man/abuser polarities may have been only partially helpful constructs in analysing the cultures of violence. This is not meant to dismiss the complex processes within which women are indeed victimized. Numerous researchers from varying parts of the world report that in approximately 90 to 95 per cent of the cases of family violence, crimes against women are indeed perpetrated by the current or former male partner (Brush, 1993; Browne, 1987; Dobash and Dobash, 1979; Berk et al., 1983; WAC Stats, 1993). Nevertheless, women *are* social agents. Sometimes women are extraordinarily resilient, sometimes provocative, sometimes assertive or passive, or sometimes even abusive themselves – but in all cases they are social agents. Even under the most extraordinary conditions, women weigh alternatives, make plans, try out strategies, often but not always protect themselves and their children, and combat sheer helplessness. Sometimes, they call the police or contact other social agencies. At other times, they run away, often taking their children with them. Women are social actors. It is no wonder that researchers are increasingly emphasizing the resilience of women through terms such as 'survivors' (Hoff, 1990), 'empowerment' (Fine, 1993), and the like. However, the latter terms also bring numerous assumptions, some adequate, others unjustifiable. One problem is that not all women survive the violence of their intimate partners. Some are killed. Some others take their own lives. Some suffer lifelong health effects, and some others develop dependencies on drugs and alcohol (Cory and McAndless-Davis, 2000; Petersen, Gazmararian, and Clark, 2001). Does this mean that those who did not survive did something wrong or different from the ones who did survive? Does this mean that survival is totally up to the women rather than being sometimes determined by the actions of their abusers? Do those who die or get mutilated fail in some way? The point is that the 'survivor' term presents an unfair divide between those who came through the mayhem and those who did not or could not. I believe that a great deal of sensitivity is required to be mindful of this difficulty and to remember that violence was inflicted on these women and not necessarily because of something they did or did not do. There must be a careful balance in emphasizing the 'agency of women' without total disregard of the 'victimization' they have suffered in the past or perhaps continue to suffer even now.

Some useful recent developments have emphasized the behaviour and responsibility of men, a shift spearheaded by the Duluth project. The Duluth model emphasizes a multilevel pattern of intervention summoning some punitive and some rehabilitative measures for the offenders through the criminal justice system (Pence, 1983; Pence and Paymar, 1993). Moreover, there is a growing insistence that partner abuse must be placed within the sociocultural and historical vortex of overall violence, since it is rooted in and ultimately contributes to the continuum of violence (Counts, Brown, and Campbell, 1992; Davidson, 1977; Gordon, 1989; Kelly, 1976; MacKinnon, 1993a 1993b; Sev'er, 1999; WAC Stats, 1993, Walker, 1990).

Types of Abuse

As the above discussion demonstrates, there are different ways of defining abuse and violence. To further complicate matters, there are also different types of abuse. Physical abuse, the form that generates the most agreement, is generally defined as hits, punches, kicks, bites, or choking, which may end up in bruises, cuts, lacerations, broken bones, and disfigurement (Dobash and Dobash, 1979, 1992). Sexual abuse is generally defined as forcing a woman, against her will, to perform sexual acts, and/or endure pain and injury during sex. Sexual abuse also occurs when a person, usually a man, has unprotected sex with his partner while knowing that he is infected with a transmittable disease (DeKeseredy and MacLeod, 1997). Economic abuse occurs when the abused person (most likely the woman) is denied access to the family's money and is not allowed any power over how money is spent. It also involves monitoring what, where, how much, and when she can spend money – even on vital items such as baby food. The most controversial form of abuse is psychological abuse. It can take the form of serious and systematic neglect of a dependent spouse (e.g., in cases of chronic physical or mental illness). More often, however, psychological abuse is in the form of verbal abuse such as put-downs, name-calling, degradation, and erosion of self-worth (DeKeseredy and MacLeod, 1997; Jacobson and Gottman, 2001). It can also involve blaming, false accusations, and verbal violence against another person, child, or pet that the woman loves. It is important to underscore that abusive men often utilize some or all of these different forms in the subjugation of their female partners. In the following pages, I expand on the dilemmas that surround these definitions.

Dilemmas

Dilemmas about Methods and Operationalization of Concepts

In the realm of violence, the debates about which terms to use when referring to the abuse of women resemble the tip of an iceberg. Even more intense debates surround what constitutes partner abuse and how it compares to other manifestations of violence. A number of social scholars prefer to define abuse as the conglomeration of physical, sexual, psychological, economic, and even spiritual control and subjugation of women (DeKeseredy and Hinch, 1991; DeKeseredy and MacLean, 1990b; Hoff, 1990; Jacobson and Gottman, 2001; Kurz, 1998; MacLeod, 1980, 1987, 1995). These conceptualizations, similar to the legal definitions, emphasize the intentional nature of such abuse. The undisputed part of the conceptualizations pertains to physical injuries, such as cuts, bruises, lacerations, rips, tears, and broken bones or sexual injuries such as being forced into hurtful sexual acts against one's will. Some women are disfigured or lose their limbs, others even lose their lives (Bean, 1992; Campbell, 1992; Chimbos, 1978a, 1978b; Crawford and Gartner, 1992; Daly, 1992; Johnson, 1988; Johnson and Chisholm, 1990; Mercy and Saltzman, 1989; Radford, 1992a; Stout, 1992).

The second part of the conceptualizations, which refers to psychological abuse, remains more controversial. Debates persist about whether to include the not-so-visible effects of humiliation, degradation, and verbal assaults against one's core personhood under the definition of abuse or violence by intimate partners. As Jacobson and Gottman (2001) point out, emotional abuse is just as effective in controlling women as is physical abuse. Yet the former is, unfortunately, not against the law (2001: 480).

In the interviews I conducted for this book, the damage done by non-physical abuse never ceased to startle me. One of my respondents (Ann) is now deemed 'legally disabled' as a result of repeated physical beatings. She was calm when she described the severe head injuries that had required her hospitalization (see Chapter 5). Yet she broke down completely when she recalled the non-physical degradations, name-calling and put-downs in front of friends, family, and complete strangers. The many shocking examples of Ann's ordeal are discussed in various sections of this book. What I want to acknowledge here are the powerful effects of the psychological degradation that women suffer, leaving them emotionally crippled for long periods, maybe even scarring the way they see themselves for the rest of their lives.

Regardless of their noble intentions and commitment to the topic, some feminist scholars are reluctant to define non-physical attacks on a woman's personhood as 'violence.' They prefer to remain within the legal definitions of assaultive behaviour (Johnson, 1988, 1996; Smith, 1989; Dobash and Dobash, 1979). There is a fear that including amorphous concepts such as 'psychological abuse' will dilute the very serious nature of the social problem. There is also the legitimate fear of a backlash from non-feminist or anti-feminist segments of society. Will the inclusion of psychological abuse open the floodgates to claims of 'suffering of men' who may also be victims of words? (See Steinmetz, 1977–8, for early renditions of such sentiments, and see DeKeseredy et al., 2000, for detailed examples of an anti-feminist backlash.) Will we provide ammunition for those who trivialize and marginalize women's suffering through de-gendering their experiences? These are serious concerns, and simplistic answers will not provide satisfactory solutions. However, it is my contention that abuse of women goes beyond bruises, cuts, and broken bones. It also includes impairing self-esteem and confidence and hollowing out souls.

Not surprisingly, the choice of methods of study is also closely entwined with the current theories, paradigms, and ideological and conceptual positions. Debates about which methods are best suited to the study of wife abuse are unresolved (Bograd, 1988; DeKeseredy and MacLean, 1990a; Dobash and Dobash, 1979; Kelly, 1997; Kurz, 1993, 1998; Yllö and Bograd, 1988). Some researchers prefer 'objective' ways of counting the incidence of abuse, while making sure that the measures are 'reliable.' The Conflict Tactics Scale (CTS), developed by researchers from the New Hampshire School (Gelles, 1979, 1985, 1987, 1994; Gelles and Cornell, 1983; Gelles and Straus, 1988; Straus, Gelles, and Steinmetz, 1980, 1986), operationalizes abuse as hits, slaps, kicks, and burns. The CTS is used often. Its emphasis is on counting and ordering the incidents according to a preconceived ranking of their severity. Two of the recent Canadian victimization surveys utilized a more gender-sensitive version of the CTS (VAWS, 1993; GSS, 2000). Some researchers also use modified versions of such scales (DeKeseredy and Kelly, 1993; Dobash et al., 1995; GSS, 2000; VAWS, 1993), despite reservations about the validity of the quantitative scales. Modifications include qualitative questions about the outcome of abuse. Indeed, there is an alluring rationale for using the CTS, since numbers provide data for direct comparisons between studies, regions, and countries. They also give a mathematical or scientific 'legitimacy' to the elusive social phenomenon of partner abuse. Nevertheless, problems arise in terms of the 'validity' of such measures, even when they are modified and used with care. For example, a slap in the face may produce no visible injury or bruise or it may knock out teeth. It is almost impossible to rank-order 'a slap' without understanding its severity and outcome. This simple example shows that the responses to scales may lead to uninterpretable or even misleading results. More importantly, the propensity for the misuse of the findings that these scales generate is a serious feminist concern. For example, studies using traditional CTS measures have repeatedly found equivalence between men and women in their abusive acts (Gelles and Straus, 1979; Steinmetz, 1977–8; Straus, Gelles, and Steinmetz, 1986; GSS, 2000). Without taking into consideration the causes, severity, initiation, or consequences of violence, the scale equates a jaw-breaking hit by a man to a defensive act by a woman in assigning them the same score. Despite all disclaimers and qualifications, the gender neutrality and equivalence findings of the CTS scales have had a negative effect on perceptions and attitudes by fuelling suspicions against women targets of such abuse.

Feminists ask if abuse can be captured adequately by piecemeal counts of slaps or kicks without due recognition of the imbalances in power, strength, privilege, intent, motive, damage, and terror that precede, accompany, or follow those acts? (see Dobash and Dobash, 1979; Kelly, 1998; Kurz, 1993, 1998; Pagelow, 1985; Yllö and Bograd, 1988.) Thus, the core of the debate is much more complex than a methodological preference towards quantification rather than qualitative research. The current debate also subsumes differences in power and the need for contextualizing the suffering and its aftermath. In addition, the debate extends into taking responsibility for how research findings may be or should be used (Dobash and Dobash, 1988, 1992; Yllö and Bograd, 1988). Contrary to the insistence of the exclusively male founders of social sciences, feminist researchers in the area of violence argue that social research cannot and should not be devoid of social responsibility (Dobash and Dobash, 1992; Renzetti, 1997; Spender, 1981; Yllö and Bograd, 1988).

Dilemmas about Cultural Differences

Debates abound over whether the proclivities to abuse of some men are rooted in different cultural patterns. Immigrant women and men ascribe to norms, values, and expectations that may be woefully different from those that the host society upholds. Moreover, the dislodged individuals may lack access to social comparison processes, while relatives and kin acting according to 'old country' customs may attempt to 'preserve' marriages at all costs. Besides, the lack of language proficiency alone may reduce individual experiences to a social mystery (Dworkin, 1993; Dasgupta, 1998). Even people who are 'trained' to extend a helping hand may fail to understand the subtleties in cultural expectations or the pressures that patriarchal cultures place on women. Despite their goodwill, help providers are likely to be far removed from the realities of the immigrants' lives (see Chalmers and Smith, 1987; Dasgupta, 1998; Gogia, 1992–3; MacLeod and Smith, 1990; Nielson, Endo, and Ellington, 1992). In addition, the legal system itself may reflect the biases of domination: favouring majority against minority, rich against poor, white against non-white, men against women, intact family against other family forms, and heterosexual against same-sex unions (Dasgupta, 1998; Ferraro, 1989; MacKinnon, 1993a, 1993b). It is clear that the dilemmas about culture are intimately linked with the dilemmas about contextualization of abuse.

Unlike some homogeneous countries that are wary of cultural differences in their midst, Canada takes sociopolitical pride in encouraging its population to uphold its ethnocultural diversities. Canadian sensitivities often translate into a reluctance to classify people by race or ethnicity, especially in areas of crime and punishment. The outcome of such an ideology is two-pronged: on the positive end, no ethnocultural group (with the exception of the Native Canadians) gets isolated and scapegoated in terms of its propensity for committing crimes (general or against women). On the other hand, the special needs of immigrant women, their disproportional social isolation, often coupled with economic dependence, and their unawareness of or inability to assert their legal rights continue to pose problems for them.

Dasgupta (1998: 211) asserts that men's power and control of women do not happen in a vacuum. Different institutions such as the courts, the police, the media, social services, work, economics, and religion all play a role in setting the level of tolerance for violence in a given society. Even the state is not a benign force in this conceptualization. Through laws, immigration policies, and citizenship requirements, the state can create additional hurdles for immigrant women (Two Struggles, 1992). According to Dasgupta (1998), even institutions do not function in a vacuum. The components of culture such as norms, rituals, values, traditions, and language contribute to a milieu that will determine the kind and direction of power relationships. To exemplify Dasgupta's institutional and cultural levels of analyses, I would like to refer back to Rosie's story. Rosie was obviously dependent on the economic and social resources of her abusive husband. Her dependence was compounded by her immigrant status, her lack of integration in the host society, and her inability to speak either of the official languages of Canada. Her dependence was also fuelled by the male-dominated society she had come from, its norms about marital arrangements, and its expectations of family sacrifices from wives in assuring the continuation of marriages. When Rosie's troubles brought her in contact with the police and social services, the people who were supposed to help her were not able to understand the unique dilemmas that sprang from Rosie's cultural background. Sadly, but perhaps not surprisingly, Rosie returned to her abuser like many other women have done before her.

Despite the open crusade against intimate violence against women, educators, law-enforcement agents, and health-care and helping professionals are sometimes unwilling, and often unable, to tackle the issues that overlap with culture, ethnicity, and race. Good intentions notwithstanding, violence against immigrant women may be obscured by an oversensitivity to ethnocultural variations and diversity, on the one hand, or by ignorance or prejudice, on the other. Caught up in an ideological ambiguity, women from ethnic enclaves continue to carry a double burden as women and as immigrants. As women, they have much to fear from their abusers. Ironically, as cultural outsiders, they have little choice but to depend on the interpersonal links that bind them to their abusers (Two Struggles, 1992). For similar reasons, these women also remain loyal to their culture, which may treat them as second-class citizens. What is equally problematic is the possibility of women's own internalization of 'misogynist' norms and values. I call this possibility the 'cult of self-sacrifice' and see its manifestation as shaming other women who fall outside of the narrow definitions of submissiveness that the ethnic culture defines (see Sev'er, 1997b). The cult of self-sacrifice often translates into guilt and self-blame if the specific culture has conditioned women to define their ultimate role as that of serving men (Ofei-Aboagye, 1997).

I will use three tragedies described in the Canadian media to show the complex infusion of cultural sensitivities into issues of violence against wives. The first is the story of Nafisibibi Shaikh, an immigrant woman from India. In the mid-1990s, Nafisibibi's husband took her to India under the auspices of visiting her family. The husband made sure that the couple left their 21-month-old son with his parents in Montreal. The husband then returned to Montreal on his own, leaving Nafisibibi in a remote village in India. She had no money and no immigration documents with which she could find her way back to Canada. Without money or documents, it took Nafisibibi a year and four months to convince the Canadian High Commissioner in New Delhi that she was indeed a landed immigrant. Only after a media exposé and an ensuing public outcry was she allowed to re-enter Canada. That she returned to a husband who had repeatedly abused her in the past, to in-laws who actively took part in her subjugation, to a child who was brought up without knowing of her existence, and to a community that upholds her husband's rights as absolute were all quickly forgotten by the media (*Toronto Star*, 5 June 1995: A9). Lawyers working with immigrants claim that they know of dozens of similar cases where the wives' legal, economic, and even parental personhood are contingent upon their husbands' goodwill. Immigrant women, especially those from cultures that differ drastically from the host culture, are systematically shortchanged (see Dasgupta and Warrier, 1996; Huisman, 1996).

The second tragedy involves nine members of a British Columbia family from a Sikh community who were gunned down by the estranged husband of one of the daughters. The assailant also took his own life, bringing the death toll to ten (*Toronto Star*, 7 April 1996: A1). The marriage had been arranged, and it was abusive from the very beginning. Although there were numerous complaints to the police about beatings, threats, and stalking, the abused wife repeatedly refused a police investigation. She was reluctant to 'shame her family' in an ethnocultural milieu that shuns publicized marital discord and disintegration. After the carnage, both community leaders and a number of academics did their best to dissociate these events from any ethnocultural link. The community leaders defended the 'legitimacy' of arranged marriages within the eastern tradition, and the academics tried to prevent a backlash against visible minority groups in general and the Sikh community in particular. These attempts were made with the best of intentions. However, the low status of women, their culturally restricted choices, their expected self-sacrifice to uphold the family name, and how all these factors may have contributed to a fertile ground for the continuation of spousal abuse and femicide became buried in the cultural-protectionism nature of the debates. The rampage that cost ten lives was thus transformed into the doings of a 'crazy man' (see Caputi's 1987 analysis of individualization that obscures issues in homicide), rather than a tragedy with links to cultural patterns of patriarchy and the social silence and docility they command.

In July 2000, Vilem Luft Jr stabbed his wife Bohuslava, shot his four children point-blank, and then killed himself (*Toronto Star*, 7 July 2000: A1, A20). His family had immigrated from Czechoslovakia in the 1960s. His wife was twenty years his junior and had come to Canada after a sort of arranged marriage. Luft was domineering, controlling, obsessive, and unstable to the degree that on a number of occasions Bohuslava had tried to return to her homeland to escape her marriage. At one time, she had actually managed to get a divorce and marry another man in her country of origin. Each time, Luft had followed her to Czechoslovakia with promises of a better life and with threats of keeping custody of their children. Each time, she gave in and came back. What is devastating in this case is quite obvious: a vicious stabbing of a young woman and the point-blank shooting murder of her four children who ranged in age from 7 years to under 3 months. What is less obvious is that Bohuslava had trouble communicating her problems in a language she knew very little of. Within her own cultural milieu, which was patriarchal and secretive, her calls of alarm and anguish had fallen on deaf ears. What also received almost no media analysis was that Luft's family organized an emotional ceremony for their son and laid him to rest with the wife and children he had murdered (*Toronto Star*, 9 July 2000: A2 and 10 July A4). Thus, although Luft had many people to protect his best interests in his life as well as after his self-inflicted death, the imported wife (and her children) had no one who would speak for them. They were unable to escape their abuser even in death.

The issue of culture is very sensitive. The goal of exploring cultural links should not lead to scapegoating ethnocultural groups or communities. The intent should not be to expose any ethnoreligious community to additional stereotypes and prejudice. However, we should be wary of the pendulum swinging too far in the opposite direction. There is a real danger of systematically overlooking the cultural backgrounds of the perpetrators, which may add to the disadvantage of their victims. There is also a danger in abandoning minority women to deal with the genderized transgression of their own ethnic men, especially if their cultures of origin protect abusive men. Although violence against women occurs in all cultures, some ethnocultural patterns do provide a more fertile ground for such genderized problems than others. Thus, acknowledging a complex link between culture and the etiology of violence against women is a must if we are going to level the playing field for ethnic or immigrant women. Cultural prescriptions versus proscriptions will encourage or harness what men will eventually do, and to what degree they will be sanctioned. In some cultural contexts, men's behaviour towards their partners will feed on pre-existing negative views of women and wives and find a sanctioned and sanctified milieu for the abuse they inflict (Dutton and Van Ginkel, 1997; Viano, 1992). Political tendencies in Canada, however, minimize the role of culture in this equation, inadvertently denying an acknowledgment of the additional risks that some minority and immigrant women experience.

Similar dilemmas are configured into the workings of the criminal justice system. In Canada, for example, until the late 1970s, victims themselves were expected to lay charges against their abusers, which also meant that, like Rosie, they could drop those charges out of love, fear, or shame. Since the early 1980s, this ominous responsibility has been shifted to the police (Burris and Jaffee, 1983), a shift that feminists themselves inaugurated and celebrated. However, the issue is less than settled, since police forces remain predominantly white and male. Increasingly, advocates of immigrant women are asking for a reversal of the process (*Toronto Star*, 18 January 1996: A21). They claim that some minority women get even more severely abused if they call the police because of the profound distrust ethnic enclaves hold for the workings of the criminal justice system. Instead, it is argued, women endure very high levels of abuse, sometimes endangering their lives as well as the lives of their children without contacting the authorities. This tendency may also put into question the validity of official statistics on abuse. As I am going to discuss in conjunction with shelters, government cutbacks since the 1990s reduced the availability of cultural sensitivity programs. Thus, women from various backgrounds are being ill-served by an environment that glosses over their individual vulnerabilities.

Canada is by no means alone in the explosive intersectionality of race or ethnicity and gender. In England, for example, Krishna Sharma and Balwant Kaur suffered years of violence at the hands of their husbands. Eventually, both broke their culturally prescribed silence by asking for police protection to free themselves from violence, but neither received the help and protection they needed. Both women were eventually killed by their husbands (Two Struggles, 1992). The British version of the tension between race and gender is captured in the following excerpt from the Southall Black Sisters (Two Struggles, 1992: 313): 'For black women, challenging an issue like domestic violence within our own communities and challenging racism of the police at the same time is often fraught with contradictions. On the one hand, we are involved in campaigns against brutality, deaths in police custody and immigration fishing raids. On the other hand, we are faced with daily beatings, rape, sexual harassment. We are forced to make demands of the police to protect our lives from the very same men along whose side we fight in anti-racist struggles.'

In the United States where racial conflicts are rampant, black (also Hispanic and Native) women are much more vulnerable than their white sisters to their abusers, as well as the police and the court system (Richie and Kanuha, 2000). The latter are woefully inadequate in conceptualizing the transectionality of abuse, gender, and race. Some even hold blatant sexist and racist attitudes (Collins, 1993; Grant, 1992; Matthews, 1993). A chilling example of the divide was O.J. Simpson's trial for Nicole Brown's murder. Simpson was a sports idol of many Americans and a cultural idol of almost all black Americans. Sadly, but not surprisingly, the vast majority of the black community (including the jurors) interpreted the issue as one of racist police framing a 'successful black man.' Conversely, the majority of the white community, despite acknowledging racism among the police officials, saw Simpson as a wife abuser and killer. Defence lawyers successfully played the race card and managed a not-guilty verdict despite the overwhelming physical evidence against O.J. Simpson (*Toronto Star*, 8 and 13 October 1995, and 3 March 1996: A2, A28, A12 respectively). He was subsequently found liable in a civil trial for the wrongful deaths of Nicole Brown and her friend, but Simpson managed to remain at large, able to pursue his personal interests and relations with numerous other women. He even managed to retain custody of his children, despite the fact that he had been found responsible for their mother's wrongful death.

Different experiences that divide white from non-white also create fissures among feminists. Despite the unifying goal of eliminating maltreatment of women, feminists from different racial origins are increasingly accusing white feminists of shortchanging women of colour. In turn, white feminists who perceive themselves as diligently trying to combat violence against women feel misunderstood and unappreciated. They may even feel uneasy about being confronted by their own racism (Radford, 1992a, 1992b).

Dilemmas about the Conspiracy of Silence

An additional dilemma feminists face is whether to combat violence against women on their own or to solicit and lobby for men's help. For example, some Canadian shelters accept volunteer help from men but are reluctant to assign them to either board or counselling positions. Once, the lieutenant-governor of New Brunswick asked 'respected' men to join ranks and 'push for change' (*Toronto Star*, 7 May 1993: A3). However, the early initiatives by prominent men called the 'white ribbon campaign' (men against violence against women) received reviews ranging from criticism to suspicion (*Toronto Star*, 3 December 1992: A26). A sparsely attended march in Toronto (sixty men) sponsored by the Labour Council of Metro Toronto also sparked divided evaluations

(*Toronto Star*, 5 May 1996: A7). The tension between feminist women and pro-feminist men is real and continuing, despite the proven struggle of some men in support of women's causes. A complicating factor is that pro-feminist men also endure social ramifications from their not feminist or anti-feminist peers (see DeKeseredy et al., 2000).

It is my contention that excluding men from efforts to resolve issues of gendered violence is neither possible nor desirable. Whether we like it or not, men are a part of the tapestry of relations, on the one hand, as abusive fathers, sons, husbands, and lovers, and on the other hand, as lawmakers, prosecutors, judges, educators, politicians, and workmates. Some are loving spouses, friends, colleagues, and model teachers. Men are still overrepresented in the patriarchal medical system (Warshaw, 1993), and disproportionally dominate the military and sports conglomerates (Messner, 1989; Russell, 1989; Sev'er, 1999; also see *Toronto Star*, 12 May 1994: A2 for sexual harassment in the military; and *Toronto Star*, 23 February 1996: A26 for abuse by a sports hero). I believe that both men and women, whites, and persons of colour must play a role in trying to resolve the complex social problem of male violence if we are going to break its vicious cycle of occurrence.

Despite increased publicity, abuse remains enveloped in a 'conspiracy of silence' even among those who may personally find physical violence against women distasteful. There are many examples of blatant ignorance and escapism even at the level of the 'delivery of justice.' In 1954, G.H. Hatherill, a commander of Scotland Yard stated, 'There are about 20 murders a year in London and not all are serious – some are just husbands killing their wives' (cited in *Toronto Star*, 11 December 1995: A17). Lest we think this is dated, there are more recent examples from men who occupy key positions: For instance, Ronald MacDonald a Nova Scotia provincial court judge, resigned after assaulting his wife. Prior to a public outrage, he was given an absolute discharge for being a respectable member of the community (*Toronto Star*, 6 October 1989: A13). In another example, five federally appointed judges were reprimanded for regrettable conduct, which included telling a victim of spousal abuse that her request to attend a pretrial hearing was 'silly' (*Toronto Star*, 25 January 1995: A2). In Quebec, a Superior Court Judge, Justice Jean Bienvenue, declared that when a woman 'decides to sink, she unfortunately does to a depth that the vilest of men would be unable to attain' (*Toronto Star*, 13 December 1995: A2). And in Toronto, Judge Walter Hryciuk appealed his removal from office despite the fact that he had French-kissed one and made lewd remarks to another assistant crown attorney (both women). He had also grabbed the buttocks of a female judge and penetrated a female stenographer's vagina with his finger. Hryciuk's behaviour was referred to as 'tantamount to sexual assault' (*Toronto Star*, 8 November 1994). Joel Gehrke, a court judge in Michigan, 'told a man convicted of spousal abuse to roll up his shirt sleeve, then punished him with a three-finger "slap" on the wrist and said "Don't do that"' (*Toronto Star*, 18 January 1996: A13). In 1998, a trial judge acquitted a man who had sexually harassed and assaulted a 17-year-old. Judge McClung's reasoning in that case was that the victim 'was not on her way to the nunnery,' and she did not 'present herself in a bonnet and crinolines' (*Toronto Star*, 26 February 1999: A7). How can women seek justice from a system that may be riddled with deliverers of justice who themselves are consumed with contempt for women? There are simply too many of these incidents for them to be written off as isolated cases. Dismissing the importance of women's personhood and trivializing the abuse of intimate female partners are part of the matrix of abuse. Regardless of the surge of information about violence against women, there has not been a concomitant change in the attitudes and behaviour of the guardians of the justice system or among members of other patriarchal institutions, including the police.

Tensions between Activism and Academic Approaches

Perhaps, our best accomplishment as feminists, intellectuals, and activists is that we have given words and numbers to women's screams. Gains have been made in the emphasis on women's capacity to survive and on the race, gender, class, and sexual orientation multiplexities rather than on a one-dimensional analysis of 'patriarchy,' and on women's own agency and empowerment rather than their sheer victimization. In addition, increasing numbers of pro-feminist men have joined in denouncing all kinds of violence against women.

The opposite side of the coin involves the trials and tribulations encountered in this relentless pursuit of speaking with intellectual authority, while at the same time repairing the lives of women who are caught in violence. Here lies the source of tension between the academics and educators versus the front-line workers, activists, and the victims of abuse. The issues of abuse that fuel feminist passions also kindle divisions in practice, abstract theorizing, and research. Among the general public, there may be an unintended satiation of interest in aberrant and abhorrent behaviour (such as partner abuse) once the magnitude of the aberration is unearthed by national studies. The emphasis in the 1970s on sheltering the victims of abuse may have inadvertently resulted in ignoring the perpetrators and the patriarchal nature of the institutions that tolerate their crimes. The shift, in the following era, towards increased criminalization of the abusers may have deflected from a social investment in the prevention of abuse. Engulfed in the day-by-day survival needs of many, the activists may have little time or energy left for seeking rupturous reconfigurations of the oppressive systems. Academics, on the other hand, may seek solutions in more abstract social and structural domains, at the cost of being seen as removed from the actual and ongoing suffering of women. Consolidated solutions to any of the above dilemmas remain out of reach.

Contextual Stance of This Book

I have so far tried to give an overview of the conceptual complexities and the methodological and social dilemmas of violence against female partners. As is true with the majority of complex issues, the dilemmas surrounding this issue are hard if not impossible to resolve. We each have our own locatedness on the conceptual continuum. This book is no exception. As a feminist researcher, as a feminist sociologist, and as a human rights activist and social advocate, my own vision and biases are reflected in this book. For example, without locking myself into any subcategory of feminism, I will highlight the historical, economic, and patriarchal roots of the violence continuum rather than the personal characteristics of the abusers or the abused.

In this book, the focus is on the violence perpetrated by men against their female intimate partners simply because it is the most frequently observed type of violence (Lupri, Grandin, and Brinkerhoff, 1994; DeKeseredy and Hinch, 1991; Dobash and Dobash, 1979). I use the term 'violence' within its broadest context, which incorporates acts carried out with the intention to cause pain, injury, or even death (Brinkerhoff and Lupri, 1988; Kennedy and Dutton, 1989), as well as controlling and degrading behaviours that target the personhood and psychological well-being of the woman (DeKeseredy and Hinch, 1991; Dobash et al., 1995; Kirkwood, 1993; MacLeod, 1987; Tifft, 1993). More than anything else, my aim is to bring to light the stories of how the thirty-nine women that I interviewed have survived. I use the terms 'partner abuse' and 'intimate partner abuse' interchangeably to refer to the violence my participants have suffered. I use the term 'survivors' to refer to the women in my study. My intention, however, is by no means to ignore their suffering and victimization at the hands of their partners. These women are indeed victims of one or a combination of physical, sexual, and psychological types of abuse. My intention is not to undermine the current difficulties that many of them have, whether in relation to their friends, family, children, or new intimate attachments. As the chapters progress, the reader will realize that these women's battles are far from over, even though they have distanced themselves from their abusive mates. I do not want to underemphasize or ignore the difficulty some of them have in cyclical patterns of self-blame, distrust of self and others, troubled relations with their children, and even self-hatred. What I do want to emphasize, however, is that despite all of these problems and difficulties, these women have made relentless efforts to cling to life, to search for better living conditions for themselves and for their children, and to live day by day. Their resilience exists despite their legitimate fears about their past and the often unclear vision they have about their futures. There are many reasons that my participants are survivors rather than mere victims. As the following poem from one of them (Ava) so eloquently elucidates, these women hope for a better future despite the crushing realities in their past and the difficult circumstances of their current lives.

Ava's Poem: Loneliness, Stay, while I'm Still Down

Loneliness, stay, let me learn while I'm still down
Loneliness, stay, let me feel while I'm still numb
Loneliness, stay, let me cry while there are any tears
Loneliness, stay, because someday you'll be gone
   and you will never return.
Loneliness, hit at my heart, pound in my head
Pinch at my nerves, immobilize my thoughts
Let me live in fear
Keep me angry at love
Because someday, you'll be gone
   and you will never return.
Loneliness, come back
Accomplish your task
You have lots to do
You are busy as a bee
This is my turn
So I can grow
Because when you leave, you shall never return.

Chapter Two

Incidence of Violence against Intimate Female Partners

The New Hampshire group of researchers call the marriage licence a 'hitting license' (Straus, Gelles, and Steinmetz, 1980, 1986; also see Gelles, 1987, 1994). As national surveys in Canada and the United States show, this attribution is often a very accurate one (WAC Stats, 1993; Canadian Panel, 1993), since almost one in three women (29%) report at least one incident of physical abuse in their long-term relationships (VAWS, 1993; Johnson, 1996). However, thinking about marriage as a hitting licence is misleading in at least three ways. First, it insinuates that intimate relationships that are not legalized are free of violence. Second, it implies that only heterosexual pairs can be affected by intimate violence, overlooking that same-sex couples are also affected by violence (Merrill, 1998; Renzetti, 1998). Third, it suggests that once the marriage (licence) is terminated, the violence will cease. I will unequivocally show that these implications are erroneous. Like legal marriages, common-law and dating relationships are also infested with violence (Crawford and Gartner, 1992; DeKeseredy, 1989; DeKeseredy and MacLeod, 1997; DeKeseredy and Schwartz, 1997; Koss and Cook, 1993). Moreover, termination of the relationship often fails to guarantee the termination of violence against the female partner. On the contrary, relationships that were not previously violent sometimes become violent at the onset of separation. More often, there is a continuation or even an escalation of violence after separation. In the worst-case scenario, women who leave their partners may be murdered. According to a recent Bureau of Justice Statistics press release (BJS, 1995), the number of intimate-offender attacks on women separated from their husbands was three times higher than attacks on divorced women and about twenty-five times higher than attacks on married women. Although these statistics may reflect separations resulting from already existing violence in relationships, they nevertheless underscore the extremely troubling correlation between violence and separations and divorce (Bean, 1992; Block and Christakos, 1995; Crawford and Gartner, 1992; Ellis and DeKeseredy, 1997; Jacobson and Gottman, 2001; Johnson and Chisolm, 1990; Kurz, 1996, 1998; Okun, 1986; Sev'er, 1998; Wilson and Daly, 1992). Some of the women in this study are certainly survivors of their partners' post-separation violence.

In the most recent Canadian General Social Survey (GSS, 2000), it was estimated that 1.2 million men and women had faced some form of intimate violence between 1995 and 1999. Although almost identical percentages of polled women and men (8% and 7% respectively) reported at least one incident of violence, the consequences of violence were disproportionally more severe for women. For example, almost five times more women than men reported that they feared for their lives. One-quarter of women who reported violence said that they were beaten, and 13 per cent reported that their partners either threatened them with or actually used a gun or a knife on them. Four out of ten women reported experiencing some form of injury, and 15 per cent claimed that they required medical attention as a result of the violence. The above are very sombre figures even though the report showed a slight overall decline in these trends since the 1993 Violence Against Women (VAWS) survey (from 12% reporting violence down to 8%). The apparent decline may also be an artefact of methodological differences, such as polling only women (VAWS) versus polling both men and women (GSS), since women are more likely to suffer violence.

Problems with Numbers

In the previous chapter, I tried to summarize the problems with conceptualizing violence against women and the methodological dilemmas about whether to restrict abuse to either a physical or a combined physical and psychological definition. In addition to these difficulties, we must now consider other difficulties relating to recording and reporting violence in intimate relationships.

Privacy of the Family and Problems with Official Reports

Especially since the Industrial Revolution, family and familylike relationships have been increasingly designated as a 'private sphere.' This means that, at the social and political levels, there is a selective dismissal of or even ignorance about what goes on behind closed doors, and at the personal level, an enthusiastic effort to keep one's problems to oneself. In one of his legendary statements, the former Canadian Prime Minister Pierre Elliot Trudeau claimed that the state had no place in the nation's bedrooms.

In healthy and well-functioning family arrangements, the social and personal privacy accorded to families works by gently shielding men's and women's intimacies from an unwelcome social, legal, or political gaze. However, in families where violence is a common occurrence, expectations about and insistence on privacy may inadvertently shelter abusive men and isolate and trap their female partners and children. Indeed, in the area of criminology, four of the most underreported crimes are crimes that are committed within the boundaries of family or familylike arrangements (Finkelhor, 1993; Gartner and Macmillan, 1995). These crimes include incest, child abuse, elder abuse, and abuse of women.

In addition to the attitudes and perceptions of family privacy, other issues also affect reporting of abuse. Fear of the perpetrator, feelings of shame, lack of social support systems, lack of knowledge or distrust of the workings of the criminal justice system, and the visibility of white and/or male dominance in police departments are all factors that interact to reduce the probability of reporting. As already discussed in relation to cultural variations (Chapter 1), immigrant women and women from visible minority groups may show even more reluctance in reporting their experiences, thus contributing to the underrepresentativeness of the police statistics. Victimization studies consistently show that only a small proportion of abused women ever report their experiences to the police (Finkelhor, 1993; Johnson and Sacco, 1995; Koss, Gidycz, and Wisniewski, 1987). According to the findings of a national survey, only one of four women said that they ever disclosed the abuse they had suffered (Rodgers, 1994). Even women who call the police do so only if the attack is very severe or only after many incidences of violence (Finkelhor, 1993; Without Fear, 1994). Bain (1991) argues that, on average, women call the police after thirty-five incidents of physical abuse. The existing reluctance is exacerbated by the incremental erosion of social safety systems and cutbacks to shelters that house women and children who flee violence (Kurz, 1998; OAITH, 1998, 1999).

In Canada, similar factors may have had an impact on the reporting rates. Since the early 1990s, there has been a systematic dismantling of social safety systems carried out by the ever-burgeoning conservative political atmosphere and governments (OAITH, 1996, 1998). Even the Liberal governments have increasingly focused on balancing budgets and giving tax cuts over pouring money into much-needed social programs. In the general election of 2000, which gave Prime Minister Jean Chrétien his third mandate, none of the political parties gave primacy to women's issues in their campaign platforms. Instead, the election was run and won on negative campaigns, personality contests, photo opportunities, and promises of economic affluence and tax cuts. Even the New Democratic Party, which is the predominant protector of the ideals of social responsibility, restricted itself to health care and education debates.

It is unfortunate that like numerous minority groups, women are severely disadvantaged in these leaner and socially meaner times. According to the media reports, in 1995, the Conservative Ontario government cut $2.5 million in annual funding from second-stage housing, $25,000 from the Assaulted Women's Helpline, and $66,000 from the Ontario Association of Interval and Transition Houses (OAITH, 1996, 1998, 1999). An across-the-board cut of 5 per cent was also made to women's shelters (*Toronto Star*, 25 July 2000: 17). Such cuts to welfare, women's skills and educational programs, child care, women's centres, hot lines, and shelters have eliminated or reduced the already meagre options for women in general and abused women in particular. For example, despite the cuts, the Assaulted Women's Helpline in Toronto was able to handle 26,000 calls in 1997, but because of the high demand, it missed another 50,000 calls (OAITH, 1998). In 90 per cent of cases, the callers were likely to get a busy signal (*Toronto Star*, 25 July 2000: A17). Toughening up the laws to deal with abusers also may have deterred women from calling the authorities. According to criminologist Ruth Mann 'If a woman thinks her partner, her husband, the father of her children might face severe consequences ... often they [sic] won't report abuse and numbers seem to go down' (*Toronto Star*, 25 July 2000: A17).

In sum, no one knows whether the slight decline in violence against women is reflective of an actual decline or is an unintended artefact of the declining support systems in the social and political topography.

Problems with Data from Women's Shelters

Since the 1970s, the number of shelters for abused women in Canada has grown to about 500 (Juristat, 1999; OAITH, 1998) with thousands more scattered across the United States. For research purposes, shelters have always served as a convenient source for compiling information on the characteristics of the women and their children who seek refuge. However, although the reliability of shelter data is very high, the generalizability of shelter-based findings is questionable at best. Information from shelters often reflects a relatively narrow range of characteristics of the women who are most likely to use such help, severely underrepresenting women who may deal with the violence they suffer in other ways. In Canada, one of the very first shelter studies to look at intimate partner violence against women was carried out by Linda MacLeod (1980). The following are the (possibly overrepresented) characteristics she observed:

- Relatively young, with young children
- Generally literate, but not highly educated
- Generally unemployed or employed in transient jobs
- Generally from lower socioeconomic status
- From urban areas

What these data underrepresent are women who do not have young children, are older, better educated, from a higher socioeconomic status and/or employed, and women from rural areas. Findings from shelter-based studies do not necessarily mean that women from the higher social strata are not abused by their intimate partners, but they do indicate that such women are less likely to be found in shelters. Alternative responses to seeking refuge in a shelter may include a private therapist, taking a vacation, or a stay in a hotel. The latter are options for more affluent women, who can thus hide their turmoil from the official statistics. These data do not say that women from rural areas are not abused. A more plausible explanation could be that rural women may not have easy access to shelters. Shelter statistics either totally omit or underemphasize the racial or ethnic characteristics of their clients. Moreover, there is a lot of speculation about whether immigrant women feel comfortable using shelters (OAITH, 1996).

Despite the aforementioned methodological drawbacks, shelter statistics do provide a unique window into intimate partner abuse. Using statistical information from shelters, MacLeod (1980: 1) has estimated that one in ten women in Canada are subject to some form of intimate abuse. Although this estimate was considered to be unrealistically high at the time, and methodologically questionable for the above-stated reasons, more current findings both from the United States and Canada suggest that it may actually have been overly conservative.

In 1999, the Canadian Centre for Justice reported findings from all existing Canadian shelters (Juristat, 1999). According to its report, there were 470 shelters in Canada, the majority being in Ontario, Quebec, and British Columbia, in that order. Between 1997 and 1998, these shelters served a total of 90,792 people (47,962 women and 42,830 children). Thirty-six per cent of the residents were between the ages of 25 and 34. Women aged 35 to 44 (26%) formed the second-largest category. Most women (56%) had their children with them (Juristat, 1999: 6). Another interesting observation in the report was that the majority of shelter stays were short, but women were likely to have stayed in a shelter more than once. This is a problem that reflects the tendency of women to return to their abusers without being able to secure either a behavioural or an attitudinal change in their partners. Thus, both the probability of more violence and the probability of returning to a shelter are high. What also contributes to this revolving door of shelter use is the decline in social safety networks in this era of conservatism and fiscal restraint, as I discussed above. Women who have a hard time securing alternate, affordable, and adequate housing for themselves and their children may be particularly vulnerable to returning to their abusive partners. Their return then sets in motion the vicious cycle of more abuse, and it may culminate in future shelter stays (OAITH, 1998).

Survey Findings and Problems with Standardized Conflict Tactics Scale

In Chapter 1, I touched upon the difficulties related to the CTS. It is now time to revisit the difficulties with quantification of abuse in an in-depth manner. The CTS was developed by researchers from the University of New Hampshire, and it remains the most frequently used tool of measurement in the family violence field (Gelles and Straus, 1979, 1988; Straus, Gelles, and Steinmetz, 1980). The instrument defines violence in gender-neutral terms 'as an act carried out with the intention or perceived intention for causing pain or injury to another person' (Gelles and Straus, 1979: 554). In its original form, the instrument lists eight violent acts, in a presumed ascendance of their severity. The items are: (1) throwing something; (2) pushing, grabbing, or shoving; (3) slapping; (4) kicking, biting, or hitting; (5) hitting or trying to hit with something; (6) beating up; (7) threatening with a knife or a gun;

and (8) using a knife or a gun. Respondents (both sexes) are asked whether any of these have happened to them within an identified span of time (e.g., last year or last five years, ever). The introduction to the scale never uses the term 'violence,' instead couches the issue as a routine form of 'conflict resolution' among intimates. Again, in its original form, the CTS does not take into account either the context (e.g., who hit whom first or whether the act was an offensive or a defensive one), sexual predatoriness, or the consequences of the injury (e.g., a slap may leave a bruise or break a jaw requiring hospitalization). The original CTS does not measure the frequency of abuse either, thus potentially leaving chronic abuse of women undifferentiated from a random hit or slap (Currie, 1998; Kelly, 1997).

What are some of the consequences of using CTS-type scales? Studies using the original version of the CTS have systematically shown a symmetry between men's and women's violence against one another. Inadvertently, these findings have given ammunition to traditionalists and to anti-feminists who want to ignore or grossly minimize violence against women as a social problem. Revised versions of the scale, which are slightly more context specific (Gelles and Strauss, 1988) and which include additional items, have done little to reverse the original weaknesses. Findings with the revised scale have also led to observations of symmetry between male and female partners. Disturbing terms such as 'equal combatants' have emerged as a result of CTS findings that are designed to count and aggregate the reported incidents. When the context-sensitive version of the scale is used, however, Gelles and Straus (1988) report that three-quarters of the women who use violence do so in self-defence. Moreover, women are more likely to be seriously hurt as a result of their partners' violence. It seems, then, that violence among intimates is far from symmetrical, and men and women are hardly equal combatants (see Kelly, 1997, and Propper, 1997, for detailed discussions of the CTS measures). When findings about killing of spouses are taken into account, what becomes obvious is that the vast majority of women who kill their spouses do so in self-defence, whereas the majority of men who kill their spouses do so in a premeditated way. Yet careless or blatantly anti-feminist use of the 'symmetry' findings has usually omitted the more complex interpretations of a scale that is biased towards decontextualized acts and degenderized use of aggression.

Surveys of the CTS type have many problems with validity, especially in terms of the arbitrary rank-ordering of the severity of acts, the omission of a long list of other acts that may be just as abusive, and disregarding the context or the consequences of abuse (Kelly, 1997). Nevertheless, surveys are quite powerful mechanisms for generating data from large, generalizable, national samples. A quick perusal of some of the key findings from representative samples suggests that abuse rates reported for the year preceding the survey range from 24.5 per cent (Brinkerhoff and Lupri, 1988) to 2 to 3 per cent (GSS, 2000; VAWS, 1993). The majority of studies report rates of abuse in the last year to be between 10 and 15 per cent (Kennedy and Dutton, 1989; Smith, 1987; Straus and Gelles, 1990; Straus, Gelles, and Steinmetz, 1980, 1986). However, when we look at rates of ever having been abused by a partner, we generally find a much higher and a more stable percentage. In a national study carried out on 12,300 women, the Violence Against Women Survey (VAWS, 1993) reports 29 per cent, while Smith's (1987) finding on 604 currently or formally married women is even higher (36.5%). Data from the most recent General Social Survey (GSS, 2000) show that an estimated 690,000 women (and 549,000 men) had experienced at least one incident of violence in the previous five-year period.

Another interesting observation in the VAWS (1993) findings is the frequency of victimization. Thirty-five per cent of ever-married women report one incident of abuse, 22 per cent report two to five incidents, 9 per cent report six to ten incidents, and 32 per cent report eleven or more incidents. The shockingly high proportion of women (41%) who have suffered violence from a former partner report 11 or more incidents of such violence (VAWS, 1993). In the more recent GSS (2000), 65 per cent of assaulted women stated that they were victimized more than once. Twenty-six per cent were victimized more than ten times, again indicating a slight decline since 1993.

Other findings point out that approximately 10 per cent of women who report abuse claim that the abuse was severe (Smith, 1987; VAWS, 1993). Younger women and women in common-law relationships report both more frequent and more severe abuse (GSS, 2000).

Woman Abuse during and after Termination of Intimate Relationships

Violence as a Precursor in Divorce Statistics

After conducting in-depth interviews with divorced women, Kurz (1996; also see Kurz, 1998; Jacobson and Gottman, 2001; Sev'er, 1997)

concluded that separation and divorce are times of heightened vulnerability for women. Kurz interprets this connection to be related to
men's desire to control their partners' decisions and behaviour. She
notes that any indication of independence on the part of the women
short-circuits the controlling tactics of abusive men or of men who are
prone to be abusive. What can be more threatening to a controlling
man than his partner's decision to leave?

In Canada, divorce statistics prior to the 1985 Divorce Act provide
one of the most visible links between violence and the break-up of
legal marriages. Under the 1968 Divorce Act, physical and mental cru-
elty categories accounted for 60 per cent of all alleged grounds (see
Sev'er, 1992: 84–90 for an analysis). Of course, these statistics are open
to errors of underreporting because of fear and shame, as well as the
availability of no-fault categories such as a three-year waiting period
before the liberalization of the Divorce Act in 1985. The actual link
between divorce and abuse may even be higher than the percentage
suggests since most women (as many as three-quarters) are reluctant to
report their victimization (Rodgers, 1994). As mentioned earlier, on
average, a woman is assaulted thirty-five times before she contacts the
police (Bain, 1991: i). Thus, one can assume that this underreporting
also mars the validity of divorce statistics.

In the most current GSS (2000), termination of relationships was
again shown to be a very strong predictor of violence. Twenty-six per
cent of men and women who have had contact with a former partner
reported having been beaten, 19 per cent sexually assaulted, 19 per
cent choked, and 17 per cent threatened with a gun. However, the violence committed against women was in more severe categories (e.g.,
they had been beaten or sexually assaulted) than the violence against
men (e.g., they had been kicked or hit).

Victimization Surveys and Homicide Data

Survey research provides more direct insights into the link between
separation and intimate violence against women. For example, an
Alberta study (Kennedy and Dutton, 1989) found that more than half
(approximately 55%) of separating or divorcing people reported physical violence, whereas the percentage among still-cohabiting partners
was lower (approximately 40%). Smith's (1990) and MacLeod's (1980)
findings also attest to the increased risk of victimization of women at
the time of separation (also see Canadian Panel, 1993; Fleury, Sullivan,

and Bybee, 2000; Kurz, 1993, 1996; Sev'er, 1997a; Wilson and Daly, 1993). Moreover, in a major national survey, approximately one of five women (19%) who reported violence by an intimate partner claimed that the violence occurred during or after separation. In one of three cases (35%), the severity of violence increased at the time of separation (Johnson, 1995; Rodgers, 1994; VAWS, 1993).

In my Introduction, I mentioned a woman who was attacked in a most brutal way while she was trying to break off a nine-year relationship. About 80 per cent of her body was burned when her estranged partner doused her with a litre of sulphuric acid. The irony in this case was that the partner had abducted her for a few hours in the previous week, but the woman had chosen not to report the incident to the authorities. What was also extremely unfortunate was that her 6-year-old son witnessed the attack as well as the corrosive disintegration of his mother's flesh (*Toronto Star*, 25 July 2000: A17). Although this may indeed be an extreme case, serious attacks against women who are trying to get out of relationships are very common (Ellis and DeKeseredy, 1997; Fleury, Sullivan, and Bybee 2000; Sev'er, 1997a, 1998).

In the most extreme situations, women are killed by their partners during or shortly after they separate (Campbell, 1992; Daly, 1992). In their analysis of Canada's homicide data between 1974 and 1992, Wilson and Daly (1994) report 1,435 cases where women were killed by their husbands. This translates to slightly more than 75 Canadian women each year. However, the risk of being murdered by a husband was not randomly distributed. In general, married women were nine times more likely to be killed by their spouses than by strangers, while separation presented a six-fold increase in risk to women in comparison with women who continued to reside with their partners. Wilson and Daly (1993; see also Gartner, Dawson, and Crawford, 2001) also draw our attention to the fact that the increased risk after separation occurs *despite* the estranged husband's decreased access to his former wife. Unfortunately, the coding of other types of long-term co-residing relationships is ambiguous, and thus the link between their dissolution and violence is less clear. For example, GSS (2000) reports that violence against common-law wives is more severe and more frequent than violence against wives in legal marriages. Could it also be the case that women dissolving common-law relationships are more vulnerable than women leaving formal marriages? We know that women are at a higher risk for violence in common-law relationships and that the dissolution of such relationships may also be more violent.

Crawford and Gartner (1992: 38, 44, 51, 57, 101) point out that although Canada's rate of woman killing is approximately half that of the rate in the United States (which they cite as the most violent developed society in the world), this should not obscure the parallel fact that the rate at which Canadian women are killed is about twice as high as the rates in most other developed countries. Until the early 1990s, although overall homicide rates – as well as the rate of husband killings by partners – had declined, the rate of women killed by their intimate partners had actually increased (Crawford and Gartner, 1992).

Crawford and Gartner (1992; also see Gartner, Dawson, and Crawford, 2001) also found that the *number one risk factor* in intimate homicides was separation. The most current GSS (2000) shows a slight decline in spousal murders, but whether this change is indicative of a new trend is not clear. The fact remains that between 1979 and 1998, 1,468 Canadian women were killed by their spouses, and this amounts to more than 75 women per year. Moreover, women are three and a half times more likely to be killed by a spouse than men are. Women under the age of 25 are found to be at the greatest risk of being the victim of spousal homicides (GSS, 2000). In the United States, every year approximately 1,500 hundred women are killed by their husbands, former husbands, or boyfriends, and the rate of male partner killings more closely approximates the rate of female partner killings (BJS, 1995).

In sum, whether shown through divorce statistics, general surveys, victimization studies, or intimate femicide statistics, the elevated risk of murder or violence that women face during or after separation is an irrefutable fact. To develop a better appreciation of the magnitude of the problem, I invite my readers to understand and appreciate the survival of the thirty-nine women in this study in light of the disturbing backdrop of the violence statistics.

Chapter Three

Theories about Violence against Women

Theories are sets of logically interrelated statements that attempt to order, describe, and explain the causes and consequences of personal, social, or other relevant events. Powerful theories also try to predict the occurrence of events before they happen. Their power is measured by the robustness of their predictions under as many varied conditions as possible. This means that theories are generally abstract and use the interrelationships among general concepts rather than concrete variables. The more abstract a theory gets, however, the less it can be applied directly to any phenomenon that needs to be explained. Conversely, the more concrete a theory gets, the less it can be applied to complex phenomena under different social conditions. Thus, the level of abstraction of a theory needs to be balanced very carefully if we want to understand the general conditions within which interpersonal violence against women takes place and how it is the same as or different from any other type of violence. Because violence against women is a narrowly focused social problem, it is difficult to find a theory that will explain just this type of violence and nothing else. Indeed, such a theory would be so concrete and so truncated that it would at best be only a model. Therefore, work in the area of violence against women in intimate relationships draws from more general theories that are related to psychological, social-psychological, or sociological fields of deviance and crime, but tries to apply their causal insights to the social problem at hand.

Psychological theories that look into deviance and crime are generally not gender-specific. They seek the causes of behaviour within the individual's traits and dispositions. General social-psychological theories are also not gender-specific. The latter seek the causes of violence within interpersonal interactions, modelling and imitation processes, and other types of learning. There are more recent and more gender-applicable variations of social-psychological theories that differentiate between what is learned and how it is learned. Sociological theories seek the roots of violence in the structure of the society and the functioning of its institutions. Critical and feminist versions of sociological theories highlight the interconnectedness between capitalism and patriarchy in establishing a fertile ground in which genderized power flourishes and is condoned. With this general overview in mind, it is now time to take a closer look at the causal sequences in violence suggested by different theories.

Non-feminist Explanations of General Violence

Individual Pathology Models

Individual pathology models of general violence gained prominence in the late nineteenth century through the medical efforts of Cesare Lombroso (1911). Lombroso's work is generally considered to be dismissive of social and structural conditions. Working as a physician at the Turin prison, Lombroso tried to link the physiological and individualistic characteristics of long-term inmates to their patterns of criminality, as if these characteristics were the causes of such criminality. Most inmates in the Turin prison actually died during incarceration as a result of a combination of factors such as long-term sentences and inhumane, dungeonlike prisons. Thus, Lombroso had a unique opportunity to conduct autopsies and often study the post mortem pathology reports of deceased inmates to augment the evidence for his physiologically based theory of criminality. Although his findings and generalizations have been repeatedly challenged, his quest to explain violence and criminality through intrapersonal characteristics is still alive and well among some theorists. Myths expressed through personal biases, folk tales, and popular media coverage also fuel the perception that there is something different, 'sick,' or in Lombroso's terms, 'atavistic' about those who perpetrate violence on others.

Indeed, there are many gender-neutral theories of violence that see violence against women as stemming from the personal weaknesses or failures of the male perpetrators. In other words, the roots of violence are sought in intrapersonal characteristics, shortcomings, or outright pathologies. Indeed, theories that look into explosive or antisocial personalities, aggression, and psychopathology are quite capable of explaining violence perpetrated by a few sick individuals like notorious serial killers (e.g., Son of Sam). Such theories, however, have very little explanatory power in understanding a widespread gendered phenomenon like men's violence in intimate relationships. Gelles and Straus (1988) inform us that only about 10 per cent of intimate violence against partners is the manifestation of some kind of clinical pathology of the abuser. This leaves approximately 90 per cent of the cases of wife or partner assault wanting a better explanation. Thus, intrapersonal theories of violence underemphasize or completely disregard structural factors such as distribution of power, wealth, and resources and some groups' historical disadvantage in relation to these resources (e.g., women, people of colour, or people with disabilities). Therefore, except in very rare cases where troubled men may hurt, maim, or kill their partners, psychological theories of violence are usually mute as to why so many men who do not seem to have any identifiable pathological traits repeatedly hurt their wives, girlfriends, lovers, partners, and even their own children or family friends (Bograd, 1988). From the Introduction, the reader will recall the gruesome murder in which Vilem Luft Jr stabbed his wife more than thirty times, shot four of his children at point-blank range, and then took his own life (*Toronto Star*, 7 July 2000). It was argued that Luft had been in therapy for severe depression (a pathology model explanation of his gruesome deeds). Even if that was the case, Luft did not attack his employers, neighbours or friends. As a matter of fact, the most vicious form of his attack (stabbing thirty times) was on his wife, while he reserved a quicker form of death for himself and his children. As it turns out, his wife was getting ready to leave him, suggesting the probability of a power and control explanation which I will introduce in the following pages.

Single-trait explanations such as alcohol or drug dependencies of the abuser are the most commonly used intrapersonal explanations of wife assault. When we look at cartoons, movies, television shows, novels, or even the printed news, it is easy to find depictions of close links between addictions and both general violence and violence against women. The bar-hopping Andy Capp, a widely popular cartoon character for decades, is an unabashed example of this link. In the cartoon, Andy's wife constantly nags Andy about his drunkenness, and Andy occasionally reverts to hitting and slapping to let his wife know that he is the boss. This link is also present in carefully conducted research, both in the United States and in Canada (Dugan and Hock, 2000: 21;

Flanzer, 1993; Jacobson and Gottman, 2001: 478–9; Johnson, 1996). For example, a large survey on a national Canadian sample showed that alcohol was involved in approximately 50 per cent of all violent relationships. Moreover, men who were heavy consumers of alcohol were six times more likely to assault their female partners (see Rodgers, 1994; Johnson, 1996). Although this link is not easily disputed, sociological studies also repeatedly show that alcohol consumption cannot be considered the cause of intimate partner abuse for very obvious reasons (Gelles and Straus, 1988):

- Not all men who drink abuse their partners.
- Abusive men do not abuse their partners each time they drink.
- Abusive men do batter their partners when they are not drinking.
- Some men who are non-drinkers also abuse their partners.
- Some alcoholics who stop drinking continue to abuse their partners.

None of these observations challenge the strong link between substance dependencies and the propensity for violence. As Jacobson and Gottman (2001) suggest, maybe there are intrapersonal flaws in men that push them to abuse drugs and alcohol as well as to abuse their wives or partners. Still, none of these findings proves that alcohol consumption causes violence.

Other intrapersonal theories of violence concentrate on creating a typology for abusers. One such psychological model classifies the victimizers as 'Cobras' and 'Pit Bulls' (Jacobson and Gottman, 2001). Cobras are men who are antisocial, cruel, egotistical, and take special pleasure from hurting a variety of people who they come in contact with. They exploit, hurt, and abuse women with no remorse, and they lack the capacity to empathize with others. Cobras are also seen as capable of severe forms of assault and even murder. One of the most striking characteristics about Cobras is their charismatic personalities, which make it much harder for women to leave them. Pit Bulls, on the other hand, confine their violence to their family members. They are jealous, possessive, and fear abandonment. Although it may be easier for women to leave Pit Bulls in the short run; in the long run, they may become more dangerous than the Cobras. As the authors argue, once Pit Bulls sink their teeth into their partners, it is extremely difficult to get them to let go (Jacobson and Gottman, 2001).

Other intrapersonal theories of violence have concentrated on the victims of violence rather than the perpetrators. The genesis of 'blaming the victim' theories stems from Freud's perception of women as 'masochistic,' emotionally immature, and deviant. The details of Freud's convoluted logic about women's psychosexual development fall outside the general outlook and orientation of this book. Nevertheless, given that his psychoanalytic views have had decades of influence on general perceptions and probably still exert their impact on stereotypical judgments, a short summary is in order.

First, what I have to emphasize is that Freud's theories were *not* about women. Women as mothers and socializers were presented as 'deficient' men, since men were the norm. Likewise, the developmental stages of girl children were an ad hoc category in Freud's longwinded theorizing about the most crucial stage in male children's lives. The phallic stage was presumed to play out between 4 and 6 years of age, and its resolution was hypothesized to determine the mental health and social adjustment of men. Despite Freud's general lack of understanding about and interest in women, he nevertheless made some damaging assertions about them. One such assertion is that little girls have an unconscious sexual desire for their fathers. Moreover, girls were purported to hold equally unconscious but equally strong aspirations for having children from their fathers. This was tied to women's recognition that they lacked penises. In attempting to fulfil their unconscious desires, Freud claimed that at least some women come up with fantasies about incestuous relationships and rape. What Freud probably did was twist the reality of instances of incest that his female patients reported to him into something that these women conjured up, or worse, were guilty of. In his view, 'normal' women were those who could transform their desire for their fathers into desire for another man and a desire to have a male child from him. In either case, women were seen as weaker and less trustworthy than men in psychological development and morality. Ironically, strong women were also seen as maladjusted and as taunting and 'castrating' the men in their lives. In recent years, there has been a disturbing resurrection of these damaging ideas cloaked as a questioning of the legitimacy of accusations made by victims of incest (for details; see Kelly and Radford, 1998; Russell and Bolen, 2000; Steed, 1994).

In the 1960s, psychoanalytic ideas about women's masochism were applied to women who were battered and/or raped. Rather than being seen as victims of men's aggression, women were seen as 'controlling' and 'castrating,' in other words, the engineers of their own demise. The following are short excerpts from what was considered to be a successful psychiatric intervention into a man's overdependence on alcohol and violence towards his wife: 'He took it as confirmation that she had been the "cause" of his behaviour; she felt that it was because she was learning how to "handle" his behaviour. We [therapists] felt that the initial improvement was due to the venting of the wife's hostility and manipulative behaviour out of the marriage, taking pressure off the husband ... The essential ingredient seems to us to be the need both husband and wife feel for periodic reversal of roles; she to be punished for her castrating activity; he to re-establish his masculine identity' (Snell, Rosenwald, and Robey, 1964: 109–10; also see Pleck, 1987, for a review).

Other researchers argue that women who were battered were likely to be promiscuous (Gayford, 1975) or trying and hostile (Faulk, 1977), again suggesting that there was something terribly wrong with the behaviour or the morals of the victims themselves.

An innocent spin-off of the Freudian victim-blaming can be found in assertions in the 1970s about 'learned helplessness' (Walker, 1979a, 1979b). In a nutshell, Lenore Walker argues that finding the roots of violence against women in the shortcomings or deviance of the woman herself was misguided or insufficient, which reflected her feminist concerns. Instead, she claims, the lack of will, moral conviction, or pathology that the abused women demonstrate may be the result of severe abuse that they have endured, but not its cause. Walker observes that women do not like abuse and very rarely provoke it, thus dispelling explanations based upon women's masochism. On the surface, then, Walker's assertions appear to have moved the discussion about women abuse light-years ahead of the more judgmental assertions about women's moral failure of the Freudian era. However, her emphasis on 'learned helplessness' has not moved the focus away from intrapersonal factors to those that are socially and structurally determined. It has also contributed, albeit inadvertently, to the oversimplified view of women as dependent, childlike, and lacking agency or initiative of their own. In short, Walker's (1979a, 1979b) learned helplessness proposition have contributed to a sociology of victimization and a social interventionism in the form of simple protectionism rather than demanding a social-structural change.

The dangers of the types of intrapersonal assertions discussed above are obvious. First, by either blaming the victim or by seeing her as a total victim, they direct the social gaze away from the perpetrators. They may even attempt to switch the roles by depicting the abusers as victims of their wives' 'castrating' behaviour. Second, by concentrating on women's own weaknesses, whether real or imagined, they create new or fuel existing negative stereotypes. Third, by personalizing the problems, they remove the need to challenge the social and structural aspects of violence, especially violence against women. The status quo is never challenged. Fourth, they impede any serious social or structural remedies to violence as a social problem by concentrating on intrapersonal dimensions. In short, we need to take into account theories of violence that go beyond intrapersonal factors and must seek the causal explanations of violence elsewhere, namely, in interpersonal, social, and structural realms (DeKeseredy and MacLeod, 1997: 34–5).

Social-Psychological Theories

Social learning theories are also gender-neutral in approach and make the argument that aggression and violence are learned behaviours. They search for the causes of violence in the interaction of individuals with their immediate surroundings and significant others and in the rewards and punishments they attain in engaging in certain types of behaviour. The classic social learning models date back to Bandura's (1973) ingenious studies with children. After watching videotapes of adult models hitting blow-up dolls, children were found to closely imitate the aggressive behaviours they had watched. Imitation was more frequent and more complete if these adult models were shown to get away with or get rewarded for their aggressive actions. Bandura's insights have been somewhat successfully applied in efforts to shield children from exposure to television violence.

With regards to violence, early results from large surveys show that learning is gender-specific. For example, Gelles (1979) observed that women who experience violence as children are more likely to become victims of partner violence in their adult lives. Male child witnesses of violence are also shown to have a higher propensity to become abusers themselves. Buttressed by such results, the intergenerational transmission theory (Levinson, 1989) was formulated. It is a variation on social learning theories and attempts to show the gendered learning processes in intimate abuse situations. According to the theory, male children who may have been targets of parental abuse in their childhood or who may have seen their fathers abuse their mothers are predicted to be inclined to repeat these patterns of violence when they reach adulthood. In line with the same logic, female children who have been violated as children or who have seen their mothers victimized may turn out to be either abusers themselves (e.g., child abuse) or passive victims (Scully, 1990). Thus, intergenerational transmission is extremely important when one considers that children witness violence against their mothers in 40 per cent of violent marriages (Rodgers, 1994: 1; also see Juristat, 1999; OAITH, 1998; Ney, 1992; Wolfe, Zak, and Wilson, 1986). Women whose fathers-in-law are violent report more frequent and more severe abuse from their partners than women with non-violent fathers-in-law (Rodgers, 1994; VAWS, 1993; also see Egeland, 1993, for history of abuse as a risk factor).

Children, especially (but not exclusively) female children, experience violence themselves. For example, in a recent national Canadian survey, 50 per cent of the female respondents reported that they had experienced at least one incident of sexual molestation before they had reached the age of 16 (Canadian Panel, 1993). According to a recent report, 60 per cent of all assaults in Canada were committed against girls, one-third of them committed by close family members (Pottie and Levett, 1998). If intergenerational transmission of violence is true, the future implications of these findings will be bewildering. In separate studies, Reppucci and Haugaard (1993) and Wolak and Finkelhor (1998; also see Bagley and King, 1991; Fantuzzo et al., 1991; Fantuzzo and Mohr, 1999; Jacobson and Gottman, 2001; Jaffee, Wolfe, and Wilson, 1990; Russell and Bolen, 2000; Zima, Bussing, and Bystritsky, 1999) conservatively estimate that 10 to 11 per cent of America's female children are subjected to some form of sexual assault and abuse. Levinson's (1989) theory suggests that such transmission of violence is vertical (violent fathers and sons, victimized mothers and daughters).

A more sophisticated application of learning theories focuses on male peer support (Godenzi, DeKeseredy, and Schwartz, 2000). It highlights the intragenerational or horizontal transmission of violence (violent peers, subcultures of violence; see Baldwin and Cain, 1980; Bowker, 1983). For example, DeKeseredy (1988, 1989, 1990) has shown how male peers cultivate unrealistic expectations among themselves, especially in stressful interpersonal situations. DeKeseredy's work shows how peers may actually push men to develop standards of hurtful, degrading, and destructive interaction patterns in dealing with female partners. Peers may also reward those who act according to the peer culture and punish those who deviate from such macho expectations (also see DeKeseredy and MacLeod, 1997: 37–40 and Godenzi, DeKeseredy, and Schwartz, 2000). There is substantial support for male peer support models, especially in youthful groups such as college students (DeKeseredy 1988, 1989, 1990; DeKeseredy and Kelly, 1993).

On the other hand, there are legitimate questions about causality in learning theory arguments. Kaufman and Zigler (1993) argue that although there are numerous studies that support the intergenerational transmission of violence thesis, a more diligent analysis of these findings shows that there are also many mediating factors. Some of these mediating factors may be biological, others socioeconomic. Other challenges to the intergenerational transmission hypothesis also exist. For example, although a large proportion of abusive men were either witnesses to or victims of violence in their childhood, an even larger proportion of those children do not become abusive towards their mates. Moreover, some men who were never abused nevertheless become abusers. As Dobash and Dobash (1979) explain, some people who observe or experience violence may learn how horrible violence is and thus do not engage in it, while others may learn how to become abusers. A woman respondent in the Dobash and Dobash study explains (1979: 154): 'It's had the opposite effect on the boys. It's had the effect I'd hoped for ... They're just normal blokes. They never have any trouble. They would not hurt anyone ... I've a great satisfaction in knowing that all the time I did spend trying to teach them the things that their father should have taught them. I've won in the end.'

Feminist Explanations of Women's Sexual and Reproductive Control and Violence towards Women

There are numerous feminist explanations of men's violence towards women and intimate partners (Dobash and Dobash, 1979; Okun, 1986; Yllö and Bograd, 1988). These theories converge to seek the roots of violence in social structures without disregarding the confounding role of interpersonal or intrapersonal processes. What is emphasized is the central role of the unequal and gendered distribution of power and resources, a differentially valued division of labour and a patriarchal system that fuels and protects these inequalities. Feminists underscore the fact that even men who do not directly harass, abuse, or otherwise subjugate women benefit from the status quo in which women's chances and choices are compromised. Thus, in feminist explanations, gender, power and control triangulation determines relations in work, politics, law, health, and education, as well as the domination patterns within coupled relationships.

Traditional Marxism

According to Marx and Engels, the roots of women's subjugation can be traced to men's patriarchal attempt to control women's sexuality and reproduction. This subjugation followed the structural changes in the society, especially changes in the material conditions such as the accumulation of wealth and advent of private property. In his exceptionally insightful (and controversial) analysis, Engels (1993) argued that gendered relations were balanced in primitive hunting-and-gathering societies. If and when any deviation from this general balance occurred, it was in women's favour (i.e., matrilineal or matriarchal) because of their advantaged position in relation to their offspring. However, when rudimentary technology as well as knowledge about farming and domestication of animals allowed agrarian settlements, the accumulation of wealth became a social preoccupation. As a consequence of their physical strength and the skills developed in times of hunting wild animals, men were considerably more advantaged in these new agrarian settings. They accumulated wealth, and they wanted to make sure to pass it on to their legitimate offspring. There is a long lapse between the sexual act and childbirth, and in the absence of biological knowledge or technological skills, the only way to assure paternity was to control the sexual behaviour of women. Engels also argued that women themselves colluded in the transformation of multiplicity of sexual partners to a monogamous situation. In this transformation, 'the overthrow of mother right was the *world historical defeat of female sex.* The man took command in the home also; the woman was degraded and reduced to servitude; she became the slave of his lust and a mere instrument for the production of children' (Engels, 1993: 120–1, emphasis in original).

According to Engels, the process of industrialization and the ensuing accumulation of capital have not been kind to women either. In his view, the practice of monogamy and the equality it connotes is nothing but a sham, because monogamy 'clearly reveals the antagonism between the man and the woman expressed in the man's exclusive supremacy' (1993: 131). In capitalism, marriages among the wealthy are merely a contract to preserve capital and to ensure its smooth and undiluted transmission across generations. Moreover, bourgeois law makes sure that capital remains intact by monitoring work relations and inheritance (1993: 135). For women, marriage is like prostitution, where she 'only differs from the ordinary courtesan in that she does not let out her body on piece-work as a wage-worker, but sells it once and for all into slavery' (1993: 134). In short, in the intergenerational transmission of wealth and power within a capitalist system, women are seen as mere vessels. The capitalist machine also exploits women's nurturing proclivities by making sure that they recondition men each night after a gruelling day of labour (Seccombe, 1980). Engels believed the salvation of women lay in their full participation in the labour force. 'The emancipation of women will only be possible when women can take part in production on a large, social scale, and domestic work no longer claims anything but an insignificant amount of her time' (Engels, 1993: 221).

In these challenging arguments, violence is not directly addressed, although general exploitation and control are. Moreover, it remains to be explained why women's increased participation in the labour market has not ameliorated their subjugation and eliminated violence against them. For better insights on the latter, we will now visit other feminist theories.

Radical Feminism

Radical feminism is a response to some of the weaknesses of more traditional Marxism: more specifically the weakness of not putting due emphasis on a global pattern of patriarchy. Radical feminists define patriarchy as a universal propensity of men to dominate women and they see patriarchal control of women as *the* most important subjugation. See, for example, Fox's critical and insightful article (1988) on different conceptualizations of patriarchy. Moreover, patriarchy is seen as invasively institutionalized within cultural rules and practices and openly manifested in all aspects of everyday life (O'Brien, 1981). The worst manifestation of patriarchy is seen as being centred around the control of sexuality and reproductive powers of women (Brownmiller, 1975). Thus, radical feminism differs from a strictly materialistic analysis of power relations in a number of ways. First, radical feminists claim that patriarchy preceded the advent of private property and continues to exist in all realms of micro- and macro-gendered relations regardless of wealth, property, or historical period (O'Brien, 1981). According to Charlotte Bunch (1975: 37), men 'conquered' women in prehistorical times. 'We do not exactly know how this conquest took place, but it is clear that the original imperialism was male over female: the male claiming the female body and her service as his territory (or property).'

Second, radical feminists see marriage and the family as 'twin pillars' of all patriarchal cultures (Dworkin, 1989). This is quite different from the Marx and Engels focus on the relations between those who own the means of production and those who sell their labour power in exchange for wages. Third, radical feminists link the subjugation of women to their childbearing, not to their relation to capital (O'Brien, 1981). Fourth, radical feminists do not see the 'state' as mostly a benign power protecting and serving the accumulation of capital (Tucker, 1978). Instead, they see state authority as masculine authority actively and forcefully defending male rights and privilege (Brownmiller, 1975; MacKinnon, 1982; Russell, 1989). In Dworkin's (1989: 18) words, 'We see the joining together of politics and morality, coupled to produce their inevitable offspring – the oppression of women based on ... a rampant sexual fascism.' Fifth, radical feminists disagree with Engels's suggestion that full employment is a sufficient condition to emancipate women. Instead, salvation is deemed possible if and only if the chains of traditional, heterosexist marriage are broken down. A revolutionary change in reproduction, which currently enslaves women, is also considered a must (Firestone, 1970; O'Brien, 1981). Others prefer establishing strictly female units and communities to countervail male power and to shelter women from male domination (Bunch, 1975; Dworkin, 1974, 1989; MacKinnon, 1982; Rubin, 1975).

Sixth, radical feminists recognize a dimension of patriarchal force that is totally omitted in materialistic analyses of gender relations. They argue that in times of social change and upheaval (examples might be economic upheaval, ethnic wars, or globalization), patriarchal forces will tighten their control on women to re-establish historical male privileges (e.g., increased violence against intimate partners around economic slumps or mass rapes during ethnic wars such as Bosnia, Chechnya, Kosova, and Rwanda, see MacKinnon, 1993b), or to eliminate possible competition from women (e.g., violence inflicted on women workers in Mexican border towns where U.S. multinationals have set up shop to exploit cheaper labour; see *Toronto Star*, 23 May 1999: B1–B5). Contrary to Engels's thesis, radical feminists claim that social change such as an increased female participation in the labour force in traditionally patriarchal societies may increase violence against women rather than lead to their emancipation. This does not mean that radical feminism is against social change. It merely highlights the costs of social change and upheaval under the patriarchal hegemony.

Socialist Feminism

Other feminists argue that both Marx and Engels's theories and the exclusive reproductive labour focus of the radical feminists fall short of developing a theory that fully accounts for the interconnectedness of productive and reproductive activity (Flax, 1976; Gravenhorst, 1988; Mitchell, 1973). In socialist feminism, both the patriarchal and class components of the social order are considered to be 'inextricably intertwined' in understanding any social problem with the social order, including problems such as violence against women (Jaggar, 1983). For example, according to Mitchell (1973), women's problems can be analysed in terms of four focal points:

1 Production of goods and services to meet basic human needs
2 Sexuality and sexual domination
3 Reproduction as an insurance for the continuation of the species
4 Gender socialization, especially in terms of the division of labour relating to production, reproduction, and sexuality

As in traditional Marxism, socialist feminists see the importance of class in determining men's propensity towards violence. Men who occupy the lowest rungs of the economic system, men who have very little power or say in the workplace, or who are cast outside of the economic system (the unemployed) may indeed have a much higher propensity for conjugal violence. Like radical feminists, socialist feminists see the interaction of patriarchal patterns in the forms of male camaraderie. On the one hand, they see male bonding among equally oppressed men (such as all male labourers, lowest-rung fighting soldiers, drinking buddies, male gangs, or fraternities). Not only are such men likely to be socialized into discerning violence as a legitimate form of action, but they are also likely to subscribe to the belief that men are superior to women (Schwartz, 1988). Men's perceptions of the superiority of men and the vulnerability that they personally feel in a capitalist and imperialist system that subjugates them are seen as an explosive mix for the lower classes. On the other end of the continuum, privileged men who occupy much higher rungs in the society may not be as prone to committing more blatant forms of sexism, because they feel much more secure about their own positions in the system. Nevertheless, they are also in power positions that allow them to preserve the continuation of the historical privileges for all men, which legitimizes some of their own privilege (such as male lawmakers, judges, clergy, politicians, and police).

Unlike traditional Marxists, socialist feminists do not see the employment of women as a solution to all their power disadvantages, although they see economic independence for women as one of the key factors. Socialist feminists acknowledge that both private and public spheres pose problems for women. For example, layers of inequalities in pay, promotions, child care, and housework issues need to be resolved before women's work can bring them on par with their male counterparts. Unlike radical feminists, socialist feminists do not see the dismantling of the family or very intimate relationships as a solution. Instead, they seek a commitment by the state to relieve some of the problems families (especially women) face, in the form of universal access to child care, generous maternity leave benefits, and equal pay for work of equal value for women who work for pay. They also seek societal recognition and support for the motherwork of all women.

Other variations of feminism (such as liberal, cultural, or eco-feminism) also focus on the disadvantaged status of women. However, their foci and insights are more directly relevant to social issues other than to intimate violence.

Power and Control Model of Violence

There is also a very specific model to explain physical and sexual violence against women, although it is not abstract enough to be considered a theory per se. It is a sophisticated model of physical and sexual violence. Through groundbreaking work known as the Duluth project, Pence and Paymar (1993) propose this conceptual model to explain the interrelated dimensions in the cycle of violence. Since its inception, the model as well as the general insights from the Duluth project have been widely accepted and used in treatment programs with abusers (Dobash et al., 1995). According to the model, physical and sexual abuse of women are products of a vicious cycle. The hub of the cycle is power and control (see Figure 3.1). The model suggests that power-seeking men use intimidation, emotionally abuse and degrade their partners, isolate them, minimize their complaints, or blame them as the instigators of their own demise. They also use children against their partners or hurt them as additional targets to get back at the women. Abusive men also benefit from established and unquestioned forms of male privilege, including sexual demands and control of

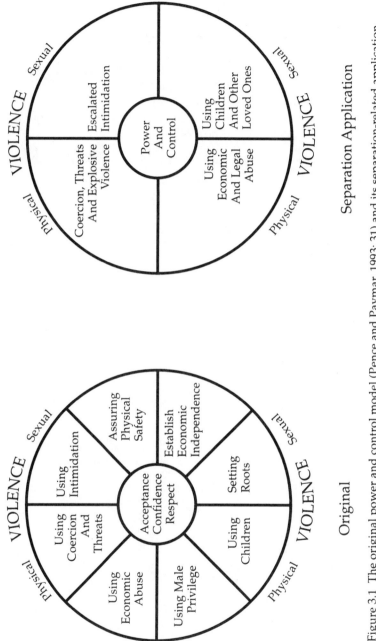

Figure 3.1 The original power and control model (Pence and Paymar, 1993: 31) and its separation-related application (Sev'er, 1997: 574).

resources. They use coercion and threats to get their way and silence their partners.

What the power and control model highlights is the systematic nature of the web of abuse as opposed to seeing abuse as separate, isolated outbursts. The model has been supported by a vast number of studies, and with slight modifications, it has been applied to violence in separation and divorce situations (Sev'er, 1997a). Dasgupta (1998) has expanded the power and control model to cover violence against women among ethnoreligious minorities.

Chapter Four

Methods of the Study

This book is based on findings from face-to-face interviews with thirty-nine survivors of partner abuse and violence. When applicable, results from an entirely different study, a five-year (1995–9) collection and content analysis of articles published in the *Toronto Star* on violence against women will be used to augment the discussion (Sev'er, 2001). First, I will explain the methods used for the interviews with the thirty-nine survivors of violence that form the basis of this book. Then, I will highlight some methodological points about the study based on newspaper articles. The analysis of the newspaper articles is used sparsely to add a backdrop to the major themes that emerge from the interviews.

Participants

Between February 1996 and June 1997, I conducted interviews with eleven survivors of partner violence to test the feasibility of the interviewing techniques and the interviewing instruments (see Interviewing Schedule in Appendix A). Between July 1997 and December 1998, I conducted an additional twenty-eight interviews. I sought participants from various sources. For example, notices were posted on local women's centres and women's health centres. Oral announcements about the study were made in large first-year introductory sociology courses held at the University of Toronto. I also used a snowball technique of asking those who had already participated in the study if they knew about other women 'who may have experienced similar problems with their former partners.' On five Sundays in the second half of 1998, advertisements to recruit participants were placed in a local newspaper (see Appendix B).

Procedures

At all times, the study was presented as voluntary and the strictly confidential nature of participation was highlighted (see Recruitment Letter, Appendix C). The notice calling for participants included the telephone number of the principal researcher. Prospective participants were assured that only the researcher had direct access to this phone number. Participants were contacted only after they took the initial step of contacting the researcher by telephone. Participation was completely voluntary, and the participants were clearly informed of their various rights about not answering questions they felt uncomfortable with and/or terminating the interview whenever they chose. Participants were urged to choose a pseudonym for themselves for their own privacy and safety. Three names (Lisa, Nancy, and Susan) were chosen more than once. Despite the redundancy, this small degree of 'participant control' over choosing a name for herself was deemed important in allowing the participants to feel comfortable in the initial stages of the interview about a very difficult topic. Therefore, any name the participant chose was accepted regardless of how many times the same name may have been chosen before. However, to differentiate between the repeated pseudonyms, later on, I assigned names of cities in Ontario as last names to these individuals. Thus, the first Lisa became Lisa Algoma, the second became Lisa Kingston, the third became Lisa London, and so on, in coding and analysing the data. Just like the pseudonyms, the city names were chosen for convenience and do not mean that these women were from the mentioned cities.

Participants were also asked to sign a 'consent' form prepared according to the stringent requirements of the Research Ethics Review Committee of the University of Toronto (see Consent Form in Appendix D and Cover Letter in Appendix E). Most participants signed the consent form with their 'pseudonyms,' but a few felt comfortable enough to use their real names. All participants provided an accurate telephone number.

Participants were asked for permission to audiotape the interviews (see Appendices C and D). All participants were assured that only the principal researcher and her carefully selected research assistants would have access to these tapes. Although all participants gave their consent for taping the interviews, the tapes turned out to be more problematic than had originally been anticipated. This issue will be discussed in the following section about problems with methodology.

Instead, what proved to be most helpful were the detailed notes taken during the interviews.

All participants were offered $25 to compensate them for their time and transportation. Interestingly, only thirty-one of the thirty-nine participants accepted this money. This observation is quite unique when we consider that most of the participants were not affluent. Those who refused the fee insisted that they wanted to help other women. Some claimed that they were happy to have someone listen to their problems without 'judging them' as their reason for not wanting the money. One participant insisted that I forward her fee to a local women's centre, which I did. I think many women wanted me to believe that they were trying to help other women and felt uncomfortable accepting money for their altruism. Another reason for rejecting the modest reimbursement may have been that the participants had to sign a receipt to get paid. Although they were allowed to sign their 'pseudonyms' (real phone numbers were required), they still may have felt uncomfortable accepting payment. They may also have felt that the fee I was able to pay was quite small.

Place of Interviews

At all times, the utmost care was given to the safety and the comfort of the participants, and to their preferences for the time and place of interviews. Approximately equal numbers of interviews were carried out in my office, either at the suburban campus or downtown, or the participant's home. Participants with small children were the most likely to want the interview to take place in their own homes. I conducted only four interviews in my home.

Questions

The interviews had a number of closed-ended questions to establish some status and demographic characteristics of the participants. Of these, the most noteworthy are the age of the participant; current marital status; number of marriages and/or number of common-law relationships; their duration; and number, age, and sex of their biological and non-biological children. Additional closed-ended questions were directed towards the education and previous and current work patterns of the participants. Where applicable, similar demographic information about their parents was also gathered. Aside from providing a detailed demographic profile of the participants and their families of origin and procreation, a reason for these questions was to help establish rapport between us.

In the interviews, race, ethnicity, and religious affiliation of the participants were not asked for. However, cases where participants referred to themselves as non-white or where they were of a visible minority group were recorded in a post-interview research note. These observations were analysed as a dichotomous white or non-white category. What needs to be immediately noted is that no woman from the far east or southeast Asia participated in this study. This is an interesting but not a surprising outcome. The few research findings that exist show unquestionably that violence against women from these portions of the world is rampant. Yet research also shows that women from these regions are particularly likely to remain silent about their predicament because of the strong patriarchal norms in their communities (Dasgupta, 1998; Dasgupta and Warrier, 1996; Huisman, 1996). Thus, the non-white attribution in this study covers only black or Hispanic women.

The major portion of the interviews was based on open-ended questions. Participants were asked about their relationship with their parents or guardians, their siblings, and their marital or common-law partners. The majority of the discussion was centred on the abusive partner(s), because some women had been in more than one violent relationship. Although the participants determined what and how much to reveal, probes were used to bring the discussion back to the abusive partner(s): type, frequency, and intensity of abuse; and the presence or absence of support systems (see Appendix A). Participants were asked about their experiences with the type and quality of support from family members, friends, police, shelters, and paralegal and legal agencies during their victimization ordeals. Of special interest was their effort to leave their abusive partners. The majority of respondents who had children were also asked about the impact of their partners' violence on their children. Throughout the interview, they were reminded about their right to terminate the interview whenever they chose.

The last portion of the open-ended questions asked about the women's insights into their own lives, if and how they have changed, what they would do differently, and what they would recommend to other women caught in abusive situations. Interviews ended by thanking the participants for their time and courage in participating and by again assuring them of the confidentiality of their responses. Respondents were asked whether they wanted to be informed about the findings of the study. The ones who expressed an interest received a compact summary of the findings (Appendix F).

Analysis

The demographic variables were entered into a database. Descriptive statistics such as frequencies, means, standard deviations, and the range for the pre-test and test participants were calculated and compared. Once it was established that the differences between the pre-test and test participants were mostly insignificant in terms of their demographic characteristics, these data were combined to generate descriptive statistics on the sample of thirty-nine.

The emphasis in this study, however, is not on the quantitative observations but on the qualitative analysis of the long interviews. For these, the data from the audiotapes were partially transcribed. The determination about what to transcribe was based on reading the handwritten notes immediately after each interview. During this crucial first reading, portions deemed particularly interesting or important in the interview were colour-coded. Where the tapes were not viable (see the part about difficulty with methods), the handwritten notes were analysed. Moreover, a short summary sheet for each interview was written and attached to the first page of the interview package. This summary sheet flagged the type and the approximate location of the crucial parts of the interview, including any disruptions (e.g., crying or interaction with children). These flags also eased the search for the complete text of the quotations that are frequently used to add the women's own voices to the unfolding of the findings reported in this book.

Pre-test Participants (N = 11)

Appendix G lists some general characteristics of the pre-test participants according to the alphabetical order of the pseudonyms they used. As the list indicates, the average age of the pre-test participants during the interview was 42.4 years (range 24–55), and the average duration of interviews was 2.4 hours (range 1.5–4.0). Nine of the eleven participants had married at least once (three of the nine twice). The mean age at first marriage was 20.7 years (range 17–27), and the average duration of the first marriage was eight years (range 1–17). Ten of the eleven participants reported at least one common-law relationship. These common-law arrangements may have preceded a marriage, turned into a marital relationship, been independent of marriage, or followed a marriage. Five of these ten reported two common-law relationships. The reported mean age at first common-law relationship was 25.9 (range 17–45), and the average duration of first common-law relationship was 3.8 years (range 1–9).

An analysis of the visible racial characteristics of the eleven participants reveals that three were non-white and eight were white. Their educational backgrounds were as follows. Two women had completed elementary school, two high school, four college, and two an undergraduate degree. One had a graduate degree (Master's). In general, the mothers of these women were less educated than the participants were. Three had attended or completed elementary school. Seven had finished high school, and one had finished college. Of the fathers, two had attended or completed elementary school, three had completed high school, and three had completed college. Two fathers had an undergraduate and one a graduate degree (Appendix G).

Of the eleven women, three were not employed at the time of the interview. Eight women had full-time or part-time employment. Of the eight, two had professional, five had skilled, and one had a semi-skilled occupation.

Together, ten of the eleven pre-test participants had a total of twenty-six children biologically related to them (mean 2.4, range 0–7).[1] The reported age for the oldest child was 33 years (mean 20.3) and the youngest child was a newborn (2 months old). The pre-test participants also had four children who were not biologically related to them. The oldest of these non-biological children was 26 years old, and the youngest was 14.

Test Participants (N = 28)

Appendix H lists some general characteristics of the test participants according to the alphabetical order of their pseudonyms. As the list

---

1 The fact that one of the participants (Amber) had seven children is a statistical outlier. This observation is capable of effecting the measures of central tendency (such as the mean) in a small sample.

indicates, the average age of the test participants during the interview was 37.1 years (range 21–51), and the duration of interviews was 2.2 hours (range 1.5–4.0). Twenty-five of the twenty-eight participants had married at least once (ten of them twice and three of them three times). The mean age at first marriage was 20 years (range 17–25), and the average duration of the first marriage was 5.3 years (range 1–14). Twenty-three participants reported at least one common-law relationship. These common-law arrangements may have preceded a marriage, turned into a marital relationship, been independent of marriage, or followed a marriage. Eleven of the twenty-three reported two and four of the twenty-three reported three common-law relationships. The mean age at first common-law relationship was 25.8 years (range 16–48), and the average duration of first common-law relationship was reported as 2.9 years (range 0–8).

An analysis of the visible racial characteristics of the twenty-eight test participants reveals that fourteen were non-white and fourteen were white. In terms of their formal education, the women were divided as follows: nine had completed elementary school, nine high school, five college, three an undergraduate, and one a graduate (Master's) degree. One other woman had taken a combination of college and university courses without obtaining a degree. Similar to the pre-test group, the mothers of these women were also less educated than the participants were. Ten had attended or completed an elementary school, ten high school, six college, and two had completed undergraduate university degrees. Of the fathers, seven had attended or completed an elementary school, ten high school, five each for college and undergraduate degrees, and one had taken numerous college and university courses without obtaining a degree (Appendix H).

Of the twenty-eight women, five were not employed at the time of the interview, three were full-time students, and twenty had full-time or part-time employment. Of the twenty, three had professional, four had skilled, eleven had semi-skilled, and one had a manual occupation. One respondent said she was working but did not clarify her type of employment.

In total, twenty-three of the twenty-eight participants had a total of forty-nine children biologically related to them (mean 1.7, range 0–4). The oldest child was 24 years old (mean 13.9) and the youngest was 3 years old at the time of the interview. The test participants also had seven children who were not biologically related to them. The oldest non-biologically related child was 20 years old, and the youngest was 8.

Total Study

As the above information attests, there are no systematic or significant differences in the general characteristics of the pre-test and test participants. The only noteworthy difference is in terms of the racial composition of the two groups (72.7% white vs 50% white). This, however, is not a very reliable measure in the first place, because the dichotomous coding was done after the interviews and was based on visual cues. As discussed earlier, race of the participants was never directly asked.

With the exception of less reliance on taping of the interview sessions, no changes were made to the general interviewing technique or procedures. Therefore, from now on, all the discussions will be based on results from a combined data (N = 39) of the pre-test and test participants. An alphabetical list of the combined sample appears in Appendix I. Characteristics of the combined sample are as follows.

The average age of the participants at the time of the interview was 38.6 years (range 21–55), and the duration of interviews was 2.3 hours (range 1.5–4.0). Thirty-four of the thirty-nine participants had married at least once (thirteen of them twice and three of them three times). The mean age at first marriage was 20.1 years (range 17–27), and the average duration of the first marriage was six years (range 1–17). Thirty-three participants reported at least one common-law relationship. These common-law arrangements may have preceded a marriage, turned into a marital relationship, may have been independent of marriage, or may have followed a marriage. Sixteen of the thirty-nine reported two, and four of the thirty-nine reported three common-law relationships. The mean age at first common-law relationship was 25.8 years (range 16–48), and the average duration of the first common-law relationship was reported as 3.2 years (range 0–9).

An analysis of the visible racial characteristics of the thirty-nine participants reveals that seventeen were non-white and twenty-two were white (43.6% vs 56.4%). Their formal education was as follows. Eleven women had completed elementary school, eleven high school, nine college, five undergraduate degrees, and two had graduate (Master's) degrees. One other woman had taken a combination of college and university courses without obtaining a degree. Mothers of these women were less educated than they were. Thirteen had attended or completed an elementary school, seventeen high school, seven college, and two undergraduate degrees. Of the fathers, nine had attended or completed elementary school, thirteen high school, eight college, seven an undergraduate degree, and one had a graduate degree. One father had taken numerous college and university courses without obtaining a degree.

Of the thirty-nine women, eight were not employed at the time of the interview, three were students, and twenty-eight had full-time or part-time employment. Of the employed women, five had professional, nine had skilled, twelve had semi-skilled, and one had a manual occupation. One did not sufficiently clarify the type of her employment.

In total, the thirty-nine participants had seventy-five children bio-logically related to them (mean number of children 1.92, range 0–7). The oldest child was 33 years old (mean age for the oldest child 15.8) and the youngest was 2 months old. The participants also had eleven children who were not biologically related to them. The oldest non-biologically related child was 26 years old, and the youngest was 8 at the time of the interviews.

Problems with Methods and Procedures of Interviews

Small Sample and Problems with Recruitment

It is quite obvious that the observations in this intensive work are con-strained by the relatively small size of the sample and its non-random nature. Despite a range of efforts including snowballing strategies, posted notices in women's centres and women's health centres, announcements in large university classrooms, and even paid ads in a local, bi-weekly newspaper, the number of volunteer participants in the study remained low. This is understandable because of the very sensitive subject matter, the continuation of society's traditional reluc-tance to address such intimate issues, and women's own reluctance (and maybe even fear and embarrassment) to share the intimate details of very hurtful aspects of their lives with a complete stranger.

In my mind, the most telling index of the double bind women may feel in participating in a study of this nature can be seen in the tele-phone calls the newspaper advertisements generated (see Appendix B). During the five weeks the advertisements appeared, I prepared and recorded a special message on a personal telephone line assuring women of the confidentiality of the study and expressing my apprecia-tion for their willingness to participate. I urged them to leave a number and either their real names or a pseudonym that I could refer to when I returned their calls. Interestingly, the ads generated numerous calls to this personal telephone line (138 in all). About a third of these calls were hang-ups (42). In a small number of the others (23), callers said they were responding to the ad in the paper, but did not leave any information to enable me to return their calls. I am not sure how many of those who did not leave their names constituted repeat callers among the 138 messages spread approximately over the five weeks that the newspaper ads ran.

Another group of women left numbers and names but were reluctant to talk to me or to make an appointment when I called them back. It was as if they had called on the spur of the moment, but then immediately changed their minds. Out of the 138 calls, twenty-one women showed a lot of interest in the study, made appointments to meet me either at my office or at my home, but then cancelled the interview a few hours before the scheduled time. Some did not cancel and did not show up to the interview at all. A few women left a name and a phone number, but I was unable to reach them although I tried many times. All in all, I was able to complete nineteen interviews from the 138 telephone calls that the newspaper advertisements generated (around 14% of the total number of calls). It is my contention that difficulties with the response rate reflect the extreme sensitivity of this topic combined with the difficulty in studying a non-captive sample of women (outside of the shelters). It is no wonder that the majority of research on violence against women is either based on shelter populations, phone surveys, or on secondary sources of data such as crime reports.

There are two additional outcomes of the newspaper ads that are not going to be included in this book but which nevertheless remain very important aspects of the methodological difficulty in participant recruitment. The first is the calls I received where nine different women gave me extremely detailed accounts of the violence they had endured at the hands of their former spouses or partners. Some told me about the violent behaviour of their current mate or male friend. They thanked me for doing this type of study. They expressed their fear, anger, frustration, and hurt. They said they would love to help other women avoid going through the pain they had endured. The longest of this type of a confessional telephone call lasted two and a half hours (equal to the average interview). Other confessional calls I answered ranged from twenty minutes to close to an hour. Two hung up in the middle of their confessions, which I interpreted to be in response to someone walking into the house or the room. I am not sure if the ones who hung up called me again. Despite their eagerness to talk, these phone volunteers did not make appointments for a face-to-face interview. It seems that all these women wanted was a non-judgmental channel for their intense isolation and hurt and someone to hear their sense of outrage. Their behaviour signals that it was not easy for these women to talk about their past experiences without risking some kind of judgment. They certainly did not want to talk in a face-to-face environment about the violence they have suffered, although they did want to talk over the phone. Since these nine callers did not sign consent forms and never told me their names or offer their phone numbers, I have not been able to use the telephone revelations as part of my research data. Nevertheless, their existence reinforces the need to tap into the frustrating life experiences of women who are not in shelters, a mammoth task that I tried to address in this study.

A second very interesting outcome of the newspaper ads was receiving calls from two separate men who had been sexually abused as children within religious institutional settings that had once served as their temporary custodians. I will call them John and Jim (one told me his real name). These men also talked for several hours, touching upon the type, severity, and frequency of abuse they suffered. More importantly, they wanted me to know how the childhood abuse affected their adult lives. John said that he had turned into an abusive person himself, exploiting anyone and everyone around him, mostly, but not exclusively, in sexual ways. He talked about his self-hatred and periods of suicidal depression. He talked about his hatred for the state (which he referred to as 'the pimp') for failing to protect him or to adequately compensate him and others like him for their trauma. Jim also talked about his self-hatred, self-destructive, and other-destructive tendencies (including numerous suicide attempts and physical assaults on others). He claimed to be one of the abused children from Mount Cashel, a very well-publicized former religious institution. After years of struggle, he and his fellow victims have managed to get some compensation from the government. In Jim's mind, however, the small settlement was like a slap in the face. He was certain that this embarrassingly small amount of money actually increased the suffering of his friends. He was not sure about where he fit in the continuum of self-destruction, but Jim insisted that without any meaningful help or intervention for the years of suffering, self-doubt, confused sexuality, and hatred, the money that was 'eventually thrown at them' had done nothing but increase their self-destructive behaviour. He mentioned drug and alcohol abuse and overdose, abuse of women and some children and at least one fatal auto accident (which he saw as a suicide).

Both of these male callers scorned me for limiting my study to the pain and suffering of women. In their minds, their own suffering was just as great, if not greater. However, both John and Jim thanked me for listening to them because they needed someone to hear them out. Out of the blue, Jim called a few weeks later and thanked me again. He told me that he was going to send me one of his friends who was an abused woman and gave me her name. However, to my knowledge, this woman never contacted me unless she contacted me under a different name. I never called women unless they contacted me first.

As interesting and insightful as these phone conversations were, and as genuine as they sounded, I had to exclude them from this book for two very obvious reasons. First, the callers did not give me any demographic information, and they certainly did not answer any of the driving questions of this work. The phone calls were long, detailed, but one-sided conversations. I did not ask questions, they talked and asked questions of me. Second, the callers did not give me their written consent.

Thus, this book is based on the thirty-nine completed interviews. Regrettably, an obvious outcome of the small sample is that the results are not generalizable to any known population of women who have been able to terminate their abusive relationships. Therefore, each individual in this study is a unique case, each voice a unique voice, and each tortured life a unique experience. Some of these women are still searching for answers that will work for them, and there are a few who seem confident that they have achieved personal growth through their past experiences. Despite the non-randomness and small size of the sample, I saw some strong threads that bind the experiences of the women together. My main goal is to weave these common threads so that a clearer tapestry of knowledge about women's survival of abusive partners will emerge. This book is meant to celebrate the lives and the sheer determination of the thirty-nine survivors without making any attempt to hide their ongoing difficulties and human frailties.

Difficulty with the Tapes

As already mentioned, recording of all interviews and transcription of the tapes were included in the original procedures of this study. However, taping the sessions proved to be less than practical in some cases, and transcribing the taped material also proved to be a difficult, if not an insurmountable task. Although all of the thirty-nine interviewees signed the official consent form, which includes permission to tape the interviews, a large portion of the tapes were either incomplete or mostly unusable for the following reasons:

- A number of interviewees actually asked me to turn off the tape recorder when they were talking about some of the intimate details of their violent relationships. In my judgment, this may have been because almost all interviewees chose to use a pseudonym at first, but then reverted to using the 'real' names of their perpetrators and children. The reader will better appreciate the unavoidability of this switch given that many women had multiple partners. Some had multiple abusers and numerous children. Switching back and forth from pseudonyms to real names became confusing for them (and for me), so most ended up using real names shortly after the start of the interviews. Although participants were assured of the safekeeping of the tapes, they may still have felt vulnerable in allowing their voices and names to be recorded on such a sensitive matter.
- At the request of the participants, roughly a third of all interviews were conducted in the participants' homes. These women mostly had small children they had to care for throughout the interview. The tape recorder had to be turned off and on many times to accommodate crying children, people coming to the door, and repeated phone calls. Noise from the television sets left on for the benefit of the children, or children's noise-making toys, or loud requests from them were problems for the quality of the recording. In a number of interviews, I did not even bother turning the tape back on after repeated interruptions.
- The quality of the tapes was also affected by the very soft, almost murmuring voices of some participants. Moreover, some women cried when they recalled their terrorizing ordeals, and a few women cried repeatedly and for a long time. The microphone of the simple portable recording machine I used for the interviews was not adequate in dealing with these trying situations.
- For the out-of-office interviews that went far beyond the expected two hours, there were two occasions when I ran out of tapes.

For these reasons, one of which reflects my own unpreparedness to deal effectively with the taping process, I have been able to make only selective use of the existing tapes, and that only for the purpose of some direct quotations that are scattered across this book. Except for this, only a small proportion of the tapes have been transcribed. Most material used in this book is based on intensive notes I took during the interviews and selected transcriptions from the tapes and handwritten notes.

Difficulty with the Emotional Content

In the formal process of becoming a research sociologist, the institutions of knowledge that oversee our professional development relentlessly teach us the desirability of 'rationality' and 'objectivity' in carrying out research. In the general social science as well as the sociological traditions, both of these terms often require putting a clear hierarchical distance between the researcher and the researched, between thought and emotion, between hard data and more subjective observations, and between knowledge and experience. Fortunately, this general insistence on undiluted objectivity has been challenged. Especially since the early 1970s, feminists and scholars in the areas of anti-racism have dismantled most of the rigidity and the superficiality of the research process that the more traditional social scientists have deemed essential. For example, feminist scholars have forcefully challenged the assumptions that masculinize the research process by giving disproportionate power to the researcher over the researched, by giving disproportionate advantage to reason over emotions, and by giving disproportionate attention to men and men's concerns over women and women's concerns (Eichler and Lapointe, 1985; Roberts, 1981; Spender, 1982; Stanley and Wise, 1983).

Because of its subject matter, this research was particularly emotional. First, let me express my deep gratitude to the women in my study who trusted me enough to display a kaleidoscope of pure emotion. Despite having worked with many thousands of people (whether graduate and undergraduate students, other research participants, colleagues, or staff), spanning more than two decades of my career, I had never seen or experienced such a wide range of 'raw' emotions displayed in my presence. I am extremely privileged to have been a witness to my participants' honest expressions of love, hate, disgust, pride, fear, shame, and, of course, triumph. I hope this book captures at least a portion of this raging humanity that moved me as a researcher, as a woman, as a feminist, and as a humanist. These feelings are also relevant to most other research carried out on extremely sensitive topics. For example, Chatzifotiou (2000) talks about a similar emotional roller coaster in her interviews with abused Greek women.

Second, let me mention the range of emotions that my participants' candid stories evoked in me. I have done more than two decades of research on women and women's issues from a feminist perspective. The topics I have addressed in the past have ranged from genderized mate-selection patterns and relative and genderized power in interpersonal interactions to topics like sexual harassment, women and divorce, and women and violence (see Sev'er, 1992, 1997a, 1997b, 1998, 1999, for some examples). In each of these previous works, I have followed the path of the trailblazing feminist scholars before me in locating myself in the research topic and process. Rather than pursuing a removed objectivity, I have always tried to give voice to those I studied. Rather than choking their legitimacy with over-intellectualized callousness, I have genuinely tried to learn from my participants. Rather than espousing the infallibility of my expertise and methodological skills, I have tried to recognize both strengths and weaknesses in my work. In short, I went into this study armed with years of research experience and intimate familiarity with feminist theory and methodology. Despite these career-long preparations, I must confess that I found myself overwhelmed with different emotions during some of the interviews. Through their tears or stoic transcendence, through their fatalism or an undeniable agency in their own survival, my participants indeed aroused very powerful feelings in me.

I did not shield myself behind a cloak of objectivity within the emotionally charged atmosphere of the long interviews. There were times when I felt tears in my eyes and a lump in my throat after hearing some excruciatingly painful life stories. Although I was cautious about never interfering in my participants' quite complex lives, I did try my best to give legitimacy to their experiences regardless of how out of the ordinary these experiences sounded in relation to my own mundane life. I tried to respect the range of emotions they expressed. I tried to be understanding and respectful when they told me parts of their lives that pushed my own boundaries of tolerance towards outrage. The powerful emotions that surround research on (and teaching) about violence against women remain a rarely discussed topic. I think this is unfortunate. In her insightful article, Elizabeth Stanko (1997; also see Chatzifotiou, 2000) highlights the emotional toll on teachers and researchers of violence. My experience in conducting the current research attests to the taxing nature of the process. I hope some of my candid observations will form a blueprint in preparing other researchers for the ordeal of studying violence.

Safety Issues

Given the extremely sensitive nature of the study, I had decided right from the beginning to carry out all the interviews personally rather than sharing or shifting the responsibility with or to research assistants. The difficulty of dealing with the outpouring of emotions time and time again assured me of the wisdom of my original decision. Moreover, feelings of general unease during the interviews, especially when the meetings took place in the participants' homes also justified the original decision. Each interview was preceded by a free-floating anxiety from not knowing what to expect. I hoped that the years of research skills I had developed would be enough to deal with unexpected situations. Crying was a frequent occurrence in interviews, and I routinely stocked up on tissues as part of my preparations. Even more difficult was the task of dealing with long-lasting crying spells, and in two cases, periods of frenzied sobbing. I chose to sit quietly during these occasions, muttering phrases like 'it is all right' or 'take your time' or 'would you like to have a glass of water?' When the participants stopped crying, I always asked them whether they wanted to terminate the session. Without exception, they expressed the desire to continue. Some of them openly admitted that they felt much better, now that they had 'got it out of their system.' Some of my respondents were surprised about how relieved they felt. One woman (Iris) told me she did not think there were so many tears left in her! Although I tried not to be overly alarmed by these episodes, I must admit that I felt quite sad and helpless in the presence of my participants' overwhelming pain. In at least two interviews, I found myself wondering about what action to take if the crying did not stop. Fortunately, it did.

On different occasions, I discussed some of these interviewing issues with some of my colleagues and friends, most of whom are well-respected scholars. I must say that I was encouraged by most, but surprised and disappointed by some of their reactions. Most encouraged me to tap into the dark side of intimate violence despite the methodological and procedural difficulties this in-depth work posed. However, I was disheartened when a few of my colleagues drew the conclusion that maybe social workers and psychiatrists should be dealing with these women, because they would be better prepared to deal with the emotional outbursts. With all due respect to the few colleagues and friends who took the latter stance, I must say that I vigorously disagree with leaving research about severely abused women in the exclusive domain of social workers and psychiatrists. First, I believe in the complex social and structural basis of intimate violence, and this is the domain of social rather than mental health related science. Second, I believe that these women are justifiably sad, angry, frustrated, and feel transgressed, rather than that they are suffering from mental or psychological disorders. Thus, as sociologists and social scientists, we have a lot to learn from collecting information on extremely sensitive topics, even when the processes involved may require great sensitivity, emotional engagement, and upheaval on the part of the researchers. The relevant question for me is how to conduct this research with the absolute minimum emotional discomfort for the respondents rather than how to avoid it altogether.

Safety was another issue I needed to consider. First, there was the safety of my participants. Although the requirement for participation stipulated that women must have left their abusive partners for 'not less than six consecutive months,' this is not always an assurance of safety from disgruntled and violent ex-partners (see Ellis and DeKeseredy, 1997; Fleury, Sullivan, and Bybee, 2000; Sev'er, 1998). As discussed in Chapters 1 and 2, the literature repeatedly shows that controlling men may become even more violent after a separation or a divorce, as they interpret the independence of their female partners as the ultimate challenge to their own control. Second, there was the issue of my own safety. Although I never questioned the goodwill and cooperativeness of my participants, their past and/or current relationships remained a total unknown to me before the interviews. As it turns out, my overall anxiety was often justified after talking to the women. For example, having ended one or more violent relationships, thus fulfilling the selection criteria of my research, a few of my participants were experiencing violence again in their current relationships. It was not such a remote possibility that one or more of these new partners may have found the feminist nature of the study 'objectionable.' Although participants were urged to keep their own involvement in this study confidential, I really had no way of knowing whether they did so or not.

These legitimate concerns were applicable to all interviews, but especially to those that took place in the participants' homes. I always expressed my preference for conducting the interviews in one of my two offices (usually after regular working hours). However, as a courtesy and an accommodation to their life conditions, I left the final choice of the location up to the participants. In fact, about a third chose their own homes. Although some of these trips took me to relatively average homes in average-looking neighbourhoods, some others took me to pockets of the city that I did not know existed. A couple of the high-rise apartment buildings I ended up in were scary. Most particularly, I remember an elevator in a high-rise building that was splashed with angry graffiti and filled with garbage from fast food outlets. Parts of the door and the walls were punched out, scratched, and broken. The lobby of the building and the elevator were reminiscent of a gang-related movie depicting inner city slums. Until that very day, I could have sworn that such conditions did not exist in Toronto. My initial feeling was to get out of there, to jump into my car, and drive away as fast as I could to the safety of my own home. Then, I reminded myself that the woman I was about to interview (not to mention the young children she had told me she had) had to live there! They did not have the option to jump into their car and run away as I easily could. If they were able to take this same elevator every day of their lives, I should be able to deal with it this one time. This rationalization did not reduce my fear, it just gave me a strong reason to try to deal with it rather than to be incapacitated.

These are indeed serious concerns for people who do any field research on difficult topics and who meet people from all walks of life. Chatzifotiou (2000) calls similar concerns 'researcher anxiety.' I will go a step further and say that doing qualitative research on violence produces a well-justified 'gnawing fear,' an emotion traditional scientific methods will neither account for nor acknowledge. The fear is real, and mostly it stems from crossing social and personal boundaries of lives that have been infested with male violence. Perhaps, the difficulty is also proportionally higher for feminist research on violence, where the survivors of violence encounter serious economic setbacks with some being forced to live under dire conditions, in unsafe, unclean, and unacceptable living arrangements. I am going to deal with some of these issues more extensively in the following chapters. In addition to the partner violence these women endure, their living conditions also violate their basic right to a safe environment. The latter is a societal failure and disgrace.

For my own peace of mind and personal safety, I developed a routine to deal with some of the issues related to interviewing participants in their homes. First, I left the phone number, the address, and clear instructions of how to get to the location of the scheduled interview in an envelope in my own home. The agreement with my spouse was that the envelope would be opened only if I was delayed significantly past the expected time that I should have been home or at my office. Second, I always called my spouse when I arrived at the interview and as soon as I left the interview. In cases when the interview took substantially more than two-and-a-half hours (the estimated duration of the interviews), I made an additional call to inform my spouse about the delay. I always used words like 'I am going to be late for our meeting' or 'I will be on time for our meeting' to avoid offending the woman I was currently interviewing. These steps may appear to be overly cautious to those who are not familiar with potentially explosive surroundings of victims of violence, but I sincerely believe that researchers who are conducting similar studies should develop similar routines to help with their physical or psychological concerns about safety. Although the chance of being injured or hurt is probably low, the spread of violence from an individual woman to the people around her is not that uncommon.

I must also confess that there was one occasion that truly frightened me. The situation involved an interview at a participant's house (Ava). When I arranged the interview, Ava told me her 'child' was going to be at home. This was something that I was accustomed to. Upon arrival, I was informed that the 'child' was a 14-year-old boy (Stan) who was sleeping upstairs, which also seemed fine to me. I was then shown into the kitchen for the interview. The kitchen was a common choice of location by numerous participants in this study. Sometime in the middle of the interview, a scantily-dressed person – more than six feet tall and looking more like a fully grown man than a 14-year-old boy – appeared in the kitchen. After banging a few cupboards and the refrigerator door, he loudly and aggressively started complaining about the food (or lack of it) in the fridge. In quick succession, he kept on opening the fridge and cupboard doors, making sure he closed them with a loud bang. Appearing to be hurt and embarrassed by her son's accusations, Ava also became quite loud and agitated. She started her own demonstration of slamming the cupboard and fridge doors and dumped all the food in the fridge on top of the table where I had been sitting and conducting the interview a few minutes earlier. Looking back on it, there is the possibility that both the mother and the son may have dealt with the same situation more casually if I had not been present. It is possible that both were seeking my attention or approval in terms of the legitimacy of their opposing claims (no food in the house versus plenty of food but an ungrateful child). I tried my best to stay calm and not to show my fear about what could happen if either of them spun out of control. I made sure to stay quiet and totally impartial throughout the angry demonstration of banging plates and food containers and the slamming of cupboard and fridge doors. Through all this, I could not help but think how big, how physically mature, and how intimidating the 14-year-old son was. If the situation turned violent, neither Ava nor myself were a match for Stan. I was also seriously concerned about Ava's agitated and exaggerated response to Stan's challenge and the tension between the two which must have been much deeper than the altercation over food. I will revisit this incident in Chapter 6, which I devote to children from violent homes, and again, in Chapter 9, which is about women's own violence.

Content Analysis of Newspaper Articles

Although most of this book is based on interviews conducted with the thirty-nine women survivors of abusive relationships, I will also use information from an entirely different study that I conducted around the time of the interviews. This second study comprises a content analysis of all articles on woman abuse or femicide that appeared in the *Toronto Star* between 1 January 1995 and 31 December 1999. As can be expected, the newspaper coverage grossly underreports abuse, because only the most gruesome cases or those committed by or against famous people are reported. However, media coverage generally approximates the official statistics on wife or partner killings and femicide. Despite its biases and an often sensationalistic stance, newspaper coverage of serious incidents often provides contextual information that is lacking in crime statistics – for example what was done, to whom, where, what time, whether other people were involved or injured, what type of a relationship the parties had, and what neighbours or friends knew, saw, or heard, are reported in detail. Some of this information is missing from official crime reports (Gartner, Dawson, and Crawford, 2001). Moreover, the type of relationship between the involved parties is presented in more detail than in the rigid definition of a spouse in official statistics. The articles often discuss the ethnic or cultural differences of the people involved and frequently make mention of other personal or social traits and of the presence or absence of previous violence. Therefore, without attempting to replace more systematic studies of crime, newspaper articles can add to our understanding of the context of some of these crimes and also give us a glimpse of how violence against intimate partners spreads outside the dyad and often victimizes children, friends, neighbours, helping professionals, and even passers-by (Sev'er, 1997a, 1998).

The newspaper study involved using a predetermined list of key words and phrases to search the electronic backfiles of the *Toronto Star*. A total of twenty key words and phrases were used as probes. These included, for example, 'husband/murder,' 'wife/murder,' 'wife/abuse,' 'spousal assault,' 'domestic violence' (see Appendix J for a complete list of the key words used in the study). The electronic search resulted in identification of 1,413 articles on domestic violence between 1995 and 1999, which equals approximately 283 articles per year. Some of these articles, however, were a repetition of or additional coverage on incidents that had already been recorded. For example, there were dozens of articles on the O.J. Simpson trial for the murder of Nicole Brown. Numerous repetitions of other famous or particularly vicious cases were also the norm. To avoid erroneously exaggerating the numbers, I flagged the original occurrence of each case (first entry) and thus was able to differentiate the first report from any subsequent articles on the same case. An analysis of the flagged cases (first entry of incident) showed that there were 648 separate cases of abuse/violence/murder against women reported between 1995 and 1999 in the *Toronto Star* newspaper. Where applicable, I am going to use information from this rich contextual source in different chapters of this book, and refer to the study as the Toronto Study (Sev'er, 2001).

Chapter Five

Women's Experience of Abuse

Perhaps there is nothing more frightening than a husband or a partner turning on his children or their mother. For our immediate purposes, I am going to concentrate on the experiences of women. Be the abuse psychological, physical, sexual, economic, or spiritual, it represents a complete breakdown of the trust and interdependence that ought to exist in any healthy relationship. One of the ways in which this breakdown can happen is in an incremental, on and off, but accelerating fashion. Generally, the pattern is set even before marriage or entering into a common-law arrangement. It may take the form of shouting, temper tantrums, jealous rages, controlling, demeaning in front of others, insisting on sex, and even hitting and slapping (Schwartz and DeKeseredy, 1997; DeKeseredy and Kelly, 1993). There is the ironic and dangerous possibility that the woman might actually have enjoyed the milder forms of such manifestations early on in the relationship, especially the ones that she may have interpreted as jealousy-based. In a culture that defines love relations as a conquest, it is easy to erroneously interpret attempts to control as 'love,' 'caring,' or 'commitment.' After all, North American society is gripped by powerful mass media that rarely dissociate love from entitlement, possessiveness, and even aggression.

Another way abuse targeting female partners surfaces in intimate relationships is related to stressful life events. Pressures can come from outside such as economic crises brought on by unemployment, economic recessions, and even war or natural disasters. Pressures can also emerge from within the family, such as personal accidents, addictions, illness, or death. Dramatic changes in the couple's life, such as unplanned or unwanted pregnancies, the birth of a disabled child, and/or real or imagined affairs can also create pressure. Abrupt status changes such as the woman starting work or school may trigger violence or escalate the existing abuse. As I have already highlighted (Chapters 1 and 2), separation or threats to separate are associated with the highest risk for women (Ellis and DeKeseredy, 1997; Gartner, Dawson, and Crawford, 2001; GSS, 2000; Jacobson and Gottman, 2001; Sev'er, 1997a).

In the present study, my participants told me chilling tales about the different forms of abuse they suffered. Before I give examples of their suffering, I would like to emphasize a number of points. First, and foremost, I would like to touch upon my own feelings and emotions. As I discussed in the methods chapter (Chapter 4), I consider myself a 'seasoned' researcher who has undertaken many studies on serious women's issues. Yet I was deeply affected by the emotional content of my participants' revelations. I must also admit that there were many times when I found myself dwelling on some of the women – their faces, their tears, their shaking hands, the scars some of them showed me, or the scars that were much too visible to miss. Occasionally, I lost sleep following an interview. I tried to tell myself that 'she is all right,' but sometimes I was not convinced by my attempt at rationalization. Fortunately, none of the women I interviewed were in immediate danger from their former partner(s) at the time of the interviews. Moreover, some appeared to be moving on in new and promising directions. Even these positive signs, however, did not dilute the fact that although the turmoil of their past was submerged, it came too close to the surface of their everyday lives. Another overpowering feeling I had during the interviews was awe. As Laurette so poignantly expressed, 'We have survived the unsurvivable.' So, they had!

The second point that I want to emphasize pertains to my subjective observations. Most women told me about their physical and even sexual ordeals in surprising detail. The words they used and the gestures they made were so clear that I could almost see exactly what had happened to them, and I felt their fear, outrage, and terror. Inadvertently, I remember thinking, 'How could they remember so many painful details?' In the literature, there are some findings about women blocking out painful memories (Bergen, 1998; Kendall-Tackett, and Marshall, 1998). This was certainly the case with some of my interviewees, as I will discuss in the chapter about coping strategies (Chapter 7). But at the time of the interviews, most of my respondents had excruciatingly clear recollections of what had happened to them and seemed eager to share their ordeals with me. I remember asking myself, 'How could they share so many painful details with a complete stranger?' Despite the respectable intentions of my research project, and my own commitment to initiating some social awareness and change, there were still times when I felt like an 'intruder' in these women's very complex and painful lives. However, these gut-level feelings, emotions, and even self-questioning did not make the research situation any less reliable or any less valid. As I interpret it, the interviews were a process where both the participants and myself as the researcher were allowed to be real, true, and human without having to hide behind artificially constructed barriers of 'objectivity' or engendering a hierarchical separation of the researcher from the researched. As Renzetti (1997) poignantly asks in relation to her study of abuse in lesbian relationships, do such circumstances make this an unbiased work? Certainly not. Does it make it good research? I sincerely believe that it does.

Women's Experiences of Psychological Abuse and Control

As discussed in Chapters 1 and 3, there is very little consensus on how to classify psychological abuse, including whether to classify it as abuse at all. Through years of working with women who have been violated in one way or another, from volunteering in women's shelters to carrying out interviews, I must say that I find psychological abuse to be just as hurtful, just as crippling, and just as debilitating as the other less-controversial classifications of non-lethal forms of physical abuse. There are other scholars who share this view (DeKeseredy and MacLeod, 1997; Jacobson and Gottman, 2001). The long interviews I conducted with these thirty-nine women reinforced this conviction. From what I heard, understood, and felt, most of these women's core sense of self was eroded through their partners' constant put-downs and criticisms. Although others may not agree, I find this relentless degradation, the hollowing out of another person's inner being, to be abuse of a high order. In the following pages, I will provide a number of examples of psychological abuse that truly outraged my own sense of fairness to other human beings in general and to women in particular. Readers are free to take their own position along this controversial continuum. I hope the following examples will contribute to the continuation of a constructive debate.

Ann's Partner Rob

From all of the accounts I listened to, I found Ann's former partner Rob to be the most destructive of the partners in this study. At the time of the interview, Ann was 24 years old and considered to be legally disabled as a result of the severe beatings she had received from Rob. However, she appeared more distraught when she told me about instances of psychological pressure, degradation, and control than when she told me about the sexual and physical violations she had endured. What was also chilling about Ann's relationship with Rob was that she saw him as a very humorous, charming, at times loving and even sexually exciting man. Despite her nightmarish experiences, Ann clearly had loved Rob, and at the time of the interview, she freely admitted to still having strong feelings for him. This iron grip that the abuser seemed to have on the woman's feelings was something I witnessed more than once. In the literature before 1970 or so, similar observations may have been misinterpreted and used to blame the victims for being 'masochistic women.' I believe that the hold these men have on women's feelings reflects the power and control of the abusers and their ability to manipulate. As already discussed in an earlier chapter, Jacobson and Gottman (2001) call them Cobras. They appear to love, but they also dominate and degrade their partners. In my interpretation, the process also shows the mutilated self-esteem of the victims, while their loyalty remains intact towards someone who violates them. Most women I talked to had stopped believing that they deserve to be loved, instead of believing that love cannot coexist with violation and/or exploitation.

In Ann's case, Rob used to invite his drinking buddies over to their house several times a week. After consuming a few cases of beer in relative civility, the gathering would almost always get out of hand. Towards the end of these binges, the party would become pornographic. As the host and the leader of the raunchy pack, Rob would make Ann squirt herself with a water bottle. Starting from her face, moving to her breasts, then to her crotch, Ann was the unwilling participant in a wet-body contest. This variation on stripping always took place in front of Rob's drinking buddies. Ann was a very modest and religious woman. The visual disrobing of her body achieved through the incremental soaking of her clothes reminded Ann of gang rapes: 'I could see their eyes, cloudy, greedy ... looking through my clothes, looking down there ... staring. You know what? It was like popping the hood of his car open, showing the engine. He liked that, you know ... show off the engine ... It was like I had no feelings ... he owned me like he owned his car or something ... he was happy to let the others gawk! ... He was happy to share me, to take me for a drive!'

Ann could never understand why Rob, her lover and partner, would want to share her body with so many other men in such a humiliating way. However, these episodes were only the tip of the iceberg in a continuum of harassment and control at which Rob was a master.

Rob also wanted to dislodge Ann from her family, and to a large degree, he had succeeded. They moved numerous times, always farther away from her parents and her sister. He was rude and insulting when her family came to visit them. He made Ann so upset that she almost always cried after her family left their house. Even telephone contact was under his scrutiny. Rob did not allow Ann to speak freely with her family when they called. He even tried to monitor her calls when he was not home by telling her that he left a secret tape recorder running all day. Ann was never sure if there was indeed a tape recorder running all day. Whether there was one or not was irrelevant; Rob's trick worked. Ann felt she was constantly being watched. Ann was intimidated.

Rob had told Ann that her family was trying to run their lives and intrude on their privacy. After a while, she really believed him and started resenting her own family members. She tried to keep them at a distance to please Rob. Rob was particularly vicious in criticizing Ann's sister. Ann started to think that her own sister was jealous of her 'happiness' and was trying to tear them apart. She started to believe whatever Rob told her. Her mental and physical subjugation was complete.

Rob wanted Ann to be docile and obedient at all times. He would do anything to achieve his goal. One of his favourite ways was to lift Ann's cat up, bringing him higher and higher towards the revolving blades of the ceiling fan. The cat would desperately try to escape Rob's hurtful grip, but Rob would squeeze him tighter and tighter. Ann would be frantic about the safety of her cat as the blades of the fan got closer and closer to her cat's head. Rob would ask Ann to swallow an arbitrary number of sleeping pills as a condition of stopping the torture, and she would comply just to end her own as well as her cat's terror. Thus, Ann would spend many hours of the day and many nights sleeping under the influence of the pills. After a while, she began to feel groggy even when she was awake. At night, she did not even have dreams that she could recall, and during the day, she was in a dream-like state.

No matter how long Ann slept, she would still wake up to the same problems and the same tortures. Towards the end of her relationship, Ann was mostly on painkillers because of the physical damage inflicted by Rob to her cranial cavity and facial bones. I will discuss these aspects in the following sections. Not surprisingly, Ann had developed a strong addiction to her prescription painkillers and to whatever else Rob had made her swallow. We will come across examples of Ann's physical and sexual suffering in many other parts of this book.

Kim's Husband Ken

Ken was a police officer and he had many police comrades. He was also a controlling and jealous man. Wherever Kim went, police cruisers would pass by. Ken's police friends would look into her car while she was parked at the curb or peer into the homes of the friends she visited. At first, Kim thought this must have been a coincidence. As Ken's jealous tantrums escalated, Kim knew that the surveillance was intentional. After work, Ken would ask her where she had been that day, and for how long. If she was not absolutely correct in her answers, Ken would correct her and demand to know what she was hiding. Kim might say something like 'I left my sister's house at noon,' and Ken would say, 'You didn't leave till 12:30, so what were you doing for so long?'

Lorie's Husband Emanuel

Lorie had never had a very high regard for herself. As the oldest of three sisters and two brothers, she only remembers being asked to do things for others. Moreover, throughout her childhood, Lorie had been told that her younger sisters were prettier and cuter than she was. The way she put it, she was 'indistinct' with whitish skin, dirty blonde hair, and almost colourless eyes. Suffice to say, 'I felt like the ugly duckling of the family who never grew out of my ugly feathers.' Over the years, the men Lorie chose or those who had chosen her to be intimate with did not help her low self-concept either. At best, she has felt invisible and unloved; at worst, she was constantly criticized and put down.

Among all the dysfunctional men in her life, Emanuel was the worst. When Lorie met him, he was as an illegal immigrant from Mexico trying to obtain Canadian landed immigrant status, possibly to obtain an easier passage to the United States. To fast track his aspiration for permanent Canadian residency, Emanuel asked Lorie to marry him, and she accepted in a heartbeat because 'he was so dark and handsome.'

The trouble was that Emanuel was also six years younger than Lorie, a fact he never let her forget. He made brutally hurtful remarks about the lack of youthfulness in her hair, skin, breasts, belly, and practically every other part of her body. Although Lorie loved Emanuel, he made her feel 'like the dirt under his shoes.' Yet Lorie never had the core self-respect to challenge Emanuel's put-downs and degrading remarks. As far as she was concerned, Emanuel was doing her a favour by accepting her as a marital partner. She did not think she was doing him a favour by saving him from deportation.

Even when Emanuel stole her money, or slapped her in the face, Lorie's feelings of gratitude towards Emanuel did not change. As far as Lorie was concerned, she was old, she was very ugly, and she was ashamed. Lorie has had an unquenched thirst for love all her life. Emanuel made her feel she was not worthy of love. Lorie's already low self-concept plummeted to dangerous levels. 'Every day, I thought about death! ... not having to deal with this shitload of pain looked pretty good to me, I tell you! Silly me, I didn't have the courage even for that ... I just thought about it, thought about it, thought about it, but I couldn't even off myself! Can you imagine that? Lorie, the sucker, Lorie the total loser!'

Daisy's Husband Al

Al was jealous of Daisy from the day they set eyes on each other. He called her 'slut' more often than he called her by her name. When Daisy returned from visiting a friend or even after buying a few groceries, Al would be pacing the floor; interrogate her, asking why it took so long to come back, whom she had seen or talked to, was she alone, and on and on; and question her about the clothes she was wearing.

'Not that we had any money to buy nice clothes,' Daisy said. 'I had half a dozen of T-shirts, some blouses, and a couple of jeans. Some were already faded. They were old. It wasn't like I was going to a fashion show!'

For her sister's wedding, Al and Daisy fought about the possibility of her being one of the bridesmaids. Daisy loved the idea of being in the wedding procession. She loved the idea of being able to intimately share her sister's wedding day by standing beside her. But she was determined to make every sacrifice possible to keep Al's jealous rages at bay. Although her own heart was breaking, Daisy gently dissuaded her sister from including her among the bridesmaids. However, 'being my sister's wedding and all, I managed to buy a nice dress. It was not expensive or anything but it was something like a melon colour which I liked and which looked really nice on me. People told me I looked like an angel, nice dress, flushed cheeks, shiny eyes ... I felt happy, that's all.'

To say the least, Al was miserable all night. He insisted that they leave early and shouted at her from across the table. He even accused her of 'flirting around' right in front of the other wedding guests. When they returned home, Al refused to go to bed with her. As on many other occasions, Daisy cried herself to sleep that night. In the morning, her pretty melon-coloured dress was spread over a chair right in front of her side of the bed, ripped into shreds. Daisy distinctly remembers two thoughts. The first being that 'he is still angry' and the second that 'I am in trouble.' She did not have the luxury to feel bad about her pretty dress. Daisy was in trouble. Al was going to make her pay. Indeed, the following days brought nothing but more degrada-tion, more insults, more name-calling, and even sex against her will, which Daisy never called rape. 'He pushed himself on me ... I think, he was trying to prove himself to me or to himself, or something. It hurt but I didn't say nothing. This was the price for going to my sister's wedding, he knew it and I knew it. I paid.'

Elly's Husband Stephan

'Stephan played mind games with me, you know the kind which screw you up, makes you think you really lost it? For a long time, I really fell for it, it was so bad. I felt like I cracked up ... lost my trust in myself ... Did I say that? Did I do that? Did I hear that? Do you know what this means? It is going right into the looney bin and back. It is like a bad movie where people are zombies ... they shuffle around without know-ing what they are doing and you are one of them.' The games Stephan played were numerous. He would ask for things, simple things like a cup of coffee. He would drink his coffee, put away the cup, and then scold Elly for not bringing him the coffee. He would forget to take out the garbage, but tell her that she brought it back in because she is crazy. 'It wasn't like a joke you know, he would be so serious that after a while I thought maybe I do those things, who knows? He would insist I did this, I didn't do this, on and on, with a straight face.'

The worst mind game was about hearing things. Stephan would move his lips, and pretend to say things to Elly. When she didn't hear him, he would accuse her of being deaf and stupid. Elly said he did this so many times that she actually believed that there was something wrong with her hearing. 'I ended up going to the doctor. He put me through tests, all kinds of tests. Surprise, surprise, my hearing is perfect, nothing is wrong with it! Nothing!' Once Elly got the confirmation from the doctor and caught Stephan at his mind games, Stephan stopped pretending she couldn't hear him. On and off, he continued with his other games. 'He wasn't crazy, you know! Oh! No! He wasn't crazy at all. He was mean! He was evil! He was trying to drive me crazy. That's what all this was about ... and I almost did [go crazy], who wouldn't?'

Amber's Husband Guy

Amber is from Jamaica and she has very light skin for a black woman. She liked dating men who were 'white,' and they seemed to think she was quite exotic. Amber got pregnant at 17 and ended up giving up her baby. Fortunately, for the baby, Amber's older sister adopted her. 'I was a partier, I liked a few joints, and I liked my booze. I was no mother. I liked the boys, too, but they just wanted me. Nothing else, just desire to get it on!'

The year she gave up her firstborn baby, Amber was almost gang-raped at a party. 'It wasn't like the other times, I mean one guy at a party. It was like a pack of wolves. Well yeah, I was blown away by that time [drunk] but not blown away enough. I was scared.' One of the men at the party saved her by taking her out of the volatile situation. He placated the others by declaring that Amber was his fiancée. Soon after that incident, Amber married her saviour, her 'hero' (Guy). In reality, Guy was no hero. He was jealous, controlling, and possessive. He had a mean temper. Moreover, Guy was an alcoholic, and he physically abused Amber when he was drunk. In Amber's words, 'I felt like a mouse,' and he told her she looked like a mouse. This is ironic because Amber was a good-looking woman, and she knew that many men had found her attractive before she hooked up with Guy. Nevertheless, after being told that she looked like a mouse, she ended up feeling like one. She figured that, maybe it was because of her skin colour – she was not white!

What Amber remembers the most are not the physical beatings and the put-downs. There were so many of those to remember. What she remembers with terror are the verbal threats. Guy told her, 'If you are not with me, I'll mark an X on your face.'

At the intuitive level, Amber knew that Guy was capable of carving her face up. She also knew that Guy could shoot her right in the middle of her eyebrows. The threat of the X on her face terrified her until she found the courage to run away. She fled to British Columbia and did not return to Ontario until she heard that Guy had been killed in a traffic accident. 'Call me sick, call me mean ... I don't care ... I was relieved, boy was I ever relieved!'

Laurette's Husband Sam

For many years, Laurette believed that she was stupid. Her husband Sam told her so. Sam also told her she was a lousy mother, a lousy cook, and a lousy wife – and she believed him. For years, Laurette lived like a shadow, trying to do the right things but always being told she had failed. 'I tried,' Laurette said. 'I tried to cook better, I tried to clean better, I tried to be a better wife, but it was no use.' When the principal of her children's school started to tell her that she was very good with children and was a good organizer in children's activities, Laurette was stunned. How could she, the clumsy Laurette, be good at anything? For the first time, Laurette started to wonder if Sam had lied? Maybe, just maybe, she might not be so stupid after all. After years of unappreciated housewifery, Laurette decided to take a few night courses from a local college. Sam hit the roof. When she actually enrolled in a college course, Sam burned all her notes and all her books.

There was another way Sam played with Laurette's mind. He would subject her to long silences. The silences sometimes lasted for days, sometimes as long as a week. He would say nothing, and if Laurette spoke to him, he would pretend she was not there. These times were hard. 'In my mind, I would go over and over ... what did I do ... what did I do? How can I make him speak? How can I make it up to him? When is he going to speak to me? ... These [questions] would just circle in my head until I felt exhausted ... In all those years, I never asked myself what he was doing to me ... I always asked ... "What did I do?" He was destroying me yet I took all the blame, isn't that something?'

Women's Experiences of Physical Abuse

Without exception, the women in this study suffered physical abuse at the hands of at least one of their husbands or partners. Moreover, all of them experienced physical abuse more than once, most of them many times. Thus, the incidents of abuse that the participants recalled are much too numerous to be included in a book of modest intent and length. I am going to relate only a few examples to highlight the many convoluted ways in which these men hurt their partners. I am neither trying to suggest that the ones I chose are the worst cases of abuse possible, nor am I saying that the experiences I omit are any less important than the ones included. Regardless of what may have happened to them, the women I talked to were frightened, hurt, and often terrorized by their experiences. In other words, the abuse they suffered was real for them, and thus the consequences of the abuse were just as real. I will select only a few cases to represent the women's suffering to avoid overwhelming my readers.

Erika's Husband Tony

Tony routinely pushed Erika around, called her 'stupid,' 'fat,' and 'ugly.' He often beat her up, especially when he felt jealous. It did not take much for him to feel jealous. It could be a phone call from a friend. It could be coming home a few minutes late from work or from shopping for food. Erika worked and paid all the bills, but that was never enough for Tony. He wanted to control every aspect of Erika's life, monetary and psychological. He also wanted to control the life of their only daughter Abby. One time, during a jealous rage, Tony picked up the decorative Samurai sword from their living-room wall and jabbed it at Erika's throat. His face was so contorted that Erika blacked out with fear. Although she was not cut, 'My life passed in front of my eyes, it was so fast that I blacked out. That day, I also learned to get out of scary situations by just blacking out ... I guess, that saved my sanity.' To this day, Erika wonders why she is still alive. To this day, Erika blacks out when she feels threatened, a coping strategy that I will revisit in Chapter 7.

Nancy Sudbury's Partner Roy

Nancy Sudbury's partner had pretty rough friends. Roy would go out and sometimes not come back for a few days. Nancy never knew where he went, and she never knew why she was not included in these escapades. When she complained, Roy would ignore her. If she continued to complain, Roy would get aggressive. A number of times she was slapped right on the mouth. 'Close that trap, you bitch!' he would say. More than once, Nancy was choked and pinned to the door or the wall. One time, Roy pulled out a gun and stuck the barrel right between Nancy's eyes. That was the first time Nancy had seen a real gun and the first time she saw Roy with a gun. Nancy thought that this was going to be the last time she would see anything at all. Drawing from an animalistic power she did not think she possessed, Nancy scratched Roy's face, shouting for help at the top of her lungs. No one came to her aid, but by some miracle, Roy spared her life that night. By another miracle, she moved into the local shelter the next day, taking both of her young children with her. By yet another miracle, this time she did not return to Roy, as she had done numerous times before. Nancy had dealt with being hit, slapped, kicked, and called names. Nancy could not deal with the gun in her face that she knew would one day kill her if she ever returned.

Lou's Husband Ralph

Lou married Ralph when she was 23 and working as a waitress in a small, greasy-spoon restaurant that served alcohol. Ralph was the waiter. At first, life was good. They would work late hours and have a couple of drinks after closing, at the owners' expense. The owners probably knew about the missing drinks, but did not confront them. The few drinks soon became many drinks, and that was also when the hits and slaps started. Soon after, there were kicks and punches as well. Ralph would hit Lou in her chest, stomach, and groin areas the most. Her face and arms, the most visible parts of her body, were almost never touched. Ralph did not want witnesses to his after-hours violence. Lou also did not have the courage to tell anyone because she was afraid they would both lose their jobs. The money was not great, but the job was steady and they ate free food and helped themselves to free drinks. When their alcohol consumption rose to problematic levels, Ralph got fired. When the beatings got worse, and she had to miss work numerous times, she got fired too! Lou did not blame the owners. 'They had to fire me, I was a mess! They had a business to run. Ralph said they were racist pigs [Lou and Ralph are black]. They were no racists, we blew it!'

Unemployment exasperated Lou's troubles. It also allowed Ralph more freedom to attack all parts of her body, including her face. He once attacked her with a kitchen knife. Lou thought that it was her last day on this earth, but amazingly Ralph did not stab her. He just made scratch marks around her neck and ears. Lou bled, but the cuts were not deep. Nevertheless, seeing her face and neck covered with her own blood frightened Lou out of her wits. The incident kept her awake for many nights. 'It was ... how do you say it? Well, it was like marking me, like branding cattle, so that I won't go anywhere. That's it, I think that's exactly what he did! He branded me.' When Lou slept, she saw herself as cut and branded, like a farm animal.

Even that was not the whole story. The worst attack Lou remembers took place on their old, bladder-style water bed. She does not even remember the content of the argument; it was probably something very trivial, as usual. In a drunken rage, Ralph pinned Lou's head between the wide side boards and the corner of the water bag and punched her face until she was black and blue. One of her eyes swelled shut and her mouth filled with blood from a gash in her lip. 'With each punch, I heard the water swooshing in the bag ... like swoosh, swoosh, swoosh. With each punch, the water went away and then came back to squeeze my head more. I couldn't get it out, I felt trapped. I thought, if the bag breaks, I would just drown.' Lou prayed that she would pass out; the reality was much too scary.

Lou's marriage to Ralph lasted twelve torturous years and two trips to the hospital. Eventually, she developed severe arthritis in her jaw, which she attributes to the beatings. Then she left and went back to school, but the terror she lived through never left her. Although they are declining in frequency, Lou still has dreams about drowning in the water-bed and getting branded like an animal.

Ann's Partner Rob

Rob used to beat Ann to a pulp. The beatings were so ferocious that Ann would lose consciousness. 'When I passed out, he would get angry, as if I failed to please him or something. He wasn't satisfied, he wasn't done with me ... He would drag me to the bathroom, lean my head against the cold [bath]tub, sprinkle water on my face till I come to [regain consciousness] and punch me some more ... when I told the police about the tub, they didn't believe me. Who would believe such a thing? What kind of a monster would do that! When you looked at him, he was no monster, he was good-looking ... Hell! He was great looking. Police thought I was making these things up.'

When Ann was down, Rob would stomp on her head. Ann would just hope that she would pass out soon because when Rob was like that, the safest state for Ann was unconsciousness. After a while, Rob's anger would dissipate, and he would carry her to bed whispering words of sorrow and remorse. He would promise never to do anything to hurt her again. Rob would nurse her back to health. He would bring her flowers. Flowers are a small comfort to a 24-year-old woman who is now wearing partial dentures and is already on a disability pension.

Debbie's Husband Ron and Partner Gary

Debbie never had a partner who treated her well. Among numerous problematic relationships, her husband Ron and partner Gary were the most abusive. First, Debbie had numerous partners. Then she met Ron and got pregnant before they were married. Ron did not want her to have the child. Debbie had a strong objection, on religious grounds, to getting an abortion. Moreover, she desperately wanted a child to love, a person who would love her back. Her own childhood had been a disaster – totally devoid of love or affection, and full of put-downs and abuse.

Whether because of jealousy of the baby or fear of the commitment that the child would bring, Ron was particularly vicious during Debbie's pregnancy. He often 'kicked the shit out of me ... He kicked me right in the stomach, with heavy work boots.' Perhaps unbelievably, perhaps not so surprising at all, similar scenes were repeated on a future occasion, with another partner and another pregnancy. All types of violence, including physical violence, have been chronic companions in Debbie's troubled life.

Like most other men and women (including herself) Debbie has ever known, Ron was an alcoholic. He would go into rages about almost anything when he was drunk. Once, he beat her up in their driveway, made her crawl around, and then tried to run her over with his van. Debbie hated Ron and hated herself so much that, at one point, she actually wished he would run her over. She challenged him to run her over and 'finish the job!' Ron did not kill her, but eventually ended up getting killed himself in a single-car traffic accident. Debbie thinks he must have been drunk. Although her memories of the time are 'foggy,' Debbie was happy and relieved. She drank herself 'silly' to celebrate the occasion.

Debbie's freedom from Ron's abuse did not last long. Shortly after Ron's death, Gary, who was also an alcoholic, walked into her life. 'It is more like stumble, we were pretty messed up. Besides, he was into heavy drugs, not just pills, needles and shit like that.' Gary was the one who introduced Debbie to hard drugs. Gary was the one who went in and out of jail, for stealing money and for beating her up. He even assaulted other inmates while he was in jail. 'He had a short fuse,' Debbie said. 'Always ready to blow!' Gary also kicked her in the stomach when she was pregnant. Debbie's little boy Mark was born prematurely, and he has serious learning disabilities. Debbie feels responsible, and she is condemned to a life full of guilt.

Women's Experiences of Sexual Abuse

Almost half of the women (18) I interviewed told me about incidents of non-consensual sex. Although only two of them actually used the term 'rape,' their stories made it clear that they were indeed describing marital rapes. Some of these rapes were injurious and violent. In the following section, I provide a few examples from the sexual experiences my respondents have endured, and I highlight the injury to their self-esteem resulting from these sexual transgressions. There is the general misconception that women who are raped by strangers are the ones who need society's protection. These sentiments have long been reflected in societal norms as well as legal statutes (Estrich, 1987; Finkelhor and Ylló, 1985; Kelly and Radford, 1998). However, numerous studies have found that women raped by men who were close to them have reported higher levels of distress than women who were raped by total strangers. Other findings indicate that the closer the relationship of the woman to the sexual assailant, the more likely she is to blame herself rather than the perpetrator (Kelly and Radford, 1998). What is even more frightening is that sometimes abusive men rape their partners while they are pregnant or rape them in front of their children (Bergen, 1998: 239, 247). In these regards, the sexual assaults and rapes my interviewees reported need to be seen as serious assaults to their personhood as well as to their bodies.

Sonny's Husband Theodore

Sonny felt like 'a rabbit in a corner' in her violent marriage. She felt 'like I was walking on eggshells, all day, all night.' Theodore was not always violent. There were days when he was calm, and there were times when he was affectionate. The trouble was that Sonny never knew when he would 'explode,' and explode he often did!

Theodore was very strange and wiry. He had been physically abused as a child. Although he would never admit to it, Sonny believes that he may have been sexually abused as well. Theodore always claimed that his father raped his sister, but Sonny thinks it may have been him instead. It is possible that both were molested.

Theodore had unusual requests when it came to sex. He often liked to cross-dress before sex, wearing Sonny's panties and bra. Sonny did not like these rituals, but she originally thought they were strange but innocent sex games. Then she found out that Theodore's cross-dressing was not innocent after all, since he went into extreme guilt trips when it was over. Frequent rages and hysterical tantrums often followed these so-called innocent cross-dressing rituals. When Sonny started refusing to play a part in his games, he raped her. Each time, Theodore said he was very sorry and he would not do it again. But he did repeat the aggressive rapes.

Sonny talked Theodore into seeking counselling. They went into couple's therapy, but after the first two sessions, he dropped out. After that, he became worse. In Sonny's words, 'He went into a "fugitive" state.' He wanted more sexual games, longer periods of cross-dressing, and there were more after-the-act explosions. 'He became a totally different person ... Who am I kidding, he may have been bizarre from the beginning ... I was in love, I didn't see. I always needed somebody to take care of, so I guess, when I found Theodore, I thought, "that's it, he needs my help."' Sonny wanted to be needed, she needed to be needed, and Theodore definitely needed help. 'Unfortunately, he needed a lot more help than what I could give him.'

Sonny and Theodore had serious money problems. Both of them liked to spend more than was coming in. At one time, Theodore wanted Sonny to strip in a bar. When she refused, he beat her up, and pulled a gun on her. Sonny called the police and obtained a peace bond, which he violated on three occasions. He also threatened their son and that is when Sonny realized that enough was enough. That was when Sonny decided to really break off the relationship and got herself into a small house shared by two other couples. Sonny would have never felt safe living on her own.

Ava's Husband Greg

Ava is from Jamaica and so is Greg. At least they had that in common. Greg was Ava's first boyfriend and first sexual partner. Starting early on in their relationship, Greg wanted simple, uncomplicated sex every night. At first, Ava did not mind this routine very much, but after a while the ritualized sex got to her. Ava said, 'I was like food for him! He had to have me, he had to eat me at least once a day. Not that he loved me, not that he showed any care, he just wanted sex, every night!' She never felt loved and she was never satisfied with this meaningless, routinized, compulsory sex. When she refused him, Greg became pushy. He would start pushing and shoving her. If Ava continued to refuse, Greg would become violent and end up on her anyway (Ava never used the word 'rape'). So, Ava learned not to refuse, to open up her legs, almost like a limp rag doll, and wait for him to finish.

Greg would come home late, usually in the early hours of the day. Ava would pretend that she was asleep, hoping Greg would leave her alone. He never did. 'He would just jump on me, just like that. Never ask, "how are you?" just jump on me.' Ava felt empty, hollow, and used when he was finished. She could not sleep, whereas he just turned over and fell asleep. She had to get up, go to the bathroom, and masturbate. She wished for someone who would care about her, who would enjoy her body. Ava also learned to dissociate from reality, a response that victims of sexual abuse frequently report (Bergen, 1998).

The following is one of the two poems Ava wanted me to include in my work. She wanted to share her thoughts and feelings and thus regain some of her individuality. I think she also wanted others to know about the depth of her loneliness.

Ava's Poem: Cloudy Days

> Lonely, cloudy days
> Dark, sad, cold nights
> Endless loneliness
> Constant grief
> Fondly, I know what a human touch feels like
> Yet, I
> I crave, I long, I search for that fulfilment
> I fear the setting of the sun
> Because, I am sure before midnight
> *My body will be used and discarded once again*
> With no regard for my being
> Why should though? [sic]
> Made into the confines of my childlessness[1]
> Hold me so captive to the strain [sic].
> (my emphasis)

---

1 Although Ava refers to her 'childlessness' in this poem, she was not childless but had a 14-year-old son (Stan, discussed in Chapter 6). Ava did not explain this reference to me, and at the time I was so absorbed in the interview that I did not think to ask her about it. Perhaps the poem was written before she had Stan.

Lisa Kingston's Partner Lynford

Lynford would beat Lisa Kingston if she said she was tired or if she did not want to have sex with him. The beatings would not come as soon as she said she was tired. It could take a few hours or even days. But they would come, and they would be bad. One time, Lynford beat her up and threw her out on to the snowbank in front of the house where they rented the basement. The property owners who lived upstairs were not home and she had nothing but her nightgown on. It was cold. She was afraid, she was shivering, but most of all, she was embarrassed. She could not bring herself to ask for help from the neighbours. 'My nightgown was old. It was dirty because he dragged me on the floor. I just couldn't do it [ask for help]. If it were the Sullivans [pseudonym for the property owners], it would be alright. They knew I was being pushed around anyways. But it wasn't, they were not home.'

Eventually Lisa crawled back into the house through a basement window that she managed to pry open. She knew that the window was loose, and she was thankful that the property owner had not fixed it when she had asked him to do so. Lisa felt like a thief sneaking into her own apartment. She was shivering uncontrollably. The first thing she did was to change her nightgown and her underpants, just in case Lynford threw her out again. Lisa thought that she had to have a clean nightgown if she was going to seek help from the neighbours.

Lisa Algoma's Husband Randy and Her Partner Gerard

Lisa Algoma had a very troubled life. We are going to see bits and pieces of her troubles in different chapters of this book, especially in the chapter about children (Chapter 6). Lisa married Randy when she was 21. Randy was much older than Lisa, and had already been married a couple of times. He had children who were close to Lisa's age. She thinks she must have wanted a father figure in her life when she married him. He only wanted sex. In her own words, Randy treated Lisa 'as a whore.' Again, in her own words, 'Why not, I enticed him, lured him, tempted him to have sex with me. I did everything I can think of to take him away from his wife. I pursued him like a dog in heat, I broke up his marriage ... Well, he didn't say no neither, if you know what I mean! But, at the time, I did not understand that ... I just thought it was all me.'

Although Randy was obviously a father figure for Lisa, in reality he was the furthest thing from fatherly. Randy had sex with her whenever he wanted, and Lisa just let him do it. Sometimes he hurt her during sex. He pinched her nipples till she had tears in her eyes. He bit her buttocks till she bled. But worst of all, Randy brought home his drinking buddies to have sex with Lisa. He sometimes participated; sometimes he only watched. He called her 'a piece of meat.' More than once, he stuck household objects in her, such as bottles. Lisa felt like 'a piece of meat,' just flesh that men liked to feed on. No wonder she ate herself into a size 18. 'I was trying to hide my loneliness and hatred behind the folds of my flesh.' Lisa felt 'caged' in her life, in her house. She felt trapped within her own body.

Randy was only one point in Lisa's long list of troubles, most of them both physical and sexual in nature. As I will discuss in more detail in the chapter about social support (Chapter 8), Lisa was molested by her stepfather when she was only 10. At 12 her own brother had sex with her. In her late teens, her sister's husband raped her. When the sister found out about what had happened, she blamed Lisa. Lisa's sister still blames her for the shower incident, even though she has been divorced from her husband for many years now; she still accuses Lisa of destroying her marriage. Lisa is so confused about her own sexuality that she also blames herself for all the sexual and abusive episodes. 'I might have done it, I don't think I did, but who knows, I might have enticed him too! Well, maybe not, he was a real creep, but I was not Ms goody-goody. The only thing I knew was to lie down and open my legs.'

Lisa's partner Gerard was also very abusive to her. 'Why should anyone be different?' Lisa asked. 'I catch the worst, like a magnet. I am like rotting meat, I attract all the flies!' Gerard was heavily into drugs and alcohol, and he was heavily into hurting Lisa during sex. She thinks that maybe this was because Gerard was not really sexually potent. 'The drugs did it to him, he just would try and try and plop! It won't work ... The more inadequate he felt, the more he turned on me.' Gerard raped Lisa by sticking things in her. He bruised her flesh and, sometimes, the bite marks he left on her breasts were so deep that they got infected. 'I just opened my legs, like I did for so many other men. I kept totally still but I *screamed* inside my head. See, how I am talking to you now, kind of nice and quiet ... Don't be fooled, I am still *screaming* inside my head.' Lisa knows that she has a very long way to go to reclaim her body. She may have a longer road to travel in reclaiming her bruised soul.

Ann's Partner Rob

As I have already mentioned, although the stories I heard from all of my participants hurt and troubled me as a woman, I was affected by Ann's experiences in a much deeper way than by the others. Perhaps this was because Ann was so young during our interview (although not the youngest one). Perhaps it was because she was so severely hurt and disabled. Perhaps it was because Rob's tactics of violence were so glaringly premeditated and vicious. The reader will recall that, in Chapter 3, I questioned the intrapersonal theories of violence against women, including those focusing on typologies of abusers. The reader will also recall the Cobra typology of men who were cruel, calculated, self-centred, and capable of inflicting enormous pain without feeling remorse (Jacobson and Gottman, 2001). The one who most closely approaches that typology in this research is Rob. Here is one of the numerous gruesome incidents Ann told me about during our long interview.

Towards the end of their two-year common-law relationship, Rob's extreme violence had pushed Ann to start considering a separation. No matter how much Rob tried to keep her docile by pumping her full of sleeping pills (see the psychological abuse section, p. 82), Ann was preparing to leave.

One of Ann's attempts to leave resulted in her being taken for a ride to a remote nature conservation area, some hours' drive north of Toronto. Rob's stated goal was reconciliation. Ann had gone along with his offer because she took it to be genuine. The ride was not smooth, because Ann did not immediately give in to Rob's reconciliation request. This was quite unlike Ann. Previously she would have readily given in to whatever Rob wanted. Ann was generally obedient, but on that hot and humid summer day, she did not immediately comply. Ann complained and asked Rob to treat her better. For her resistance, Rob's revenge was quite merciless. He stopped the van in the middle of the road, dragged Ann out into the bush, and violently raped her. The brush was sticky, and they were in the middle of the wilderness.

The rape was only the beginning of the hours of torture that Rob inflicted on Ann. He ripped off all her clothes, jumped into his van, and started to drive away. Ann chased the van, totally exposed while he drove ahead watching her anguish from the rear-view mirror. Ann ran for seven miles. 'It was a marshy area, the road was full of slithery things; he knew I was deadly afraid of slithery things! I was hysterical.' When Ann collapsed from her ordeal of the rape, coupled with her fear of the bushland and heat exhaustion, Rob picked up her nude body, drove back into the city, and dumped her on the front lawn of her parents' home. When her parents got her safely into their home, Ann was still totally nude and covered with dirt. Although her parents made sure that Rob was charged and eventually got convicted for his sexual and physical assault, he served less than a month in jail. Moreover, his cousin happened to be a night employee at the local jail. Through his cousin, Rob was able to make midnight telephone calls to Ann, some of which were apologetic, begging her to return to him. Most of the calls, however, were harassing and threatening. Ann's parents made sure to tape these calls, but they were not able to get Rob's sentence increased.[2]

Elly's Husband Stephan and Erika's Husband Tony

Elly's husband always put her down. As far as he was concerned, she was a 'tooth-pick,' 'ugly,' 'a bitch,' and a long list of other undesirable things. Yet, the extremely negative attributes he pinned on Elly did not prevent Stephan from showing extreme control and jealousy over his wife. For Stephan, who spent most of his life unemployed, a relentless need to determine Elly's whereabouts was a full-time job. Elly always worked, sometimes in more than one job, to make ends meet. She also worked to help out her parents, who were immigrants from an Eastern European country.

Stephan did not allow Elly to stay around with other employees after work, go out for lunch or dinner with them, or attend other company functions. Stephan would beat her up even at the mention of any social activities like those. Elly often worked overtime, however. This meant more money, and Stephan did not mind that. What he did mind was 'fun.' He was pathologically obsessed with the possibility of Elly's infidelity.

Once, Elly went to a company Christmas party simply because she had to. She had run out of excuses, and her absences from work-

---

2 Since 1993 stalking is a criminal offence under the Criminal Code of Canada; Rob's harassment of Ann occurred before this legislation was enacted.

related occasions were starting to be construed as a negative attitude towards work. Knowing that she would pay for it in more ways than one, Elly went to the party without Stephan's permission and still managed to have a good time. 'I wasn't fooling around or anything, it was just so nice to be out of the house. It was so nice to talk to people, hear them talk to me. It was like meeting these people for the first time in my life. Before the party, it was all work, work, work. The party was really really nice!'

When she arrived home, Stephan was waiting at the door. He choked her and pinned her to the door as soon as she walked in. 'As silly as it now sounds, I was thinking, let me take off my shoes first. Just let me take off my shoes, then you kill me.' Then, Stephan ordered her to remove her underpants. Stephan inspected her underpants and asked her why there was a stain, why the crotch was not totally dry. Stephan smelled Elly's underpants. Stephan then had sex with Elly right at the doorway. Elly wished she was dead. Elly wished she could kill him. She could taste her own hate.

As Erika explained, her husband 'Tony was a needy man.' He wanted things, he wanted to be the centre of interest. He beat her when she was pregnant. Once, he put out his cigarette on Erika's palm. Tony was pathologically jealous of Erika and constantly feared that she was going to have affairs with other men. Once Erika got a severe beating when she said Tom Selleck was good-looking. If Erika was a little late coming home, Tony would conduct what Erika called 'body searches.' He would strip her down and go through her belongings. He would check her underwear for smells and stains.

Elly and Erika are two different women from two different cultural and racial backgrounds with two different partners, but they both had very similar experiences of unimaginable scrutiny and degradation.

Women's Experiences of Economic Abuse

At the time of the interviews, twenty-eight of the thirty-nine women were employed (about 72%). However, during the period when they had experienced partner abuse, the proportion who held jobs was much lower (16, or about 41%). With the exception of one, all were low-paying, sometimes transitory jobs. Women like Elly had two jobs, but no control over the money they earned. This is not uncommon, because abusive men often prevent women from participating in financial decisions (Kurz, 1996, 1998). Most women in this study did not have a reliable, steady source of income they could call their own or access to resources even when they worked. Most were economically dependent on their partners; some were dependent on the state. This dependency gave their abusive partners yet another area within which to misuse their power and to demean, degrade, and control them.

Vicky's Partner Jerry

Vicky had no say over money matters. Every week, Jerry would give her $40.00 for groceries and ask for the grocery bill. 'We didn't have visitors or nothing, but odd times, people show up, but no cash! Still 40. I'm telling you, 40 don't entertain much. Any change, he'd take it back!' Vicky was allowed to go bowling with her friends, once every two weeks. 'He'd give me 10, five to get in, a buck for a drink. He'd ask for 4 back. Once I got two drinks, the hell broke loose! I says, "girls have two or three, so what's the big deal?" He says, "You'll have one, money don't grow on trees! Have water if you want more!" He has 10 beers a night with his buddies, for me one damn pop ... and water!'

Elly's Husband Stephan

I just finished providing a summary of what happened to Elly on the night she went out for a Christmas party. Now, I would like to summarize what happened to her pay cheques. As will be discussed again in the chapter about social support systems (Chapter 8), Elly worked all her life. From early on, she had to help out her immigrant parents, who lacked the marketable skills to properly fend for themselves. When she married, Elly turned in her pay cheque to Stephan just as she had turned in her pay cheque to her parents before. Stephan was difficult about every penny she needed to spend, including the money for groceries. Elly never had nice clothes, never had a decent vacation, and rarely had enough money for an extra cup of coffee at work. Elly could not have called a cab had she wanted to leave, so she didn't even think of leaving. When Elly tried to buy a car for herself with the money she was earning, she almost lost her life. I will expand on the incident in Chapter 8 when I discuss Elly's in-laws.

Iris's Husband Alex

Throughout her twelve-year marriage, Iris never had to work. Alex made enough money for a house in the suburbs with two cars, and he bought every other status marker for a middle-class life. Alex was a good provider for their daughter Elisa. However, Iris was not happy within the marriage and was increasingly restless within her traditional housewife role. When she wanted to go to work and when she wanted to go back to school, Alex started to flex his patriarchal muscles. When Iris wanted to leave, Alex refused all material support for her as well as for Elisa. The day they separated, Alex cancelled the health and dental care coverage for Iris, although his company paid for family coverage. Because Iris was just starting to go back to school, she had no income of her own. The first thing that had to be sacrificed was the extensive dental treatments she needed and was in the middle of receiving. By the time Iris graduated and found a relatively good job, her dental problems had deteriorated so much so that she lost a number of teeth.

Iris had to move out of the affluent neighbourhood she and her daughter enjoyed when she was married. The two of them moved into a one-bedroom apartment with dark walls, few windows, and lots of cockroaches. There were times Iris could not find the money to send Elisa on school trips. Then there were times when the money ran out before the days in the month did. Iris would skip meals to make sure that the few leftovers would stretch to feed Elisa. During the years following her separation, which Iris refers to as 'the hard years,' there were many nights Iris cried herself to sleep.

Chapter Six

Children: Reluctant Targets and Witnesses

As feminist theories of violence suggest, violence that targets women also spreads to the people and things that are important in their lives (Sev'er, 1998, 1999). The literature on violence against women shows that abusive men frequently damage property, hurt pets, and harass friends and relatives, in addition to the direct violence they inflict upon their partners. It is sad, but not at all surprising that men who inflict violence on their mates frequently inflict similar violence on their children (Wolak and Finkelhor, 1998). The most extreme form of this violence is multiple homicides, where the abuser kills his partner, his children, and himself. As discussed in the Introduction, in one of the most gruesome cases recorded in the Canadian family violence literature, Vilem Luft Jr stabbed his wife to death, shot his four children point-blank, and then killed himself (*Toronto Star*, 7 July 2000: A1). The youngest victim was less than 3 months old.

Effects of Direct and Indirect Violence

Child murder is the ultimate extreme, but acts of violence towards children take on many different forms (Health Canada, 1996). Sometimes, violence starts before the children are born. Prevailing estimates of violence during pregnancy range from 7 to 20 per cent (Kaufman Kantor and Jasinski, 1998: 32). Numerous studies report that existing violence escalates during pregnancy (Campbell et al., 1992; Campbell, Harris, and Lee, 1995; McFarlane, 1992; Stark and Flitcraft, 1996). McCue (1995: 83) asserts that battered women are not only more likely to get pregnant more often, but they are also significantly more likely to have miscarriages or induced abortions. More frequent pregnancies may be an artefact of the woman's lack of say in birth control methods used or the timing and the nature of the intercourse. Physical attacks during pregnancy are centred on the women's abdomen, breasts, or genitals in many cases (McCue, 1995; McFarlane, 1992). Again, in extreme cases, men kill their pregnant wives and their unborn children, as in the murder of a pregnant woman who was poisoned on Mother's Day (*Toronto Star*, 16 July 2000: A5).

Violence during Pregnancy

In this study, more than half the women (21) talked about the increased difficulties they faced during pregnancy. These ranged from increased put-downs and drinking and shouting binges to increased physical and sexual violence. In ten cases (Ava, Debbie, Elly, Laurette, Lisa Algoma, Nancy Niagara, Rose, Sonny, Sue, and Terry), physical attacks during pregnancy were particularly severe. Sue's husband Ed repeatedly got drunk and asked her to 'kill the baby.' Sue knew he was not joking. Debbie, Elly, Rose, and Terry claimed that they were kicked or kneed in the stomach and the groin. Lisa Algoma's husband Randy was wearing heavy work boots when he kicked her, resulting in hospitalization. Her common-law partner Gerard also kicked her when she was pregnant. These women were absolutely sure that the goal of the beatings and the kicks was to induce a miscarriage or to force an abortion. These suspicions were realized in at least a few cases. Rose miscarried shortly after receiving a kick in the stomach. The youngest of Debbie's children, Mark was born prematurely and required long-term hospitalization. Elly's delivery was extremely complicated, requiring hospitalization both for herself and for her newborn. However, she said, 'I liked it. I liked staying in the hospital, I felt safe there. I wanted to stay longer, I didn't want to go home. I didn't want to take my baby home.'

Indirect Violence towards Children

Sometimes, violence towards children is an extension of violence towards their mother. In such cases, children get hurt because they happen to be around when their mothers are being attacked (Wolak and Finkelhor, 1998). In a content analysis of 648 cases covered in the media between 1995 and 1999, I found that eighty involved biological children of the women who were injured or killed (Toronto Study, see

Sev'er, 2001; also see Chapter 4). In seven additional cases, stepchildren were also injured or killed. Although the media reports are selective and biased, the sheer number of children being victimized along with their mothers attests to the spread of violence beyond the partner.

In this study, Laurette claimed that her husband Sam frequently threw things around. Sometimes, these objects hit one or more of her four children. Suzan Toronto is a petite woman who weighs about 100 pounds. Her husband threw her out of their first-floor window, leaving shattered glass all over the living room. Suzan does not remember how many cuts she received in this terrifying incident. However, she does remember that Joseph, only a toddler at the time, was crawling on the broken glass to reach her. Debbie said that her partner threw things at her, sometimes hitting the baby who was playing beside her. Amber claimed that her husband Guy was particularly fond of hitting her when she was holding one of their newborn babies. This was his way of making sure that she could not defend herself. Amber gave birth to a total of seven children, probably contributing to her own dependency on the numerous untrustworthy men in her life.

Witnessing Violence

Even more frequently, children witness the violence, although they may not be the target of it (Fantuzzo et al., 1991; Kelly and Radford, 1998; Jaffee, Wolfe, and Wilson, 1990). I have already discussed the case where a Toronto man poured a litre of sulphuric acid over his partner who was in the process of breaking up their long-term relationship (*Toronto Star*, 4 July 2000: B1). The woman was in critical condition with caustic burns to 80 per cent of her body. Since witnessing the ghastly attack, her son, who was 6 years old at the time, has been repeating the blood-curdling details of the incident like a mantra (*Toronto Star*, 25 July 2000: A17).

The most recent national survey (GSS, 2000) also identifies children as witnesses to family violence. It must be emphasized that the witnessed violence is disproportionally against women. For example, children were twice as likely to witness violence against their mothers as against their fathers. In the five years preceding the survey, 37 per cent of all victims of spousal violence claimed that their children witnessed at least one violent event. Moreover, the violence was often severe. For example, in 45 per cent of the households where children had witnessed violence, the victims had suffered physical injuries (GSS, 2000).

Children also accompany their mothers to shelters, if their mothers flee the violence. Confinement to less than adequate living quarters, concerns about safety, and exposure to other children who may have suffered and witnessed violence make these children's lives less than tolerable (Sev'er, 2002). In one study, 70 per cent of children in a shelter were found to demonstrate clinical-level behavioural problems, and 53 per cent were found to be clinically depressed (Wolak and Finkelhor, 1998; also see Terr, 1990; Zima, Bussing, and Bystritsky, 1999).

The significance of these types of events is that the witnessed violence is taking place in children's core relationships. Children may see their fathers hitting their mothers or siblings. They may hear bodies or objects being thrown around, and they may feel helpless to respond to cries for help or grunts of pain. They may see cuts, bruises, and blood. Some children observe sexual assaults or even the murder of their mothers (Eth and Pynoos, 1994). Surveys asking adults about their childhood memories of witnessing violence have found that anywhere between 11 and 20 per cent of adults recall such incidents from their childhood (Wolak and Finkelhor, 1998: 75; Fantuzzo et al., 1991). Adults who have witnessed violence as children recall an average of nine such incidents. Thus, there is the possibility that exposure to continuous violence may have compounding effects (Terr, 1990).

In Canada, the Violence Against Women Survey (VAWS, 1993) indicated that children witnessed violence between their parents in 39 per cent of violent marriages. Moreover, much of this violence was serious since 52 per cent of abused women said that they feared for their lives. In addition, 78 per cent of women who stay in Canadian women's shelters report that their children observed the violence that they endured (Juristat, 1999, vol. 6). This observation may mean that the VAWS (1993) findings underestimate the problem of children witnessing violence against their mothers, or it may show that women are more likely to seek shelter support if their children witness the violence. Whatever the case may be, it is clear that children often form an unwilling audience to one of the most awful crimes imaginable.

Effects of Witnessing Violence

Wolak and Finkelhor (1998: 81) group the symptoms shown by children exposed to partner violence under the categories of behavioural, physical, emotional, and cognitive. Other researchers also point to severe psychological and behavioural problems (Kelly and Radford, 1998;

Zima, Bussing, and Bystritsky, 1999). Examples of behavioural symptoms are aggression, tantrums, acting out, and delinquency. Sleeping and eating disorders, psychosomatic symptoms, and regressive behaviours such as bed-wetting are examples of physical symptoms. Emotional disorders include anxiety, depression, withdrawal, and low self-esteem. Cognitive disorders are related to poor academic performance, language lag, and poor social skills in managing conflicts. Beyond Wolak and Finkelhor's (1998) classification, what I would like to emphasize is that the effects of either witnessing or experiencing violence are at least two-pronged. One possibility is that when such children reach adulthood, they may externalize their fear, anger, frustration, and lack of social skills by trying to control others. These are the ones who contribute to the cycle of violence by transforming themselves from victims into perpetrators (Jaffee, Wolfe, and Wilson, 1990). Another possibility is that some children will internalize their fear, anger, and frustration. Their problems may be compounded by a lack of social skills. These are the ones who will contribute to the cycle of violence by becoming easy targets for abuse by making poor decisions, by allowing other people to make decisions for them, by choosing problematic partners, or by engaging in forms of self-deprecation that may range from low self-esteem, eating disorders, drugs and alcohol use, self-mutilation, or even to suicide (Bagley and King, 1991; Kelly and Radford, 1998; Steed, 1994; Zima, Bussing, and Bystritsky, 1999). There is no proven one-to-one correspondence between observing violence as a child and becoming either a victimizer or a victim as an adult. Yet there is enough research to suggest that the correlation is significant.

As discussed in Chapter 3, social learning theories make strong predictions about children's propensity to imitate the behaviour of adult models in their lives (Bowker, 1983; Walker, 1984). Accordingly, children who watch their parents acting in violent ways may learn that violence is 'acceptable.' They may learn to use certain types of weapons, such as belts, hockey sticks, or baseball bats. They may also learn ways of violating another person, such as through verbal put-downs or psychological taunting (Pottie and Levett, 1998). Gender-based applications of the social learning model suggest that male children may learn techniques of violence from their violent fathers and female children may learn submissiveness, docility, and helplessness from their victimized mothers (Arias, 1984; O'Leary, 1988; Jaffe, Wolfe, and Wilson, 1986; Kaufman Kantor and Straus, 1989). Indeed, there is some support for the occurrence of genderized forms of transmission of violence. Information gathered from VAWS (1993) indicates that violent men are three times more likely than non-violent men to have witnessed violence in their childhood. Women raised in violent homes were twice as likely to fall victim to spousal violence compared with women raised in non-violent homes. These are disturbing patterns of intergenerational transmission of violence. These are also the patterns that emerged in the lives of some of the women I interviewed, such as Clara, Debbie, Elly, Erika, Kim, Lisa Algoma, Lisa London, Lorie, Sue, Terry, and possibly others.

According to the social learning theory, if role models get away with violence, or actually receive symbolic or tangible rewards for behaving the way they do, the propensity for learning and/or imitation of the violent behaviour is much higher. This assertion has many implications for children observing their father's violent behaviour, because the fathers frequently get away with such conduct. Since the original laboratory experiments of Albert Bandura (1973) and Robert Sears (1961), there has been substantial support for the social learning model of transmission of violence (Health Canada, 1996; Jaffee, Wolfe, and Wilson, 1990; Lehmann, 1997; Graham-Berman and Levendosky, 1998).

For Children's Sake

In the current study, only six women (15%) had no children. The remaining thirty-three (85%) had a total of seventy-five biologically related and an additional eleven biologically unrelated children. At the time of the interviews, the age of the oldest biological 'child' was 33 years (Olga's son) and the youngest was Amber's 2-month-old baby. The oldest biologically unrelated 'child' in these women's lives was 26 years old (Olga's sister's son, who has lived with her since childhood). If we aggregate the numbers, there could have been an average of three possible child witnesses for each incident of abuse. Given the negative effects of experiencing or witnessing interpersonal abuse on children's lives, our attention now turns to what may have happened to some of these children.

First, I must strongly underscore that the women I interviewed expressed a lot of warm feelings and care for their children. Words like 'I am living for them' (Laurette), 'without them, I would have killed myself' (Elly), 'I will do anything for them' (Sue and Suzan Toronto), 'I will never let anything happen to them' (Debbie and Lisa London), were extremely common. Another common declaration that was expressed in similar if not identical words was 'I didn't leave because of my children.' Some women (like Laurette) had put up with all types of abuse themselves, but had found the courage to leave only when their children were also abused. Some women (like Carmen and Erika) had extremely strained relations with their children, but had not given up on them. Three women (Debbie, Elly, and Lisa Algoma) had their children under the care of the Children's Aid Society for periods of time. At the time of the interviews Debbie and Elly were trying to get them back, which they claimed was an uphill battle.

Many women shed tears when they mentioned the difficulties their children have had or continue to have. Many women expressed a profound sadness and grief at not being able to erase the turbulent events from their children's memories. In Debbie's words, 'If I could change one single thing in my life, I would make my children have a normal life.' I have absolutely no reason to doubt the authenticity and sincerity of the expressed sentiments. Despite this deep maternal love and commitment, I sadly heard and recorded many serious problems with the children of my participants. In my mind, there is no doubt that most, if not all, of these difficulties are related to exposure to sometimes serious and often repeated violence. I am going to summarize my findings under general problems, self-directed problems, and other-directed problems that these children displayed.

General Problems

One of the very clear messages I got from these interviews is that children react in very different ways to the violence in their lives. Regardless of the trauma they experience through their fathers' violence, some children seem to prevail against all odds. Some, however, carry the burden of physical or emotional scars right into their adulthood. At one time or another, almost every mother I interviewed expressed serious concerns and doubts about at least one child's future. Most were worried about poor school performance, poor relations with peers, not listening, poor hygiene, sleeping or eating disorders, or bed-wetting and nightmares. Occasionally, school counsellors, social workers, therapists, and legal professionals were also involved.

Debbie's Son Mark
As discussed in the previous section, Debbie was one of the women who was kicked in her stomach while she was pregnant. Her son was

born prematurely and was hospitalized for months afterwords. As it turns out, Mark's development is much slower than children of a comparable age both at the cognitive and aptitude levels. He is still not toilet-trained, and his vocabulary consists of a few simple words and grunts. His understanding of abstract terms seems to be dismal.

Debbie told me that although she never hits her kids, she cannot help but shout at them when she is under a lot of pressure. Unfortunately, Debbie's life is constantly under pressure. Mark is 4 years old, and he goes into hysterical shakes when she shouts, and she feels much guilt when her son uncontrollably shakes. She said she promises him (and herself) that she will never shout again. Sadly, she does shout again, perpetuating the destructive cycles of fear, guilt, and self-hatred in herself and of fear and terror in her son. 'You should see the little thing, just staring into my eyes, shaking all over. When I see the fear in his eyes, I often stop, but I don't really know when I catch his eyes ... I might be screaming for a long time ... screaming, screaming ... who knows? You should see him shivering, shaking. It is pitiful, he is so tiny. I hate myself! I really hate to see him like that. I hate doing it to him! I would do anything for him, anything at all ... but I still scream, isn't that horrible?'

Laurette's Son Tom

With tears in her eyes, Laurette told me that her 13-year-old son Tom was the only one of her four children who had been frequently targeted by her abusive husband. At one time, Sam had tried to choke him. At another time, Sam pushed Tom hard. When Tom fell on the floor, Sam stomped on his head. 'It was not just an act. He was actually trying to crush his head. I thought, he was going to kill him! Jesus, help me, he is going to be squashed ... I was terrified. I was shouting: *stop, stop, stop!* He did stop, but not before he kicked Tommy a few more times.'

According to Laurette, Sam's targeting of Tom could have been the result of Tom's close resemblance to Laurette. She thinks that Sam always detested this close resemblance. It could also have stemmed from Tom actually trying to intervene a few times when his father was beating up on Laurette. Of their four children, Tom was the only one who was protective of his mother. Sam resented this challenge. Of their four children, Tom was the only one who got abused.

Whatever the real motivation may have been, the violence has taken a toll on Tom. Laurette told me that Tom sleeps in a closet, with the door securely shut. He has stashed a radio, a few pillows, and a blanket in his closet. As if Laurette's troubles were not enough, Sam has involved the Children's Aid Society in this matter. Sam has tried to have Laurette declared an 'unfit mother' to obtain full custody of all four children. Laurette said: 'He blames me for Tom's peculiar behaviour. He unleashed his dogs [Laurette's term for lawyers] on me for this. My case for custody is jeopardized by all these vicious accusations. It's not that he gives a hoot about the children ... He doesn't! He even told me he doesn't want them. But, he'll fight for them just to turn my life into hell. He's been dragging me through a nasty custody fight ... Doing everything to prove I'm crazy ... I'm unfit ... I'm making Tommy crazy! The court sent us to the shrinks. Tommy told them he loves me and wants to stay with me. But who knows ... [Since he is a corporate executive] ... he has money, power. He has an army of high-priced lawyers. I try to make my case through Legal Aid. It doesn't matter who's right in this world, Sam has the money, I am scared.'

In the meantime, Tom is still sleeping in his closet. At least in her own mind, Laurette has a 'logical' explanation for Tom's unsusal behaviour. She explains that he learned to sleep in a closet as an attempt (albeit futile) to protect her from Sam's violent attacks. It seems that the closet Tom originally slept in was situated between his own and his parents' bedrooms, giving him an opportunity to hear any scuffles and run to his mother's aid when she was in distress. Although they are now separated, and Laurette is no longer in danger of being attacked in the middle of the night, she thinks Tom's behaviour just became a habit. Despite Laurette's rationalization of her son's behavioural problem, the whole family was in therapy at the time of my interview.

Nancy Ottawa's Daughter Samantha
Nancy Ottawa's 8-year-old daughter seems to have so many nightmares that she is afraid to go to sleep. At the time of the interview, she was also wetting her bed almost every night. Nancy is concerned that Samantha has a very low self-concept because of her bed-wetting problems. She does not want any of her friends to sleep over at their house, and she does not go to her friends for sleepovers. When Samantha was 3 or 4 years of age, her abusive father James used to wake her up, shake her, and sometimes even spank her whenever the little girl wet the bed. After four years, the behaviour and the fear and terror seem to persist in Samantha's life and in her dreams. Samantha's bed-wetting has turned her into a loner.

Erika's Daughter Abby

Erika's relationship with her daughter Abby has disintegrated to nothingness. She says that there is an unbreakable wall between them. For years she has done her best, but she has not been able to tear down the wall. Abby has an eating disorder. Erika blames the years of abuse she herself suffered for what she calls 'Abby's burn-out.' She fears that her daughter is an emotionally charred woman, with very few feelings for anyone other than herself. According to Erika, Abby shows no feeling, care, or respect for her mother. 'Last year, I had a hysterectomy. They took the whole thing out! There were complications. Many complications ... Some were life threatening. I was this close to death [makes a gesture of a small space with her fingers]. I almost died! People from my work came, neighbours came, some friends kept a vigil. Abby didn't show up, can you imagine that? She didn't even pick up the phone and call. It's not that she can't reach the phone, she has a cell [phone]. She didn't even send me a card ... Sometimes it hurts so much, I mean her being like that and all ... but sometimes, I say, "Girl, you are sick," hell with her, your first mission is to try to get better!'

Iris's Daughter Elisa

According to Iris, Elisa turned out to be a cold and manipulative woman. She is 27 years old and does not seem to have any female friends, and all the heterosexual relations she has had have been short-lived and superficial. Because Elisa happens to be a very beautiful young woman, Iris has seen many male friends around her. But Elisa pays attention to them only when she needs or wants something from them. Otherwise, she puts them down, finds their vulnerabilities, and says hurtful things. Elisa is also cold and distant towards Iris. There are times when she does not bother to call her mother. At other times, she calls and makes cutting remarks about Iris's weight or something she may have said or done. According to Iris, Elisa is punishing her for leaving her abusive father and destroying their family. 'This is really hard for me to say ... she's my kid, my own flesh and blood ... but, sometimes I think she would rather see me get beaten up. She doesn't appreciate my struggle. I know it sounds terrible, but this is exactly what I think!'

Self-directed Problems

Again, I would like to reiterate that not all children seem to have or continue to exhibit problems that are closely linked to the abuse they have experienced or witnessed. However, both in the literature and in the current study, this link is strongly present, as the following examples show.

Terry's Daughter Teddy

Terry described her 14-year-old daughter Teddy as a 'walking death wish.' She talked about the fact that Teddy has been smoking and drinking for a couple of years (at the time of the interview). Regardless of how many times Terry has talked to her, Teddy has just kept on doing as she pleases. Terry suspects some drug use as well, but does not know (and as she put it, does not even want to know) the extent of the problem. What Terry knows is that her teenage daughter is already sleeping around, with boys much older than herself. Terry is horrified that she is going to 'catch something unmentionable.' However, Terry is not surprised at all by her daughter's risk-taking behaviour. She suspects that her abusive husband Jack may have 'messed around with her' when she was much younger. 'I don't really know if he did it, maybe he did, maybe he didn't! I don't really know. But, Jack was real bad, you know. I wouldn't be surprised.' Terry, herself was beaten up 'to a pulp.' Many times she has thought about confronting Jack about Teddy, but she has never found the courage to find out about what else was happening 'under her nose.' She fears for Teddy and feels a tremendous amount of guilt. She thinks Teddy hates her even more than she hates her abusive father. Terry is confused and completely helpless. Teddy may be on a path of self-destruction. 'I don't want to call the cops on her, you know! She already hates me, she'll hate me more if I did that. Besides, they'll take her away or something. Just look at me ... I'm not the Blessed Mother. I'm afraid. I know she is just a baby, but she has a mind of her own. She has a temper. Sometimes she stares at me ... I see her father's mean eyes. I don't know what to do or what to say ... I'm frozen right here [shows her chest]. I tell her I pray for her ... I know pray ain't enough, but I don't know nothing else.'

Monica's Son Tim

Monica's 10-year-old son Tim has had learning difficulties for as long as she can remember. Tim has been diagnosed with attention deficiency syndrome (ADS), and the school counsellors seem to be on his case. What worries Monica the most is her son's bizarre behaviour of sitting in a high-back chair and banging his head on the back of the chair, sometimes for twenty or thirty minutes at a time. She has tried to make him stop by bribing him or offering food or toys that he likes. She has scolded him. She has sent him to bed. She has turned off the television. One time, Monica even lost control and hit him on the head. All to no avail. When her son starts banging his head, Monica feels like someone is banging on her own head with a hammer. She is afraid she may lose control again and beat him up. She is afraid that Tim is going to have brain damage by banging himself so hard and so long. Monica wonders about what might be going on in his mind when Tim behaves that way.

Stacy's Son Leo

According to Stacy, Leo, who is 10 years old, is a bitter old man in a little boy's body. He has tried to run away from home numerous times, hiding in awkward places like behind dumpsters at apartment buildings. He has been on strong medication for clinical childhood depression. Stacy is sure that someday Leo is going to try to kill himself. She has discussed her fears with social workers assigned to his case. She has called the police when he ran away. Stacy has pleaded with them to put Leo into a facility where he can receive the help he needs. The police have tried to placate her by saying that children run away for many reasons, sometimes as a prank. After all, he was just hiding in the neighbourhood, a few blocks away from his own home. The police have also told Stacy that there is not much they can do about his depression until Leo 'does something.' Stacy is angry that they are waiting for him to actually attempt suicide. 'Can't they see he needs help now? Can't they see I need help? The kid's on a slippery slope, what do they think? He's going to wake up one day, and whooosh ... all is OK? Are you kidding me, he may be dead! He may fucking be dead!'

Stacy is also afraid for her 7-year-old Chris who is constantly exposed to his brother's behavioural and psychological problems. She said, 'Call me crazy, call it an instinct, but I can see another one coming through the dark tunnel.'

Other-directed Problems

Several women talked about their children's unruly and destructive behaviour. Some of these complaints were in the vein of 'children will be children' or 'boys will be boys.' However, some sons and daughters were engaged in behaviour that cannot be brushed off as the regular pain of growing up. As the following examples show, some of these children are on their way to becoming or have already become abusive adults.

Gwyn's Son Ronny

Gwyn says that her 11-year-old son Ronny is smart and does well in school. But she also says he has an uncontrollable temper and does not have many friends. A few times, Ronny has chased neighbourhood girls who are younger than himself and made them cry. Now the little girls seem to run away as soon as they see him. Ronny seems to spend most of his time alone, sitting, sometimes staring into space but mostly intently watching animals. Gwyn has caught him throwing rocks at the neighbour's cat who frequents their small garden. She says he throws things at the birds who try to drink from the birdbath and he pulls Bungie's (their dog's) tail and ears to the degree of making the poor animal yelp. 'He is not a baby, he knows he's hurting the poor thing!' Once Ronny kicked Bungie hard enough to make the dog lose his balance and fall. Gwyn has talked to Ronny about treating pets kindly, but it has not made much impact. Gwyn has threatened to give Bungie away if Ronny continues to be mean to him, but that has not helped either. Gwyn is afraid that Ronny has 'things bottled up in him, getting ready to come out.'

Sue's Two Adult Sons Trevor and Billy

When I met Sue, she was excited about a new relationship she was embarking on. In her past, there had been two violent relationships involving regular beatings, constant harassment, and stalking. Shortly after their separation, her former husband Ed kidnapped their son from school. Although the son was returned without harm, during the torturous hours of waiting, Sue realized that Ed had the power to hurt her and her children whenever he wanted to. This realization was yet another blow to Sue's already fragile self-concept.

At the time of the interview, Sue had just become a grandmother through her youngest son Trevor, who was 21. I sensed that this may not have been a purely joyous occasion, since Trevor has been routinely beating up his girlfriend. Even in his youth, Trevor has already gone through a number of struggles with alcoholism and has come to police attention because of his overall violence and abuse of his girlfriend. Sue is afraid that Trevor may even hurt the baby if he is 'loaded.' 'He has a short fuse, you know. I see Ed in him! Smallest thing, and booom! He goes. What's he going to do with a baby who don't listen? He might just throw him at the wall or out the window or something. Those two are not ready [for parenthood] ... Before they get their shit together, a dog is too much for them!'

Sue's oldest son Billy, who is 30, has also been arrested for abusing his current common-law partner. Billy's marriage has recently ended. Sue suspects it was for the same reason. 'Maybe I should feel bad or guilty or something ... I don't. They are like their fathers [sic]. There's a mean streak in those boys. I don't hurt a fly, they're not like me!'

Elly's Sons Jimmy and Andy

I will discuss the lack of social support in Elly's life in Chapter 8. For the purpose of the present discussion, let me remind the readers that Elly was kicked in the stomach when she was pregnant and was hospitalized. She was beaten up many other times as well. Each time, her own parents told her it was her fault. In every case, her whole family, including her sons Jimmy (age 14) and Andy (age 11) have turned against her, rather than blaming or questioning their abusive father Stephan. From all these incidents, Elly talked about one particular Christmas as being one of the most hurtful events in her life. The following is a summary of the event.

Elly comes from a very religious family of Roman Catholic background. Celebrating Christmas always had a very significant meaning for them. One year, because of a very serious beating she had received, Elly had to pack up her children and go to her parents' house during the Christmas break. Her parents were not happy about the situation. They insisted that she return to her abusive husband. 'They had company from the old country, distant relatives or something. My mother asked me to stay in my room, not to come out and talk to them. I had to keep the boys in there with me. I guess, they did not want the guests to see me black and blue. They were embarrassed. They like to pretend all is great, you know ... This old country thing, I guess! This old country lies about "my daughter married well!"'

Elly's children did not take the move away from home well either. They wanted to go back. They wanted to be at their own home to open their presents. They shouted and cursed at their mother, who is small and weighs no more than 100 pounds. On Christmas Eve, Jimmy and Andy physically attacked their mother with sticks and plastic baseball bats for depriving them of their father. Jimmy was shouting, 'I wish you were dead!' while Andy was hitting her on the head. Within a couple of days, Elly did return to her husband. After the mother-bashing Christmas incident, her two sons routinely joined their father in beating her up. Because of her inability to control her sons' violent behaviour Jimmy, the eldest of Elly's children, was at a group home at the time of our interview. I felt that Elly was quite reluctant to get him back in the near future. Clearly, she was afraid of him.

Chapter Seven

General Strategies of Survival

When I started my research, I had the strong expectation (maybe wishful thinking) that I was going to find numerous 'success stories.' At least in my own mind, I defined 'success' as breaking the cycle of violence, saving oneself and where applicable, one's children, from the physical, emotional, economic, and/or sexual violations by a male partner. After all, I had chosen to find 'survivors' of abuse, who had already demonstrated a gargantuan effort in leaving their abusive partners and not returning to them for at least six months (the criterion for inclusion in my study). In a way, that these women are alive and going on with their lives day after day, week after week, and month after month is indeed a success in itself. There are also other glimpses of hope and even some triumph in these lives. I am going to deal with such accomplishments in the following pages, which pay tribute to the strength and resourcefulness of the women in my study. I also must emphasize, however, some of the less positive aspects of what years and sometimes decades of abuse have left behind. In the final analysis, what emerges is how deeply and how seemingly irreversibly most of these women's lives have been altered, coloured, and reshaped. My interviews left me with the feeling that these women do not want to be judged – who could ever be an impartial judge of their dramas? These women do not want pity, and pitying them would certainly be arrogance on the part of those of us who cannot even imagine the strength needed to survive the horrors they have lived through. Nevertheless, their long and arduous, sometimes successful and other times failed attempts at dealing with violence have taught them some strategies for survival. I want now to focus on how some of these strategies are positive strengths, but others are social and personal traps with their own negative consequences. My interviewees shared their struggles with me to help other women who are caught up in violent relationships.

Strategies to Protect Children

As I discussed in Chapter 6, all but six of my interviewees were mothers. All expressed a deep fondness for and attachment to their children, whether the children were currently residing with them or not. Even Elly, who was obviously afraid of Jimmy's violence, and Terry, who occasionally saw a meanness in Teddy's eyes, cared deeply for their children. It is not surprising that one of the main concerns of these women had been to keep their children safe. They also worried about the psychological well-being of their children.

Strategies to protect children were mostly developed in intuitive ways. Women tried to keep the children away from their explosive partners or husbands. They fed them early. They let them play outside or at neighbours' homes till late hours, or they put them to bed early so they would not be around if their fathers went on a rampage. These strategies worked to some degree. The negative consequence was that children were removed from participating in 'family life.' Children may also have learned that family life is unpredictable and even dangerous.

Protecting children also involved instructing or teaching the older ones to gather up the younger ones and get them out of the way when there was trouble. This is a strategy many of the women used repeatedly to keep their little ones safe. But the strategy had the unintended consequence of giving adult responsibilities to relatively young children because of the unpredictability of violence at home. Children were taught to take care of themselves and to take care of others, since their mothers may not have been able to protect them. Sadly, even when children were never targeted or hurt themselves, they were nevertheless robbed of a carefree childhood. They were forced to be always on guard, to be anxious for their own safety and for the safety of their siblings.

A few women (like Suzan Toronto, Stacy, and Laurette) prepared special bags containing a few clean clothes, some dry food (chocolate bars were mentioned), phone numbers of a few relatives, and some loose change. The women I interviewed did not seem to have access to very much money during their abusive relationships. Laurette included bus tickets in the stash. These bags were hidden in various places such as sheds, garages, or under the porches where they could be found relatively easily. Most older children and even some younger ones were instructed about how to take these bags and under what conditions to do so. Most women taught their children how to dial 911, or to call a designated relative, or escape into a predetermined hiding place and stay there. Most children were instructed not to cry or shout no matter what happened, so that they would avoid being found in their hiding places. What is amazing is that most children learned not to cry or shout even when exposed to quite scary episodes of violence. At relatively early ages, these children learned to control (maybe overly so) their natural instincts and emotions, which may have serious implications for their own adult lives – Erika's and Iris's imperturbable daughters Abby and Elisa come to mind (see Chapter 6).

Like responsible fire marshals, some mothers routinely put their children through drills to make sure that these vital strategies were not forgotten. When I asked women whether their children knew about the seriousness of these drills or whether they treated them as a sort of game, they assured me that the children knew that these were not games. Starting from an early age, children in violent homes learn to walk on eggshells. They know that calm can be switched to chaos in a split second, with angry words, threats, shouts, and things being thrown around. Worst of all, some have seen their mothers get hurt. A few have been hurt themselves (Laurette's son Tom and Terry's daughter Teddy; see Chapter 6).

In very individualized ways, some children develop their own strategies to deal with the crushing burden of membership in a home of abuse. As I already discussed in more detail in the section on children, some learn to hide (like Laurette's 13-year-old son sleeping in closets). Others learn to be tough and violent and to attack others (Like Sue's sons Trevor and Billy and Elly's sons Jimmy and Andy), some learn to hurt themselves (like Debbie's and Stacy's sons Mark and Leo). A few abuse substances or their own bodies (like Terry's daughter Teddy and Sue's sons Trevor and Billy) or become cold, non-emotional, and exploitative (like Iris's and Erika's daughters Elisa and Abby; see Chapter 6). In the long run, some of these strategies of survival themselves turn into lifelong burdens or interpersonal problems.

Strategies for Mental Health

Women develop strategies for themselves to cope with the violence in their lives. Some of these strategies are positive and helpful. Others, while appearing to help them in the short run, may turn out to be quite negative in the long run.

Work as a Strategy

In the current study, twenty-eight of the thirty-nine women were employed (roughly 45% part-time and 55% full-time). Of those who were employed, five can be classified as professionals, nine as white-collar, twelve as skilled, and one as a semi-skilled employee. One woman did not clarify the type of work she did. Moreover, two women were taking university courses towards an undergraduate degree in addition to being employed. Three other women stated their occupations as full-time students (see Chapter 4).

Some of these women did not like their working conditions or their work mates, and some did. Most complained about the hours, the difficult child-care arrangements for those who had younger children, and low or insufficient pay. Nevertheless, almost all interpreted work as a positive aspect in their lives, something that gave them independence and dignity. Some even interpreted their work as a form of therapy, a welcome escape despite working conditions that were less than desirable at times. One of my respondents said that work kept her 'sane.' The following are some examples of the role of work in these women's lives.

Sonny
At the time of the interview, Sonny worked as an executive assistant in a large financial corporation that was in the process of expanding. To say the very least, she had an extremely high-pressured job. Moreover, Sonny's immediate boss was known to be a demanding and short-tempered man who acted unpredictably towards his employees. His shouting at the top of his voice and cursing were daily, if not hourly events. Sonny's job also involved long hours, and in-town or out-of-town trips related to corporate affairs. Despite these difficult aspects of her job, Sonny got along well with other employees and performed her job with a big smile. Sonny earned regular bonuses, was frequently invited to out-of-office gatherings, and had the confidence of many of her fellow workers. Sonny was very proud of herself despite the extraordinary pressures of her work.

Kim
Kim works in new home sales as a part-time sales hostess. Her job requires her to dress fashionably, keep herself well-groomed, and to act

and appear happy and pleasant at all times. Kim likes most of these aspects of her work. She feels good when she gets her hair done or when she buys herself a nice perfume to wear at work. For Kim, who is on her way to rediscovering her bubbly, outgoing personality, these are things she cherishes. Kim also likes meeting 'all kinds of people' her job brings her into contact with. She finds great pleasure in answering their questions and showing them the 'selling' features of the homes they may have missed. She loves talking to them. Kim does not earn much money, but she spends it all on herself and on going out with her female friends, which she calls her 'girlfriend time.' She likes buying herself some silly things 'just to keep up my spirits.' She is generous towards her sisters and nieces and nephews, and their appreciation makes her happy. Her current husband Rick earns a comfortable income as a police officer, and Kim refers to their life together as 'nothing to flip over, but normal. I saw some "kooky" times; now I'm a kind of gal who appreciates normal if you know what I mean!'

Amber
Amber is a caregiver (she called herself 'a nurse without papers'). Having just given birth to her seventh child, she was on maternity leave at the time of our interview. Otherwise, she works full-time in a patient care facility for older men. The men she cares for are between 75 and 85 years old, with impaired cognitive abilities. Amber's work has some shocking and difficult aspects, which she takes with a healthy dose of humour. Her clients or patients can be physically abusive at times. They kick, pinch, and try to bite or scratch their caregivers while their clothes or beds are being changed. Some spit their food during meals or resist assisted feedings. Others just spit at the nurses.

Amber's clients are sexually abusive as well. Amber says they routinely masturbate, urinate, or expose themselves in public. Verbally, they call her names, shout at her, swear, and suggest or gesture about sexual acts. Yet Amber does not seem to let these things spoil her work life. 'They are old, they are all shrivelled up. When they expose themselves, I tell them I've seen better ones [laughs really hard here]. Of course, their biting and scratching are problems but we [nurses] have ways of dealing with the worst ones. Sometimes, we restrain them during meals. They don't really mean what they say, anyways, they just say things cause they don't know any better.'

Despite its perils, I had the distinct impression that Amber liked her job. She also seemed to be quite skilled at it. Maybe having had seven children of her own (although her first baby was raised by her sister) has fine tuned her to the needs of others as well as endowing her with endless patience. More interestingly, it was not just a shallow level of tolerance. Amber actually expressed fondness for the old, cognitively impaired men, who certainly did not seem to be a pleasant or an easy bunch. She said, 'They are discards, no one wants them ... their kids don't visit. I feel sorry for them, they are not that bad really.' Amber cares for them at work, and she cares for her three youngest children who live with her at home. Amber is still trying to learn to care for herself.

Volunteering as a Strategy

Most of the women I interviewed were not engaged in any kind of volunteering at the time of my interviews. Probably, volunteering is a luxury for many of these women who seem to be overburdened by their pasts and the complex demands of their current lives. However, a few women did mention volunteering as an ongoing activity. Gwyn, Laurette, Lisa London, and Terry have been involved in the school activities of their children, including participating in bake sales, overseeing sports activities, and supervising lunches and extra-curricular activities. Lorie has been helping a blind relative and has done a little bit of volunteering for the Canadian National Institute for the Blind.

From my own work at shelters for abused women, I learned that many of the volunteers at shelters are survivors of violence themselves. This is a pattern that is well established from the very early shelter movement in England and in the United States (Dobash and Dobash, 1992; Schechter, 1982). Thus, I was a little surprised that out of the thirty-nine, only one woman, Sue, was directly involved with issues relating to violence against women. Sue was an active volunteer in women's centres and shelters. A few years ago, she decided to talk freely about the abuse she has endured in her life, hoping to be able to help other women in similar situations. Sue acknowledged that her involvement is also serving as a kind of therapy for herself. Elly also wanted to eventually have a job in a helping profession, although she was not volunteering at the time of her interview.

Creative Writing

At the time of our interview, Sue was in the process of writing a book about her own experiences with violence, not only as a possible guide for those who are caught in similar situations, but also to gain insights into her own life. She was kind enough to send me a portion of her work in progress. Reading her writing gave me the impression that she was quite masterful in analysing her own life, own thoughts, behavioural patterns, and feelings as a self-taught psychologist.[1] I found her work introspective and enlightening. Although she requested my critical comments, I was able to offer very few, because her work was extremely personal.

Creative writing was also a strategy that Ava used. As the two examples of her work show (Chapters 1 and 5), Ava used poetry as a way of dealing with her experiences in life. She also used poetry to express some hope for the future, even when she was being physically and sexually abused.

Except for Sue and Ava, I did not get any sense that any of the other women were engaged in some kind of a 'creative' pastime or hobby. This comment is not to judge them in any way or find them wanting, but to acknowledge a general emptiness or void I sensed. Perhaps the energy required to deal with the day-to-day requirements of their lives is so great that it allows very little outside interest or passion to take root.

This pattern reminds me of Abraham Maslow's (1954) theory about the 'hierarchy of needs.' According to Maslow, people need to acquire and feel safe about their most basic needs (such as housing, food, and clothing) to be in a position to aspire or accomplish higher-order needs. The higher-order needs he proposed are related to creativity, beauty, and the fine arts and literature. The highest order of need Maslow envisioned was 'self-actualization,' which is more or less an ultimate form of being satisfied with one's life and achieving an all-encompassing inner peace, comfort, and happiness. My goal is not to provide empirical support for Maslow's model or to prove the importance of his rank-ordering of the categories of need. Nevertheless, I could not help but observe that the survivors of violence were so disproportionally consumed with their past experiences and with the pressures of day-to-day living (including their children's complex needs) that there seemed to be little or no opportunity for them to pursue more abstract pleasures in life. Maybe this artefact of victimization is just as unfair as the more easily recognizable injuries of abuse.

---

1 I do not feel entitled to quote some of her work here, although it would have been interesting and appropriate. My fear is that if her book gets published, the quotations I use will give away her identity, which is something I am ethically and morally responsible for safekeeping as a condition of my study.

Sheer Survival Strategies

In the Introduction, I discussed the murder-suicide case involving the totally naked Gillian Hadley running out of her house, clutching her 11-month-old son, and screaming at the top of her voice for help. She was able to pass her son Christopher into the safe arms of her totally astonished and horrified neighbours before her estranged husband, Ralph Hadley, caught up with her and shot her dead. Shortly after this Kafkaesque murder, Ralph Hadley took his own life (*Toronto Star*, 23 June 2000: A1). A police investigation showed that Ralph had made meticulous plans and left a detailed suicide note well before his gruesome act. What is especially important in this case is Gillian Hadley's resilience even under the most unimaginable circumstances. Gillian did not just curl up, did not freeze, did not make perhaps futile efforts to plead for her own life. She showed an almost superhuman effort to save the life of her son, although she may have known all along that she could not save her own.

Fortunately, the thirty-nine women that I interviewed and their children survived their ordeals. They did not have to make a life-or-death choice like Gillian Hadley did. Nonetheless, these women's resilience, their relentless concern for their children's safety, and their ability to plan for the worst-case scenario all bespeak of their own understated heroism. Probably the greatest failure of the 1970s 'victimology' orientation to the study of violence against women is its failure to give credence to this aspect of violated women, which pushes the boundary of humanity towards the extraordinary.

Avoidance as a Survival Strategy

As Jacobson and Gottman (2001) convincingly show, the perception that women provoke violence is a myth. It is true that women can and do say hurtful things, may engage in socially undesirable acts, and may even challenge their partners in very inappropriate ways. Nevertheless, nothing they may say or do justifies either physical or sexual violence against them. Violence is a criminal act. Ultimately, the perpetrators are responsible for their violence. In most cases, however, women come to believe that they are responsible for their partners' violence, and try to make serious changes to their own behaviour. First, I will discuss some of these strategies and then I will point out their possible pitfalls.

During numerous interviews, I heard women talk about ways to avoid angering or frustrating their partners, and thus staying out of harm's way. Although the methods of these strategies were very different, the goal seemed identical. Some of these strategies involved the individual woman curbing her actions or engaging in acts that she thought her mate wanted. Other strategies involved attempts by women to curb other people's actions, such as the behaviour of their relatives, children, and even pets.

I heard many examples of each type. To reduce the possibility of a violent episode, Laurette tried her very best to cook a good meal and to act as a very gracious hostess, regardless of how many times Sam filled their home with his business associates after only a last minute call. To avoid a blow-up, Ann did her best to keep her parents and her sister at a distance, sacrificing their closeness in sometimes futile attempts to maximize her own safety. Ann also agreed to swallow sleeping pills to assure the safety of her cat from Rob's sadistic games. Sonny claimed that she always 'walked on eggshells,' and for his sake, appeared to enjoy participating in Theodore's strange rituals before sexual contact. Elly skipped almost all work-related parties and after-work get-togethers to avoid triggering one of Stephan's jealous rages. She also handed him her own paycheque. Lisa Algoma opened her legs whenever and wherever she was asked to engage in sex, although she screamed inside. Daisy talked her sister out of asking her to be one of her bridesmaids and settled for an inexpensive dress to blend in with the other guests at the wedding. DeeDee told Stuart how good he was at sex, although she often felt hurt and exploited during intercourse.

These women also learned to keep their children out of harm's way, by feeding or putting them to bed early or by sending them to friends or relatives, as already discussed. Debbie was an expert in using this strategy, especially because her youngest son Mark is developmentally challenged. Laurette was also an expert in trying to protect Tom, since Sam systematically targeted him. Other women specifically instructed their younger children to go to their room 'if daddy is upset' or instructed their older children to keep the younger ones at a safe distance.

The positive implications of these strategies are obvious. They give women a sense of control over their lives, although this sense of control may be quite misleading. These strategies may keep the children safer than they otherwise may have been. Yet the negative implications of the strategies are also obvious. No matter how much women try to change their own behaviour (or their children's), the violence eventually recurs. This pattern endlessly forces them to try harder and harder.

They also tend to interpret the outburst of their partner's violence as their own failure, which diminishes their already lowered self-esteem. In sum, avoidance strategies have the makings of a vicious cycle.

Self-defeating Strategies

In their eagerness to survive under the most adverse conditions, women also learn strategies that seem to work temporarily, but which may be self-defeating or even destructive in the long run. An oversimplification of these complex processes will reduce these women to sheer victims, which is something I do not want to do. As I have mentioned in various parts of this book, I do not see these women as just victims, although there are dimensions of their lives within which they were truly victimized. Without ignoring those dimensions, I did see these women as trying to make choices, trying to better their lives, and improve their safety whenever they could. They were actors, not totally passive victims. I also want to refrain from using psychological phraseology such as 'learned helplessness' or 'identification with the aggressor' or its more recent variation 'the Stockholm Syndrome' (Hoff, 1990; Walker, 1993). From what I could gather from my interviews, the self-defeating strategies were women's attempts to exercise some control over their lives when so much in their lives was out of their control. Even when their strategy was one of inaction, they were not totally passive in what was happening to them. It is true that some of their survival strategies did not work at all, some of them lost whatever potency they may initially have had, and some actually became destructive patterns along the way. However, what is crucial to acknowledge is that these women tried things, they made adjustments, and they managed to move from one day to the next. They have agency. They were rational enough to avoid making long-term plans, given the unpredictability of their lives, but nevertheless they did whatever they could to make sure that they survived.

Those of us whose selfhood is not tattered by violence may find some of the strategies women use unwise, inappropriate, or even immoral. But drastic lives obviously breed drastic responses. I hope my readers find ways of understanding the complex lives of these women and of learning about their strengths and failures rather than judging them. The former is what I have tried to do.

Elly's Gifts for Beatings
We have met Elly in different chapters of this book, and we are going

to encounter portions of her complex life and survival in the following sections as well. In this section, what is most relevant is how Elly learned to get things that she wanted. As you may recall, Stephan took all of Elly's paycheque, just as her parents had done before she married. Elly worked for pay, but never had anything to show for it. She did not have nice clothes, she did not have nice jewellery or belongings, and she could not go out with her work mates. She rarely had change enough for a cup of coffee. She soon realized, however, that after a vicious beating, Stephan would be exceptionally conciliatory, asking (sometimes begging) for forgiveness. After beatings, Stephan would also buy her things, nice things she would not normally have. So, Elly learned to ask for more and more things after getting beaten up. She told me: 'I can't do anything about him beating me up, he would do it if we didn't have shampoo in the house, he would do it if we had shampoo but he couldn't find it ... He would do it if I had my pink dress on, or if I wore my black pants. Anything for an excuse! ... So I said, why not get a nice dress out of it? That's fair, isn't it? Hell, towards the end, if I wanted something, I would even set him off [to blow up, turn aggressive]. If anyone wants to judge me, hey go ahead! I did what I had to do.'

Olga's Escape to the Old Country to Visit Relatives

Olga is a first-generation immigrant from an Eastern European country. She has no one in Canada except her daughter and two other unrelated children she has helped to raise. She has endured very harsh treatment from her husband Karl during the eleven years of their rocky marriage. 'One time, after, you know, he really messed me up ... he sent me to the old country. Not for a week, mind you, for three months! It was wonderful. I wanted to stay there, didn't want to come back. Next thing, he flies there to get me. My folks say, "girl, that's your husband. Do what he says. See, he wants you, he came all the way here!" A couple of years and he beats me up again. I just came out and told him: I want to go ... I want to go to [city]. You know what, he lets me! The next week, wheeey, I was on the plane ... Oh, I got beaten up pretty bad alright, but I saw my old folks cause of it!'

Kim, Erika, and Ava's Dissociations

In the early 1970s, the role Sally Field played in the Sybil film transformed multiple personality disorders and dissociative states into household terms. In the child sexual abuse and incest literature, forms of dissociative episodes are also frequently mentioned, albeit under different names (Kelly and Radford, 1998; Kendall-Tacket and Marshall, 1998; Steed, 1994). The literature also points to numerous factors that will affect whether abused children or youth will experience such states. The most obvious factors are the severity of abuse, its duration, and the age of onset. Usually the more severe the trauma and the younger the victim, the higher the possibility of developing mental strategies to separate the victim from her (or sometimes, his) ordeal. A sense of detachment from one's own body and feelings of disjunction between what is real and what is not real have been reported by about one-third of victims of child sexual abuse (Kendall-Tackett and Marshall, 1998). To my knowledge, the dissociative responses of adult victims of partner abuse have never been studied in their own right. Therefore, I was quite surprised when about 20 per cent of the women I interviewed told me about events which were so terrifying or so unpleasant that they had used some kind of psychological block to separate themselves from the events. Three women (Kim, Erika, and Ava) actually used the term 'dissociate' to describe their experiences. These three women (and a number of others) had gone to therapy sessions, and all three were continuing to do so at the time of the interviews. This is where they may have picked up the concept 'dissociate' to express what happened to them, and it is also why I chose to tell their accounts of the process. This self-defeating strategy seems to be quite common among women experiencing physical or sexual abuse, if the responses from my snowball sample have any generalizability to abused women.

Kim's second husband Ken was the one who pulled a gun on her. Although Ken had abused alcohol routinely and physically and sexually abused her, she had never thought that he would actually pull a gun on her. It was not that she had never seen guns before. Ken was a police officer, and he always had weapons in the house. What Kim had never seen was a gun pointing right at her face and Ken's face looking so malevolent behind it. That is when Kim thinks she went into a dissociative state. 'I heard screams, horrible, horrible screams. Someone was screaming far away. Screaming, screaming, screaming ... then I realized it was me.' After years of therapy and a third marriage (to Rick, who is also a police officer), Kim still hears that scream once in a while. She still has trouble believing that those unearthly screams actually came out of her own throat.

What is even more worthy of mention is that Kim's dissociative experiences have continued. 'Not all the time, mind you ... it may be once a month or it may be once in six months, you never know. It's like someone draws a thick, white curtain right in front of my eyes, I see and hear things but everything is muffled. It's like I'm in another room. My therapy helps ... I have less of them now.'

Erika experienced a similar dissociation when her alcoholic husband Tony put an ornamental Samurai sword at her throat. She could not believe this was happening. She was in a panic as soon as she felt the cold edge of the sword pressing on her neck. She forced herself to think this was just a bad dream. This was the first time Erika had ever broken away from reality and it worked. It saved her from dying right then and there. So, Erika learned to distance herself from what was happening to her in the subsequent episodes of abuse as well. In her mind, she would retreat to a safer place. The duration of her dissociations increased from seconds to minutes as she got better at this form of mental escape. The images during mental escapes got better as well. She started imagining things like standing on a bridge and watching the water flow.

Ava's dissociative feelings were connected to the non-consensual sex she had to endure each and every night. As already mentioned in the section on sexual abuse (Chapter 5), Ava learned to calmly open her legs while she imagined that she was somewhere else. Sometimes, she imagined making love to a man who loved her more than anything else in the world. Although she could not see the face of this imaginary lover, she did feel the warmth of his love.

Lisa Algoma's and DeeDee's Use of Sex

Lisa Algoma's torturous life experiences, which included rape by five different men, should already be clear to the readers. Starting from an early age, Lisa's body was an arena of exploitation for her stepfather, biological brother, two of her partners, and a brother-in-law who all raped her. In this continuum of exploitation, Lisa learned to use (or misuse) her own sexuality as well. The clearest example of this was when she lured her first husband Randy away from his existing marriage. Her strategy of using sex to establish control in her life backfired when Randy became one of her greatest tormentors, both physically and sexually (see Chapter 5). Randy also destroyed what little self-respect Lisa may have been able to preserve from her torturous childhood by bringing home his male friends to have sex with her. She is not sure, but Lisa thinks she may have used her sexuality to have a relationship with her brother-in-law as well, who took this as an open invitation to rape her. For Lisa, who had very little control over most events in her life, sex became the only 'currency' she had. But using sex also had dangerous consequences, such as marrying men who treated her badly. Her self-concept is so damaged that she likened herself to 'rotting meat' during the interview.

DeeDee used sex to calm down her raging husband Stuart. Whenever Stuart seemed to get out of control, whenever Stuart started to push, shove, and shout at her, DeeDee would assume a flirtatious role: telling him how strong he was, how charming he was, what a good lover he was, and many other sexualized variations of these sentiments. Occasionally, her tactics would work to contain Stuart's anger before it escalated into a full-blown beating. The down side was that the sex that followed this pattern of enticement was often rough, selfish, and physically hurtful. Yet because her sexual tactics occasionally seemed to placate Stuart, DeeDee could not stop herself from reverting to them time and time again.

Similarly, Sonny took part in Theodore's strange sex games, at least during the initial stages of their marriage. She did not enjoy his crossdressing, infantile postures, and strange sexual demands, but she appeared to enjoy them to keep him satisfied and content. She knew that if she refused to go along with him, there could be violent consequences. Nevertheless, even when she went along with the sexual games, there were threats and violence. She felt vulnerable 'like a rabbit,' and at her husband's mercy.

Numbing the Pain: Using Alcohol and Drugs

A destructive strategy to deal with hurt and pain that some women used was consumption of alcohol and drugs. First, I have to stress that the majority of the women in this study had been exposed to alcohol and some of them to hard drug use in their families of origin. For Ava, Clara, Debbie, Erika, Kim, Lisa Algoma, Lisa London, Lorie, Lou, and a number of others, alcohol consumption among one or both parents, brothers, sisters, and other close relatives was rampant. In other cases, such as Terry's daughter Teddy and Sue's sons Trevor and Billy, the women's own children were starting to abuse alcohol. Most husbands or partners also had excessive consumption patterns that made alcohol and drugs a complexity in these women's daily lives. Just to name a few, Amber, Ann, Camilla, Debbie, DeeDee, Erika, Kim, Lisa Algoma, Lisa Kingston, Lorie, Lou, and Sue had partners who drank heavily, and some of these men also used drugs. It is no wonder that about one-third of my interviewees sought escape in something they knew so intimately: alcohol. A few went beyond that and used drugs.

Ann's dependence on prescription drugs began as a way of controlling her pain from the beatings. Her dependence accelerated as the abuse intensified. However, the most important factor in her dependence was Rob's cruel attempts to control Ann and to keep her quiet and docile by forcing her to take drugs. At the time of the interview, it had been almost a year since Ann separated from Rob, but she was still struggling with her overdependence on sleeping pills and painkillers. She admitted that one of her 'normal' days consisted of twelve to fourteen hours of sleep. On less normal days, Ann slept close to sixteen hours. In a way, drugs were instrumental in transforming her life into one of inaction and sleep.

Lou's dependence on alcohol started in her days as a waitress, when she and Ralph had a few drinks after work. It accelerated into a full-blown dependence that resulted in first Ralph and then her getting fired. Unemployment brought harder days, and certainly escalated Ralph's abusive behaviour. Lou lived most of these days under the haze of alcohol. After the violent water-bed episode (see Chapter 5), Lou undertook the daunting task of leaving her abusive partner, curbing her own alcohol consumption, and returning to school for more education. 'I miss it,' she said! 'I really miss it. I can't give in though, a few drinks, and I'm right back to the old Lou, the old ways. I just have to fight it.'

Lisa Algoma was engaged in what she called the 'fight of her life' during our interview. She was trying to keep her children from being placed in foster homes by the Children's Aid Society. Yet, Lisa was also aware that her real battle was with her own addictions to alcohol and drugs.

Lisa Kingston has been on hard drugs. Her partner Lynford was the one who introduced her to drugs, and it spread like 'wild fire.' Lisa did not want to feel pain or feel like a loser, so she drank and took whatever drugs she could get her hands on. Lisa's memory of most of her days with Lynford is enveloped in a haze, with some sharper memories of excruciating pain. She remembers being hospitalized twice for drug overdoses. She is surprised that she is still alive.

Aggression

I am going to devote Chapter 9 to women's own aggression. As we will see, for some women, aggression is a strategy for survival, although not always a successful one. For the purposes of the present discussion, I just want to acknowledge aggression as a defensive strategy. During our interview, Ava looked right into my eyes and asked me not to think of her as a victim. She told me she was verbally expressive – even taunting at times. Yet it was Ava who was forced to have sex every night, and it was Ava who learned to dissociate from the unwanted episodes of predatory sex. In a sense, Ava's world was full of contradictions, and although she tried a few strategies to assert her agency, the strategies she utilized did not change the quality of her life. Even after she was able to end her abusive marriage to Greg, the remnants of her earlier dysfunctional strategies seem to negatively colour her relationship with her teenage son. Ava used aggression at times (see Chapter 9).

Suicidal Thoughts

Studies on sexual abuse of female and male children report very high proportions of suicidal thoughts and attempts at suicide (Kendall-Tackett and Marshall, 1998; Steed, 1994). In some studies, this proportion has been found to reach 66 per cent. Studies on woman abuse also frequently report suicidal thoughts by the victims (Mahoney and Williams, 1998). In the present study, more than two-thirds of my respondents (27) mentioned that they had considered taking their own lives on at least one occasion. Some of my respondents had repeated suicidal thoughts during their ordeals of abuse (for examples, see Chapter 9). Nine had actually attempted to take their own lives, although they fortunately managed to stay alive. Nevertheless, the self-destructive strategies have only added to the existing difficulties in these women's lives.

Some Generalizations on the Strategies

As a researcher, as a feminist, and as a woman, I cannot help but feel an overwhelming awe when faced with the sheer determination of the women I interviewed. In spite of their ineffective or even dysfunctional strategies, temporary regression, and self-destructive thoughts and behaviour, these women did not want to die. All they really wanted was for the abuse to end. They yearned for happiness and they managed to cling to any faint hope of it they could find.

More importantly, they were not passive victims but active agents.

In varying degrees, they made choices, came up with plans and strategies and sheltered their children in the best way they knew. That they are still alive is the best indication that they succeeded in surviving the violent explosions of their partners. Nothing I will say in the following paragraphs should be interpreted as a denial or dilution of their important accomplishments or strengths.

I must argue, however, that most of the strategies I listed above are problematic in and of themselves. In the long run, some of them have the potential to be extremely destructive. For example, avoidance as a survival strategy may occasionally keep women safe by temporarily reducing their proximity to the abuser. This strategy may also give women some valuable interaction skills by making them experts on looking for and interpreting non-verbal signs, gestures, and intonations. But there are at least two dangers to this relatively benign-looking strategy. First, it makes women obsessed with trying to predict what may be behind each word, each gesture, each comment, and each gaze. At least a dozen of my respondents used a term similar to 'walking on eggshells' during the interviews. One mentioned 'leaving the lights on all day,' in alluding to constantly being on the watch. Ceaselessly walking on eggshells is a taxing way of living that drains energy from the actual satisfaction of being alive. Second, constantly trying to guess the mood of the partner may provide a false sense of control over the situation or an erroneous sense of failure when their partners end up hurting them anyway. After all, the violence of the partners is rarely, if ever, under the control of these women (Jacobson and Gottman, 2001). It is something that their male partners inflict on them. The repeated failures of their meticulous efforts to avoid violence have the potential for diminishing their already fragile sense of efficacy. Although such strategies may provide a temporary sense of accomplishment, they have the tendency to become a vicious cycle.

The self-defeating nature of the dissociative states is more obvious. Each time a woman breaks away from the dire nature of her reality and escapes into an altered state is a missed opportunity to question, challenge, or change the original reality that caused her mind to flee. It is also a missed opportunity to reach out to others, to seek professional help, or to try to get away. Psychological escapes may make women feel better for a fleeting moment, but they do not remove them from or resolve the imminent dangers in their lives.

Probably three of the most problematic strategies are using sex, using aggression, and thoughts of suicide. In all such strategies, women are bound to lose. When Lisa Algoma used her sexuality as a bargaining tool, she not only made herself more vulnerable to vicious sexual attacks, but she also lost respect for herself. When Randy called her a 'whore,' the hurtful word had a double impact, because she also saw herself as one. That her weight ballooned to a size 18 and that she loathes herself are not accidental.

When women use aggression, they may get more seriously hurt than if they had not. This does not mean that women should never defend themselves. As a matter of fact, there are those who suggest that women should take self-defence courses or engage in contact sports so that they will be in a position to protect themselves. Maybe these are appropriate strategies for younger women who are so inclined and who are physically fit. There is a posibility for those who start young that these self-defence techniques may encourage a healthy lifestyle. For most women, however, counter-aggression may be more danger-ous than helpful. Women might be sailing uncharted waters while at the same time inadvertantly escalating their partner's violence. More-over, when aggression becomes common, it can have the tendency to normalize the partner's behaviour or at least provide an excuse for it.

Women also know that killing themselves is not a way out. Although some morbidly thought about death and a few attempted to kill them-selves, these women are more interested in finding a better life (see Chapter 9).

Suggestions for Positive Strategies

As I have tried to point out throughout this book, violence is a reality in the daily lives of millions of women and children. As the women survivors in this book exemplify, it is difficult but entirely possible to break the cycle of violence. But there needs to be a triangulation of strategies to break the vicious cycle. In my mind, the triangle consists of personal, social, and structural levels of change and intervention. The personal level pertains to what women themselves can do to get out of violent relationships. As discussed, some of these strategies may have unintended and even negative consequences. At the social level, families, friends, work mates, police, and health professionals must be involved to provide support, help, and protection. As the respondents repeatedly stated, abused women do not want to be judged. At the structural level, the role of the legal system, political climate, and pub-lic support for women's centres, emergency hot lines, women's shelters, educational programs, and child care services are crucial. Affordable housing, job training, and skill development programs, all of which work towards making women independent will likely be the most important factors in preventing them from returning to their abusers (OAITH, 1996, 1998; Sev'er, 2002). I will develop such a model of post-violence adjustment in Chapter 10. At the most abstract level, we must see the right to safety as a fundamental human right.

Throughout this book, I have also tried to emphasize women's agency without ignoring the hurt and devastation to their lives caused by violence. At this point, I would like to revisit the agency issue once more. Most of the women I talked to gave me the impression that they knew something was wrong in the relationship even before the violence started. Their partners' attempts at control and jealous tantrums, sometimes coupled with risk-taking and drinking binges, were telltale signs of abusive relations. Yet most women talked themselves into accepting these patterns. Justifications were different for those who had been exposed to violence most of their lives than for those who were not accustomed to violence (see Chapter 10). Yet most of these women frequently said things like 'but I love him' or 'but he loves me.' It seems to me that as a society, we are conceptualizing 'love' as something that can tolerate or even excuse bad or destructive human relations. Perhaps such problematic definitions of love are socialized into women more than into men (Cancian, 1980; Gilligan, 1982). It is a challenge for our society to develop definitions of love based on mutuality, integrity, and respect rather than on a conceptualization of power, control, and possession. It is also a challenge for women to recognize the telltale manifestations of controlling behaviour and then to either get out of such relationships or make a substantial change in the quality of relationship by seeking help early on.

The ability to have a say in the quality of the relationship requires that women have some level of confidence and respect for themselves and some resources that they can mobilize to tip the scales in their favour. In this regard, some connection with formal education, paid work, and continuing connections with friends, neighbours, and family members are essential. In the literature, as well as among the women I interviewed, the greatest dangers were experienced by women who were isolated from others. Women did themselves and their children a favour when they counterbalanced their partner's influence through cultivating resources and connections of their own.

One piece of advice my respondents provided is for women to get out of over-controlling relationships before the violence engulfs them. Mobility is easier for women who do not have children, and my respondents warned women about having children with abusive men. Yet some abused women do not have control over their sexual lives (Ava, Debbie, Lisa Algoma and Lisa Kingston are examples). They may have little or no say about when, how, and under what circumstances they will be forced to have sex. What is also ironic is that when women are not happy or satisfied in their relationships, the desire to get pregnant is common (e.g., Amber and Debbie). Through gendered socialization and a general pro-natalism (Eichler, 1997), having children is looked upon by some women as a way of smoothing problems, increasing their partner's commitment, securing his love, or of having someone to love them back. Unfortunately, in abusive relationships, pregnancy becomes a very dangerous time for women (Ava, Debbie, Elly, Lisa Algoma, Lorie, Rose, Sonny, Sue, Nancy Niagara, and Terry) and the presence of children creates additional hurdles for getting out (Chapter 5).

As we have seen in this book, and as we are reminded in the media coverage of the real life cases of extreme violence, it is very difficult if not impossible to break the cycle of violence on one's own (see Chapter 8). Violence is deeply rooted within complex combinations of the individual's past experiences, personal or social skills, current circumstances and life chances, and peer support and reward structures. At the more macro-level, media exposure, economic, social, political, religious, and legal institutions also play a role, either by providing a fertile ground for or by taking an interventionist stance against violence. In this tapestry, self-defeating strategies to end the violence are almost always doomed to fail. Even if these strategies may provide some temporary relief or escape, they are rarely sufficient to force the dramatic changes needed to alter the abusive partner's behaviour, to enhance woman's self-esteem, or to improve the quality of the relationship. From my interviews and from years of sifting through the literature, I am strongly convinced that the most effective strategies of breaking the cycle are those that link personal, social, and structural dimensions to make a more permanent, more sustainable change that allows an inner transformation where women regain self-worth. I will talk about such changes in Chapters 8 and 10.

Chapter Eight

Positive and Negative Social Support Systems

One of the insidious aspects of female partner abuse is the systematic absence or incremental dismantling of the woman's social support systems by the abuser. In the Pence and Paymar model (1993; see Chapter 3 on theory), one of the spokes of the power and control wheel is related to the phenomenon of isolation of women from friends, neighbours, and even close family members. In the case of two recent wife murder and suicide incidents in Ontario, neighbours repeatedly mentioned how 'isolated' the families were (*Toronto Star*, 25 June 2000: A4 and 8 July 2000: A1–A2).

The isolation is based on a number of simultaneously occurring social dynamics. First, the woman may already have a very small or a dysfunctional support system. Second, the abuser may actively curtail her choices and social contacts. He may control whether she can work, where and when she can work, whether she can go to school, or visit and/or go out with family and friends. Third, the abuser's control may be less direct, yet equally effective in isolating her. He may control what the woman can buy, what type of clothes she can wear, how much money she can spend, and whether she can have access to transportation or the family car. Fourth, the isolation tactics may entail psychosocial strategies that can be as powerful as more direct ones. The abuser may be rude or even assaultive towards family and friends, pick a fight each time visitors are around, and repeatedly embarrass the woman in front of them, so that she herself will want to avoid company. Moreover, as indicated in the Pence and Paymar (1993) wheel of control that accompanies abuse, the degradation against the woman's personhood may be severe. Thus, she may be so consumed with 'doing the right thing' and 'pleasing the abuser' that she may end up inadvertently contributing to her own isolation.

The fifth factor that can lead to isolation is the presence of destructive social networks. The role of negative support systems such as those found among separated and divorced women is rarely addressed in the literature (see Hillock, 1990, for a notable exception). In other words, although common sense often biases us to expect positive interaction and relations among family and friends, this may not always be the case in the experiences of abused women. In my interviews, there were several women who were or felt they were completely isolated. I also found situations where family and friends actively contributed to the continuation of abuse, rather than working towards its eradication. This is not uncommon. In the inquest following Gillian Hadley's murder, her own sister and other close relatives testified that they were colluding with Ralph Hadley by informing him about the details of Gillian's affair with another man, although the Hadleys were already separated. Their intention had been to help Ralph get Gillian back. Instead, pumped up with the information of infidelity, he shot her to death (*Toronto Star*, 23 and 24 October 2001: B1, A1, respectively).

Examples of Isolation

During their abusive relationships, women in my study had very little social contact with the adult world in general. Even those who had jobs had little opportunity to socialize with their co-workers or to go out with friends because they were expected to be home right after work. Going out with male friends was totally out of the question. A number of women also mentioned that the money they earned was not theirs, because they had to hand over their paycheques to their partners. The isolation of those participants who were mothers and full-time homemakers was even more pronounced. These women were basically left with only the company of their children. In addition to the attempts of partners to isolate their women, some other factors need highlighting.

Existing Problems with Social Networks and Parental Strife

More than half the women I interviewed (23) mentioned serious difficulties within their families of origin. These difficulties were diverse and included excessive alcohol consumption by fathers, mothers, or both (20); violence against mothers (11); stepfamily problems (5); long distance moves or immigration leading to disrupted family ties (4);

drugs (4); incest (4); suicide of close family member (3); and violence against a father (1). Because the total of these numbers exceeds the sample size, we can see that some families were plagued by more than one of these problems. The result was almost always two-pronged. First, women started to believe that these problems were acceptable or at least unavoidable in family life. Second, the family of origin was often so consumed with its own difficulties that it hardly ever served as a dependable social or economic resource for the abused woman. Some families offered no positive role models. In the following pages, I am going to provide examples of the non-functional support networks of some of the women I interviewed.

Clara's Escape from Her Own Family
Clara is from Trinidad. She came to Canada in her late teens, escaping a father who was physically abusive to both her mother and herself. In turn, her mother was abusive towards Clara and her two sisters. At the age of 20, Clara married the first man (Clifford) who asked her. She did not love Clifford, but she desperately wanted a child. Clara accepted Clifford's proposal just to get out of her undesirable and unpredictable surroundings. However, soon after the wedding, she found herself in yet another abusive situation. Clifford knew she had no place to go, as did Clara. So, she stayed and took abuse for five years. For Clara, those five years felt like fifty.

More than anything else, Clara recalls feeling all alone in this world. She had no friend, neighbour, or family to talk to, get advice from, or to call on in times of need. She remembers being crammed into an awful basement apartment – first alone with her husband, then with two young children in addition. Her children were often sick, and they always looked pale and weak. They were cranky and hard to please. Clara remembers 'being trapped as a mouse.' She remembers the physical beatings she received. The most painful thing for Clara to remember is being too harsh with her children. 'I took all my anger on them, it was horrible. It wasn't their fault that I was trapped like that ... They didn't do it ... But, they were the ones around all the time, so when I broke down, they picked up the tab. My poor babies, I was harsh ... What am I saying, I was mean ... but don't get me wrong. I love them more than anything else in this world. What's done is done, but I wish I could make it up to them ... Oh! I'm much better with the little one now [referring to her 3-year-old].'

Even at the time of the interview, Clara insisted she had no one she could trust. Her years of isolation were somehow continuing even though she had a new partner with whom she had a child.

Erika's Isolation

Erika's parents are first-generation immigrants from the Bahamas. When Erika was 6 or 7 years old, her father's best friend sexually molested her. When she told this to her parents, her father did not believe her and accused Erika of conjuring up stories. Rather than sympathy or protection, Erika got a beating. Her father was abusive to everyone under his roof, but he could also be nice and caring. He was like a 'Jekyll and Hyde.'

Before marrying her father, Erika's mother had already had two marriages and numerous affairs. While still married, she had gone for a vacation in the Bahamas and come back pregnant. After some violent confrontations over the pregnancy, the first marriage came to an end. The second man Erika's mother married just left the country one day, leaving her and young Erika to fend for themselves. Erika never had a good relationship with her mother, and her siblings were violent both with one another and towards their mother. Her brothers seem to be repeating the mistakes and the infidelities in their parents' lives. In Erika's words, 'The whole family put the fun into dysfunctional.' Yet Erika had no 'fun' in her voice as she looked back on her childhood and teenage years. Those were years of instability, disloyalty, and physical, psychological, and sexual abuse. Not surprisingly, when her own marriage turned out to be violent, Erika did not have a supportive family to turn to. She was betrayed time and time again. As Erika sees it, one of her betrayers is her own daughter (see Chapter 6).

Isolationist Tactics of the Abuser

Ann's Estrangement from Her Sister

Ann's childhood was spent within a loving family. She and her older sister were loved and cherished by their parents. Having interpreted this closeness as a threat to his control over Ann's life, her partner Rob did everything in his power to disconnect Ann from her family. They moved a few times, incrementally getting farther and farther away from Ann's family home. Rob monitored the timing and duration of visits from Ann's family, reducing them to short visits during the holiday season. He had insulted her family so much that they had practically stopped visiting them altogether.

In 1995, Ann's grandmother died. Despite the ill treatment the family had received, they allowed Ann and Rob to live in the grandmother's house for free. Their generous offer did not have a time limit either; they could have lived in the house for as long as they liked. When I interviewed Ann, she was still living in her grandmother's house. Even this act of kindness and help was interpreted in a sinister way by Rob. He accused Ann of living tied to her mother's apron strings. Ironically, after being told this so many times, Ann also came to suspect her family's motives, rather than questioning the motives and the hostile behaviour of Rob.

Rob made sure that Ann did not go out to work. Above all, he made sure that Ann and her older sister were no longer as close as they once were. Ann now thinks this may have been because her sister was the only person who sensed the abuse even before its severity and destructiveness made it a public as well as a legal matter. At the time, however, Ann was carefully brainwashed to think that her sister's efforts to help were nothing but an intrusion into Ann's private life.

At the time of the interview, I sensed there was still distance between Ann and her sister. This was sad, considering that as an outcome of a genuine concern for Ann's troubles, her sister had become an enthusiastic and committed volunteer in the women's shelter movement in Ontario. As an exceptionally interesting coincidence, I had an opportunity to meet and work with Ann's sister while I myself was a volunteer at the same women's shelter. Although I never mentioned Ann to her sister, I was able to learn about the love and dedication the sister had for Ann. I admire her unwavering commitment to making life better and safer for all abused women. I could not help but wish that Ann would find a way to heal the poisoning effects of Rob and reclaim the closeness with her sister. But as many other stories I have heard from other women show, the destructive effects of the partners' behaviour linger long after the women manage to distance themselves from these men.

Laurette's Husband's Company
In terms of North American standards of beauty, Laurette can be considered a very beautiful woman. She has a petite build, naturally wavy light brown hair, a very nice complexion, and deep green eyes. At the time of the interview, she weighed less than 100 pounds. Laurette married when she was 21, divorced, and married again within a year. She had four children in quick succession. She never worked outside the home during her second marriage, since her husband Sam was a

wealthy, established, and respected corporate executive. Sam was also extremely controlling, manipulative, and isolating. His business associates found him 'charming,' and he was often the centre of his corporate gatherings. He stretched his work life into their home, whenever he pleased. After working long hours, Sam would call Laurette and tell her that he would be bringing home anywhere between two and a dozen people for dinner. He would expect good food and cheerful service, and he would always find a reason to criticize Laurette in front of his company.

Every day, Laurette would be afraid of the telephone, not knowing when he would call, not knowing what Sam was going to ask her to do. She had no friends of her own. Sam told her that she was ugly and fat and, amazingly, Laurette believed him. Sam told Laurette she was stupid, and Laurette believed that, too. Laurette talked very little in front of Sam's company, thinking that her 'stupid words' would end up embarrassing her 'important' husband. Sam's colleagues never talked to her as a person; they would sometimes comment on the food, as if she were the cook.

Laurette's parents were systematically kept at a distance by Sam. They had to follow strict day and time limitations to call their daughter and wait long periods before they were allowed to meet with their grandchildren. Through his influential corporate and police connections, Sam would get printouts of phone calls to and from the house, and than drill Laurette about the ones that he deemed inappropriate or out of the permitted schedule.

When their youngest son went for a serious surgery, Laurette had to 'beg' Sam to come to the hospital. His reply was, 'It better be important!' When she gave birth to their fourth child, Sam was on a hunting trip. Laurette did not mind so much that he was almost always absent from her life, because his absences meant relief from constantly being judged. What bothered her the most was being unable to satisfy her 'charming, affluent, respectable' husband who kept her so isolated. At the time, Laurette did not see that Sam was also her tormentor and jailer. When Sam told Laurette that she was a lousy cook, Laurette tried to cook better. When Sam told Laurette she was a lousy mother and a lousy wife, Laurette tried to be a better one. It was like running in a race where the finish line always moved further away. 'Many times, I thought about killing myself. The only reason why I clung to life was for my children. I couldn't leave them with their cruel father for the rest of their lives. I just couldn't do it.'

Destructive Social Networks

Ann's Partner's Drinking Buddies

Ann recalls serious degradations that always took place in the presence of Rob's drinking buddies. I already discussed the shocking exhibitionism Rob forced on Ann by asking her to squirt herself with a water bottle (see Chapter 5). Ann was a very private and deeply religious person, and these incidents felt like 'gang rapes.' The physical beatings took place when Ann was alone with Rob, but they often followed these drinking episodes. Eventually, when Rob was charged with aggravated assault, his drinking buddies showed up to testify on behalf of his 'kind and gentle' nature. They portrayed Ann as a loud, promiscuous woman who would constantly entice and provoke 'poor Rob.' They presented the water bottle incidents as Ann's way of provoking Rob rather than as Rob's way of degrading Ann in front of other men. When Rob was convicted of assault, one of his cousins employed at the jail allowed him to make telephone calls to Ann's parents' home. Most of the calls were of a threatening and harassing nature (Chapter 5).

Ann is now 'legally disabled' as a result of repeated physical beatings, some of which resulted in severe head injuries requiring hospitalization. But of all the things that distress Ann, the degradation and psychological games played by Rob in front of his drinking buddies seem to hurt her the most.

Elly's Old-World Parents

As the daughter of immigrant parents from the old world, Elly has always had to work to help her parents make ends meet. Due to their poor language skills and different customs, norms, and values, Elly's parents remained on the fringes of Canadian society. Elly did not mind working hard and helping out. What has hurt her is knowing that whatever she did and whatever she accomplished were never enough for her parents. Whatever ideal of perfection they may have had in their minds, they always made sure to let Elly know that she fell far below the mark. As far back as she can remember, Elly's mother would tell her that she was 'ugly,' 'skinny,' and 'too stubborn.' Elly's mother told her that she was a 'slut' and needed a 'man to break her in,' as if she were a horse. When Stephan, a co-worker from the same part of the world, forced himself on Elly, she responded by marrying him two weeks later. Elly was desperately trying to prove to herself that she was 'not a slut.'

Shortly after the wedding, Stephan started beating her up, and cuts and bruises covered her body and her face – and her parents never asked Elly what happened. When she made a point of telling them about the violence, her mother said she must have deserved it. Her mother also told her that that was what husbands were for. When Elly was hospitalized because of a kick in her stomach during her pregnancy, her mother told her to shut her big mouth and become a 'good wife.' Her father said she should not bring shame on her family by talking about these things. Elly's parents never offered her a way out; on the contrary, they tried to force her to stay in her violent marriage.

Elly's in-laws were not much better, maybe even worse. They would ask Stephan, 'What do you see in this toothpick without any flesh to pinch?' as if she were not there. They would complain about Elly's darker skin, although they shared the same dark olive Mediterranean complexion. The following story clearly shows how Elly's in-laws treated her. Elly bought a new car with money from her employment. According to their ethnic custom, Stephan and his parents accompanied Elly to the dealer on the day she picked up the car. Judging from her excitement – not to say the fact that Elly was the one who had signed the financial documents – the salesman handed the keys to her rather than to Stephan. Her father-in-law was outraged about this transgression. He openly encouraged his son to slap Elly in the face so that she would 'know her place.' Stephan did more than that. Once they got home, he tried to run her over with the brand new car that her paycheques were paying for. Elly's in-laws joined the assault by spitting on her and kicking her while she was lying on the driveway. That day, Elly wished she would die. She challenged Stephan to finish the job. She also wished Stephan would drop dead himself.

When Elly ran away from the abusive husband who had threatened to kill her, both sets of parents made sure that she went back to him. They told her that she had brought 'shame on their family by causing these problems.' Elly's own father was the one who drove her back to her abusive husband's home. He told his daughter to apologize to Stephan. When Elly refused, her father slapped her. As we have already seen in Chapter 6 (about children), Elly's sons also turned on her and joined their father in inflicting abuse.

Lisa Algoma's Incestuous Stepfather, Brother, and Brother-in-Law
In all my years of training and research about violence against women, I have never heard of anything that approximates the horrors in Lisa

Algoma's life. On a scale of 1 to 10, the destructiveness caused her by her family network would probably register right off the scale.

Lisa Algoma was born into an abusive family, where everyone beat up on everyone else. For as far back as she can remember, her father beat her up. Lisa was sure that her mother knew about this, but either did not care or could not do anything about it. Instead, her mother also beat her up whenever she did something her mother did not like. There did not seem to be many things her mother did like; it was as if she was perpetually on the lookout for an excuse to put Lisa down.

Once Lisa's father stabbed her mother, leaving her temporarily paralysed, and was incarcerated for it. As soon as she had recovered from her injuries, Lisa's mother took up with numerous other men, while her father was still serving his sentence. Most members of Lisa's family were alcoholics and some used drugs. Eventually her mother married another alcoholic.

When Lisa Algoma was 10, her stepfather sexually molested her and her younger sister. That abuse continued for years. When she was 12, one of her biological brothers sexually molested her. She is certain that the other brother knew, but did nothing to protect her. 'It was like my bedroom had a revolving door, my step[father] would finish, and my brother would sneak in. It was just terrible ... But, you know what, I worried about my sister more than I worried about me. They were doing her too, and she was much smaller! She was just a baby.' At the time of the interview, both of Lisa's brothers were using hard drugs and had had many alcohol-related mishaps. Lisa knew of at least two occasions where they had overdosed on drugs. She openly wished they were dead. For Lisa Algoma, her brothers are already 'gone too far, they are off the humanity scale ... they are drunken beasts!'

When Lisa Algoma was in her late teens, her older sister's husband raped her while she was taking a shower. Her sister blamed Lisa for the incident, saying that she must have led him on. Lisa thinks that this may have been true, but she is not sure. Lisa feels that the only way that she can express herself is through sex. Her choices in men are as bad as her mother's.

Lisa Algoma married Randy, who was much older than herself. When they met, Randy was already married. Lisa did everything in her power to lure him away from his wife. At first, there was some hope in the relationship. They put a down payment on a house, and for the first time in her life, Lisa thought there might be a way out after all. Then Randy started bringing his drinking buddies home. He allowed them to rape his young wife. Sometimes he participated; other times he just watched. As if the horrors of her life were not enough, Lisa thinks she deserved what she got, and feels guilty. She thinks God is punishing her for seducing Randy and breaking up his marriage. Lisa thinks she needed a 'father figure' in her life and that she went after Randy like a 'bitch in heat.' She does not blame Randy for thinking of her 'as a piece of meat.' Despite the horrific abuse that took place there, Lisa loved her house. When Randy left her, it saddened her that she lost her one and only house.

The man she lived in a common-law arrangement with for a while (Gerard) also raped her, sometimes using household objects like bottles. He also introduced her to drugs. Lisa overdosed on at least two occasions. There may have been more occasions, but she does not really remember. Her memory of life with Gerard is hazy.

Almost every social contact in Lisa's life has been abusive and exploitative. Lisa says that when she sees a man 'I automatically open up my legs, but I *scream* inside my head.' (The auditory emphasis was hers. She used the term 'scream in my head' at least a dozen times during the interview.) Lisa is extremely overweight. She said, 'I'm using my fat as a shelter.' She has a very low self-concept. She also has a new man in her life, and I had the painful sense that she is repeating the negative cycle.

Lisa is afraid of losing her children, because the Children's Aid Society is involved in her affairs (see Chapter 6 on children). The CAS is keeping track of her drug rehabilitation efforts. Lisa is horrified by the prospect that her 'boys' will grow up like the men in her life. Lisa is afraid of who she is. She has eaten herself into a size 18 to fill the emotional void in her life. These are sad but frequently observed behavioural patterns seen in adults who were abused as children (Bagley and King, 1991; Kendall-Tackett and Marshall, 1998; Steed, 1994; Wolak and Finkelhor, 1998).

Professional Support Systems

Whether they have functional or non-functional affective systems, a sizable proportion of abused women eventually came into contact with various professionals. The contact could be initiated for reasons external to themselves. Examples of this could be the medical professionals or teachers whom they see because of their children's health or education. They may also have contact with counsellors because of their children's behavioural, psychological, or learning problems. They may have to deal with the police and legal professionals because of the questionable activities of their close relatives, current or former partners, or children. They may also come in contact with medical or law enforcement professionals because of their own health, injuries, suicide attempts, or dependence on prohibited substances. Thus, a number of women who are severely abused are destined to have direct contact with a range of professionals such as family physicians, hospital personnel, addiction-related counsellors, police, social workers, hot line volunteers, and shelter workers. They may also have direct contact with lawyers and judges.

The type of help (if any) and empathy these professionals provide is crucially linked to the way that the women see them and see themselves in the future. Women's ability to develop some trust and confidence in the helping professionals may be causally linked to their eventual decision to leave their domestic relationship if the situation gets dire (OAITH, 1998).

Each of the thirty-nine interviewees talked about some form of contact with professionals: either for or through their children, or more directly, as a result of the abuse and violence that they personally suffered. Approximately one-quarter of these contacts were discussed as generally positive or neutral events. A few were discussed as being clear turning points in the women's perception of themselves or in the questioning of their partners' motives and behaviour. Sadly, approximately three-quarters of the contacts were identified as negative or even extremely negative. In such cases, the participants talked about complex emotions of anger, frustration, hate, and most of all, loss of all hope, being let down, and giving up. A few participants used phrases like 'a sinking feeling' or 'felt like dirt' to express the hollowness they felt after their experience with ineffective or unsympathetic professionals. One participant used the phrase 'a kick in the head' to express the intensity of the rejection she felt.

In the following sections, I provide examples of both negative and positive contacts with various professionals. However, before I do that, I would like to re-emphasize that the reported negative experiences were three times as numerous as the positive ones. There may, of course, be a psychological tendency to remember the negative experiences more clearly or for a longer period, and this may partially explain the skew in the observations. Nevertheless, these women's experiences beg us to raise the question of how to improve the quality of services abused women receive when their long-term physical and psychological health and well-being, as well as the mental and physical health of their children, may be contingent on such help (Sev'er, 2002). In extreme cases, their children's or their own survival may also be contingent on the quality and efficacy of these front-line contacts.

Positive Examples of Contact with Professionals

Lisa Kingston's Contact with Police
Lisa Kingston admitted that she was a very disturbed woman when she was still living with her abusive partner Lynford. They were both on drugs and alcohol (in Lisa's words, 'Whatever we could find'). She remembers those days as a haze, with long periods of feeling nothing at all – occasionally spiked by the pain from beatings. Lisa had contacted a hospital for emergency services at least once, when her wrist was broken. She told the emergency staff that she had fallen down the stairs. As far as she remembers, they probably did not believe her, but neither did they bother to ask about the real reason. The real reason for her lie was to shield herself from yet another beating. Lisa lived in a basement apartment and thus did not have many stairs to fall from.

'Things got so rotten' that Lisa Kingston threatened to leave. Lynford begged her to stay. He promised to 'change,' and he actually cut down on the 'booze and the other stuff' for a while. He also came up with the idea of driving to Niagara Falls for a romantic evening and for 'patching up.' Lisa was happy about the trip with the naive expectation that things would actually turn around. Despite their troubles and regardless of the beatings, Lisa had a strong attachment to Lynford.

The trip began very pleasantly. They drove to Niagara with a lot of excitement, had a quick snack at McDonald's, and watched the Falls. They held hands and kissed beside the waterfront rails. Lisa Kingston was joyful for the first time in a long while. But, like many other occasions, the Niagara trip turned out to be a disaster. Things started to turn sour when they went out for dinner and drinks. Lisa does not remember how many beers they each had, maybe four or five. Right after dinner, Lynford got 'some extra beers' from the car, and they sat down at a relatively quiet section by the water, just past the hydroelectric plant. They hid the beer bottles in paper bags.

Lisa remembers feeling dizzy and the ground being quite wet, probably from the spray of the Falls but maybe from sprinklers. It was then that Lynford got ugly. Lisa does not remember the content of the argument – if there was a content to it in the first place. With a lot of alcohol in him, anything could have sparked the explosion. Within minutes, Lynford started punching Lisa repeatedly. He tore her blouse, spit on her face, and stomped on her when she lost her balance and fell. He left her on the ground and took off in their car. Lisa does not remember how long she stayed on the ground. After a while, she managed to sit up, but she did not have the ability to stand. She said, 'I would have given the whole world if I was invisible. Even being drunk did not help my shame. I felt this small [making a gesture with her fingers], I felt like an abandoned child. I looked like a bag lady. I wish I was invisible.'

Lisa was not invisible. The other tourists who saw the incident called the police and when the police cruiser arrived, even more people gathered around her to exacerbate her embarrassment.

Lisa Kingston cried a lot when she told me how 'low' she had felt that day. Aside from her muddied and torn clothes, she 'stunk' after a whole night of heavy drinking. Lisa expected the police to treat her like 'scum,' and she felt that she deserved to be treated like that. Lisa remembers the Niagara occasion as the lowest point in her already problematic life. 'I was at the bottom, so down, there was no place to go. I couldn't see a way out. No way! I was in a dark tunnel, alone. Shit, I was afraid.' Yet, to her amazement, one of the young constables who was dispatched to the scene treated her like a human being. 'He helps me get up, helps me walk ... not like dirt, mind you, like a nice girl. He gives me a blanket to cover. My clothes are torn, dirty. My bra is showing. He helps me clean the mud and the mess out of my hair. There was globs of dirt ... Not a pretty sight ... He knew I was drunk ... he ain't stupid, he knew I stunk like a drunken skunk! But he was nice! He was a nice gentleman. He didn't put me down no more, he treated me like a nice girl.'

The two constables drove Lisa Kingston back to Toronto. During the long drive, the one who was kind asked her additional questions and provided her with detailed information about her alternatives. The same constable showed up for the trial when Lynford was charged and eventually found guilty of common assault. For the first time in her life, Lisa felt that someone was helping her without judging her, and without ignoring or dismissing her as the pathetic creature that she felt she was. Although Lisa had made many mistakes before, and many since, this humane treatment gave her back a little bit of the dignity that she craved.

Laurette's Contact with the School Principal
Laurette's influential husband Sam was the one who repeatedly told her she was ugly, fat, and stupid (see Chapter 5). He also told her she was a bad mother and a bad wife. Amazingly, Laurette never questioned these harsh judgments about her looks and abilities. After all, Sam was a 'very respectable man' and whatever he told her 'had to be true.' Laurette spent all her energy trying to be a better wife and a better mother, but to no avail. Sam still found her wanting and 'stupid.' After years of such brainwashing, Laurette became her own harshest critic. She was exhausted from being 'bad' at everything she tried. She gave up hope; she felt like a total failure.

Laurette clearly remembers and is eternally grateful to a man who helped to break her vicious cycle of self-deprecation and self-hatred. The man was the principal of the local school that three of her four children attended. At the gut level, Laurette is certain that the principal knew something about her dire situation at home. Although he never confronted her with this sensitive knowledge, he found an indirect way of helping her. It is also possible that, like so many others, the principal did not really know about the iron cage of Lisa's personal life. Perhaps, the event that changed the course of her life was just a coincidence.

The unexpected break came when Laurette was asked to be a parent volunteer for a school outing. Having become a harsh judge of her own capabilities, she tried to turn down the challenge. Laurette thought all the children in her care would get sick or die or something, because she was such a 'bad' caregiver. She had bizarre dreams about children getting run over by trucks and being attacked by vicious dogs during the outing because 'she failed' to protect them. To Laurette's amazement, none of the children in her care was hurt. Even more amazingly, the same children specifically asked for Laurette to supervise them the next time there was a school trip. The principal said, 'Mrs [Laurette], you have a natural gift with young children. We are lucky to have parents like you to help us out. Please help us again in the near future.' At first, Laurette thought that the principal was confusing her with someone else, another woman, another mother. How could she be good at anything when she knew she was so 'bad'?

The principal was not confusing Laurette with another mother. Indeed, having four children of her own and loving each one of them more than life itself, Laurette had learned ways to relate to children, and children sensed this and loved her for her gentle manner. It took a while for this message to sink in. When it did, for the first time in over a decade of marriage, Laurette had an opportunity to question the truthfulness of her husband's cutting evaluations of her. Could it be that she was a good mother after all? If she were a good mother, could it also be that she was a good wife? Could it be that she was not so stupid? If Sam was lying about the quality of her motherhood, could it be that he was lying about other things? For the first time, Laurette started seeing a different woman when she looked in the mirror. For the first time, she started to see a dishonest and manipulative man when she looked at Sam.

Liz's Encounter with a Help Line Therapist

The day after Liz's husband Roger punched her in the mouth hard enough to loosen two of her front teeth, Liz called the women's help line. This was not an easy decision to make, because Liz had never been comfortable with making the private aspects of her life open to public scrutiny. However, Roger had hit her with a great deal of force. On top of the flash of pain in her mouth, Liz also feared for her life.

The woman at the other end of the help line listened to Liz patiently and asked very few questions. What was insightful for Liz was that as she answered the questions, a pattern that she had never seen before emerged right in front of her very eyes. Up to the time of the phone call, Liz had experienced numerous aggressive and threatening behaviours and pushes and shoves, but she had always managed to dismiss them as one-time events. She had always been able to find excuses for Roger's hurtful behaviour. Only when she was talking to the therapist on the help line did Liz realize that there was a clear pattern of intentional abuse. What Roger was doing to her was systematic; it was not just isolated events. Liz said, 'After having a blurry vision, this was like finding my pair of prescription glasses. For the first time, I saw Roger for who he was. I saw what Roger did to me. I also saw me taking all he dished out ... I didn't like what I saw.'

Shortly after the help line encounter, Liz started to look for a place of her own. Although Roger was taken aback by her decision to separate and insisted that they work things out, he did not turn violent. As a matter of fact, he started dating a younger woman shortly after she announced her decision. Liz thinks that he was trying to make her feel jealous and maybe to reconsider her decision. She did not reconsider and ended up moving into a small apartment that she shares with a co-worker who is also a friend.

Erika's Spiritual Support Group

Erika has found a support group for herself. The group has a religious leader. She says the group is the best thing that ever happened to her. She found God and learned to forgive herself. Erika has also forgiven her abusive partner. 'I wrote him a letter. Told him I forgive him. I told him I'm at peace, and I want him to forgive himself. I told him to follow God. You know what? He is in jail. His new wife put him in jail ... when he pulled the same stuff on her that he pulled on me, she put him away ... Maybe, God did not forgive him yet, who knows!'

Erika now has a family of strangers who are kinder and more considerate to her than her own family ever was. She now goes home looking forward to the friendly messages on her telephone answering machine, rather than fearing the mostly alcohol-induced, threatening messages she used to receive from Tony.

Kim's Therapist

After five years of intensive therapy, Kim calls her therapist 'the best gift I gave myself.' She likes herself now. She has overcome her fear of guns. Kim has stopped putting herself down. She has even come to terms with the impact on her life of her controlling mother and recently deceased father. Both parents were a little too much into alcohol, and Kim's mother was always too busy with her own life. But now Kim can deal with her past. When her father died, she was even able to cry and feel true sadness. These are accomplishments for Kim who has had nothing but fear and hate for a long time. Kim's philosophy now is: 'If something doesn't kill you, it makes you stronger. Well, guess what? Ken didn't kill me.' Kim laughed out loud, a genuine laugh, after this statement.

Negative Examples of Contact with Professionals

Unfortunately, the positive experiences discussed above were very few. They were often outnumbered by the negative experiences women recalled. I cannot overemphasize the disappointment some of my respondents felt when people who were expected or trained to help them failed to do so. What was more distressing was that many women felt they were being 'judged' by the people who were supposed to help. In the following section, I provide some examples of the types of negative encounters most women I interviewed experienced.

Sue's Encounter with the Judge

When Sue decided to end her relationship with Ed, he became more abusive than ever. Although he taunted Sue about her age and called her ugly and fat, Ed did not want to let her go. He stalked Sue. He also stalked their children. In Chapter 6, I already mentioned how Ed kidnapped one of their sons (Trevor) from his school. Although he later returned Trevor, unharmed, Sue was devastated. Ed also made as many as thirty phone calls a day, and left messages when she stopped answering the phone. Some of these calls were apologetic, asking for another chance. Some of them were full of threats towards Sue and the children. Upon police recommendation, Sue recorded all of these calls.

Because of the continuous threats, the stalking, and the horrifying kidnapping incident, Sue had to contact the police dozens of times. She took out a peace bond, prohibiting Ed from coming close to her or the children. Ed repeatedly violated those conditions. Police were polite each time they responded to her frantic calls, yet Sue never had the feeling that they were actually trying to help. 'I think, they saw me as a nuisance ... Maybe a bitch! They showed up, and made their appearance, but it was like a show! It felt staged.'

Because Ed was repeatedly violating the peace bond issued against him, Sue had to go to court on a number of occasions. On one of these, a male judge said, 'Oh, no! It's you again!' as if Sue was the guilty party in her own victimization. Worse yet, the judge openly trivialized the years of suffering in her life by treating her like a hysterical woman. 'He was after me, I knew it, my kids knew it, they knew it! They did nothing ... not a damn thing. You know what I think? I think they are as bad as Ed.' Understandably, Sue has lost all confidence in the police and the legal system. She feels both failed to protect her.

Lisa London's Encounter with a Crown Attorney

Lisa London had never been very close to her family. She certainly had no friends, and she did not work outside the home during her first marriage. When George, her first husband, threw a kitchen chair at her and broke her arm in three different places, Lisa ended up at the emergency ward of a hospital. Observing the extent of damage and the hard-to-explain bruises all over her, the hospital contacted the police.

Lisa does not really remember how she was treated by the police or the hospital personnel. She was too distraught and in too much pain to remember the details of that night. She does remember the crown attorney from when George was charged with assault. 'Let's not waste each other's time! You don't really want this guy to go to jail. Who is going to bring home the dough? Kiss and make-up. I think, he worried about you enough.' Lisa's arm was still in a cast when she heard these words. Moreover, 'Can you believe? The crown attorney was a woman. You'd think she'd show a little bit of understanding. No ... no such luck. She says "kiss and make-up." You think she would have kissed and made up if half of what happened to me happened to her?' Maybe the courts are different now because of the increased awareness about violence against women, but this was Lisa's experience with the attorney who was assigned to protect her rights.

Ann's Problems with the Police
The police were not kind to Ann even though she had been seriously hurt on more than one occasion. 'Although they didn't come right out and say it, I am sure they thought I asked for it. Maybe they thought I was telling lies. Rob had guns in the house. Well, they were registered and all, but still, guns are guns. He also had swords, supposed to be a collection, but he swirled them around, scared the cat, scared the hell out of me. The police let him keep the guns; they didn't bother with the swords. There were [prescription] drugs all over the place. Ann called one of the strongest sleeping pills that Rob gave her something like 'Helcion' but she was not sure.' 'They let him keep that too! It was like he's the nice one and I am the troublemaker. I even heard them talking about the hockey game at one point. There I am black and blue, drugged out of my mind ... they are talking about NHL.'

After the violent rape at the nature reserve, Rob was convicted of assault. Infuriatingly, his cousin, a night employee at the local jail allowed Rob to make harassing calls to Ann and her parents from the jail (see Chapter 5). Even when Ann's parents taped the calls, nothing came of this evidence. Police said that they may have been calls that he had made before Rob went to jail.

Kim's Husband's Police Buddies
Kim's abusive husband Ken was a police officer (so is her third husband Rick). When Ken threatened to kill Kim, she called the police. They did nothing. They answered the call, but mostly stuck around talking with Ken as if they were at a social gathering. Kim thinks they protected him rather than her. 'You know ... He could've cut me up into little pieces, right in front of their eyes, and they still won't do nothing.

Those guys protect their own, they don't protect you. They thought all was a joke, they didn't have the gun stuck right on their face.'

Kim also had problems with the first shelter that she sought refuge at. 'They wanted me to go for counselling, *with him*! What the hell is that? The guy beats me to a pulp, threatens, stalks, puts a gun on my face, and they want me to sit side by side and get counselled? They just pissed me off! I was stuck with the noise, the kids, lack of privacy ... all that. But asking me to go counselling *with him*! That's where I draw the line. I told them that ... and I just got the hell out of there' (the auditory emphasis is Kim's).

Camilla's Shelter Experience
During the fourteen years of her abusive marriage, police had to take Camilla to a local shelter on two different occasions. The first stay was short, and not so bad. Her son was small and was left behind. She was naive enough to expect change. She wanted to return home, and she did. Larry was all excuses, promises, and apologies. Soon after this honeymoon behaviour, he became just as abusive as before. The second shelter trip took place when Larry punched Camilla in the face. Her eye swelled shut, and she ended up with a detached retina. After this second major assault, which required an emergency trip to the hospital, Camilla was taken to a different shelter. 'The [shelter name] was full so they drove me to [shelter name]. This time, I had Tommy [her son] with me. The place was filthy. There were too many kids, running around, shouting, crying ... dirty diapers. Smell! Some kids were pretty sick, running noses ... I didn't want Tommy to get sick. Bunch of girls chain-smoking. When I tried to talk to the counsellor, she says, "Do you think you are in a five-star hotel?" That was not right, of course, we weren't in a five-star hotel. We weren't even in a one-star hotel. But that doesn't mean we were a bunch of animals. Some of us wanted a bit of dignity, that's all ... This was years ago, though. Maybe shelters are not like that no more.'

Laurette's Encounters with the Police
Sam, Laurette's executive husband, mesmerized the police. He also mesmerized the judge, with his professionally tailored business suits, impressive vocabulary, and high-priced lawyers.

> No one could believe that he was the abuser he was. No one could suspect he was the liar that he was. He made me look like a stupid fool, a hysterical, crazy woman. He told the judge I was spending all the money

for myself [child support] and starving my children ... He didn't even pay the support. Just some money, here and there. I was buying groceries with the money my parents gave us [she and her four children]. We had nothing! But, the judge believed him. He asked me to submit my grocery bills to the court. Every single bill ... for milk, for bread, for my tampons ... The judge asked me to go through [psychological] testing to see if I was a fit mother. No one asked him to take a [psychological] test although he was the one who beat us up [Laurette's son, Tom, was also abused]. At the beginning, even my own lawyer thought that I must be starving my children. She told me herself later ... She apologized!'

Stacey's Discussions with Social Workers and Police

As explained in Chapter 6, Stacy was worried about Leo, her 10-year-old son. Leo was on medication for depression. He had run away from home and hidden behind the garbage dumpsters of apartment buildings. Leo seemed to be far away, somewhere Stacey did not know how to reach. When Stacey told the social workers about her fears for Leo, she felt dismissed. When she talked to the police about the possibility of Leo bringing harm to himself, police told her that there was nothing they could do. According to Stacy, the system only works when people die or kill another person. The system does nothing to prevent personal disasters before they happen.

As the above examples clearly show, there were occasions where women I interviewed gained comfort, understanding, and help from their encounters with professionals. In some cases, these contacts set the stage for these women to re-evaluate their lives. Some women started to seek ways of breaking the chains of their abusive relationships. Others found ways of changing their own thoughts, behaviour, and attitudes. But the majority of the experiences were negative. Maybe my respondents were not abused by the systems they sought help from, but they have certainly felt dismissed and marginalized by them. What is curious is that none of the complaints I heard were race-related, although almost half (43.6%) of my respondents were non-white. It is possible that my respondents freely disclosed their gendered experiences with me but not their experiences related to their racial or ethnic characteristics because I happen to be a white woman. It is also possible that the negative treatment they perceived was so interrelated with abuse and its aftermath that race and ethnicity were not the most salient aspects of their discontent. Unfortunately, my findings cannot answer these puzzling questions.

Chapter Nine

Debates about Women's Own Aggression

Women's own violence in family affairs is a topic that creates an enormous amount of controversy. Feminists are passionate about not allowing the discussion of violence against women to become diluted by a reversal of the argument which puts the emphasis on the violence that women themselves perpetrate. This passion is more than justified in societies like ours where there are many negative stereotypes of women. It is also true that many men and some women do use these stereotypes to further subjugate women. Talking about women's own violence is never a simple discussion about 'facts.' It can also 'spin into' a justification of the status quo, and this is detrimental for women (Currie, 1998; Dobash et al., 1992). Thus, talking about women's own violence can be an ideological and political statement about where one falls on the pro- versus anti-woman continuum.

Debates

The genesis of the controversial views about women's role in family violence dates back to Freud's extremely androcentric and sometimes even misogynist views about the psychosexual development of women. As I have already pointed out (Chapter 3), armed with Victorian expectations and a rigid moral stance, Freud developed a theory of the female psyche based on a handful of observations of affluent but troubled female patients (1959, 1974). Rather than interpreting their troubles in relation to the suffocating and subjugating conditions of their Victorian lives, Freud chose to seek the causes of their condition in their biology and in their early childhood dilemmas. To buttress his emerging theoretical views, Freud saw his female patients as morally immature, sexually manipulative, and personally untrustworthy adults. Even when his patients were survivors of paternal incest, Freud's conclusion was that they were fabricating accusations. In Freud's view, women were driven by their unresolved passion and desire for their own fathers, albeit mostly at the unconscious level. Thus, Freud held that women act in one of two troubled ways: either they transfer their extreme anger and frustration onto other men and become 'castrating,' or they transfer their guilt and shame onto themselves and become 'neurotic.' Either way, women have the potential to become masochistic; they engage in either self-deprecation or taunt their partners. They seek punishment, preferably punishment from men (Freud, 1959, 1974).

Fortunately, not many social scholars have agreed with Freud's scenario of such blatant victim blaming, but a few have. For example, Snell, Rosenwald, and Robey (1964) were the first researchers who construed violence against female partners as something their negative, taunting, castrating behaviours had asked for. 'The periods of violent behaviour by the husband served to release him momentarily from his anxiety about his ineffectiveness as a man, while at the same time, giving his wife apparent masochistic gratification and helping probably to deal with the guilt arising from the intense hostility expressed in her controlling, castrating behaviour' (1964: 111).

In the more recent literature, the blaming of women victims of violent partner attacks is a lot more indirect and much more muted. Questioning the women's role in intimate violence continues to be a popular theme, nevertheless. One recurring question is about how women contribute to their own victimization. This question makes a subtle connection between women and the masochistic idea of womenhood. A less blatantly sexist position centres on women being equally violent to men. The third recurring theme is about how women victimize other family members, be it their children, their aged relations, or their lovers and husbands. I will now deal with each of these three themes, eventually returning to the observations in the present study.

Women's Contribution to Their Own Victimization

The argument that women willingly or unwillingly contribute to their own victimization is quite common. The source of this argument may stem from psychological or psychoanalytic practitioners who may still be influenced by diluted forms of Freudianism. Learning theorists also inadvertently contribute to the debate by emphasizing the learned patterns of behaviour that mould children to respond to interpersonal crises in non-functional ways. For example, in his model of transgenerational triangles of abuse, Ney (1992) suggests that people occupy roles as either the victim, the perpetrator, or the witness of abuse (the three corners of a triangle). According to this model, the triangle rotates over time, and those who were the victims may become the perpetrators or witnesses to other violence, or they may again become the victims themselves. What is explicit in this model of triangulation is the possibility of intergenerational transmission, which is quite well documented in the literature (see Chapter 3).

What is implicit and to some degree dangerous in this model is the assumed equal weighting of the three corners of the triangle. This inadvertently removes the weight of responsibility from the abuser by making his or her position equivalent to the roles of the victim or the witness. Even if the victim or the observer is not entirely passive in the realm of abuse, is it at all justifiable to dilute the responsibility of the perpetrator by creating a visual image of equality in the roles of witness–victim–perpetrator?

Some theorists, despite their best intentions towards women's dilemmas, such as Walker (1979a, 1979b), have inadvertently contributed to the thesis of women bringing abuse on themselves. To Walker, this is through her insistence on the learned helplessness of the female victims of abuse. Albeit unintentionally, the perception of a weak, passive, infantile, and totally subjugated victim that Walker's work projects is not far removed from the Freudian construction of masochistic women. In each case, and quite unfairly, women themselves become the targets of social analysis rather than their perpetrators or the violent circumstances of their lives.

Women as Equally Violent

When the pendulum swings to the mid-point of the continuum of blame, we find arguments that women are as aggressive as men. The most adamant proponents of this thesis are the founders and some of the users of the Conflict Tactics Scale (see Gelles and Straus, 1979, 1988; Straus, Gelles, and Steinmetz, 1980; also see Chapter 4 in this book). Just to recapitulate, the original CTS defined violence in gender-neutral terms as 'an act carried out with the intention or perceived intention of causing pain or injury to another person' (Gelles and Straus

(1979: 554). In other words, the CTS was interested in the act and the aim, but not the motive, or the consequences. Thus, the numeric count of assaults that caused severe injury were considered equivalent to assaults that caused no injury at all. Moreover, in its original form, the CTS did not deal with motive thus equating predatory violence with violence as a means to defend oneself or one's child. In a review article, Breines and Gordon (1983) characterized the CTS as an empiricist approach that can effectively count violent events but that cannot inform us about their nature or etiology (also see Dobash et al., 1992).

Moreover, the items on the CTS were pre-ranked by their severity according to the logic of the designers of the scale. For example, threatening with a knife, although no injury may have taken place, was ranked as more severe than a hit in the face which may have broken a jaw or loosened teeth. The original form of the scale also omitted all reference to sexualized violence, thus ignoring one of the main categories within which women are victimized (GSS, 2000).

Some of these obvious weaknesses of the CTS were addressed in a revised version of the scale (see Gelles and Straus, 1988; Straus, 1989). Nevertheless, studies using the CTS have repeatedly produced findings that equate women's and men's violence, showing reliability but failing on validity. Partially because of the insensitivity of the items in differentiating serious attacks from not-so-serious ones, a gender-neutral introduction of the scale (as to how people resolve their conflicts) and the omission of the motive and consequences of acts, findings of the CTS have contributed to the perception that women are just as violent as men.

Ironically, the designers of the scale are aware of the potential misuse of the mutual combat findings. Indeed, they have highlighted that women are a lot more likely to get hurt in family altercations than men are, indicating that the equivalence that the CTS produces needs to be interpreted with a lot of caution (Gelles and Straus, 1988). Nevertheless, the unscrutinized use of the CTS findings has served as ammunition for anti-feminist groups to stage a backlash against women victims. For example, Pleck et al. (1977–8) report that claims that women are also violent were used to deny funding for shelters. Stephan (1994) observes that women who resort to violence even when they need to defend themselves are likely to be held responsible for *all* the violence. Furthermore, police may be reluctant to remove the perpetrator or to lay charges if they know or suspect that the woman may have retaliated, and the judges may treat this factor as a mediating aspect in sentencing the perpetrator. Dobash and his colleagues (1992) discuss the myths of symmetry in violence that CTS findings have engendered, and the ramifications of such myths.

Women as More Violent Than Men and the Exaggerations of Husband Abuse

The probability does exist that some women will victimize men (or other women). In the extreme, some women do kill their partners, although the ratio of women who kill their partners is less than 30 per cent of men who kill their partners (GSS, 2000). Thus, there is little justification for exaggerated claims of abuse against men. Yet this erroneous perception lingers. The mass media and the entertainment industry perpetuate deceptive images that fuel this misconception. Images of violent women have proven to be lucrative for many writers and filmmakers. The film *Fatal Attraction* is a notorious example of this pattern. In the film, the love-crazed woman played by Glenn Close becomes vindictive and dangerous when her affair with a lover (Michael Douglas) turns sour. Close's character hunts him down, attempts to hurt his family (whom he had cheated on), and even kills and then cooks their pet rabbit. Given the superstar status of the actors, films like *Fatal Attraction* serve as an interesting thrill and titillation. Yet, for women in general, they fuel negative stereotypes. Another notorious example of the same phenomenon is the widely popular Steven King book and movie *Misery*. In that story, a crazed woman admirer comes across her favourite author shortly after he is injured in an accident. She kidnaps and repeatedly tortures him and forces him to alter the ending in his famous love stories. The blood-curdling attacks are interspersed with moments of care and tenderness, underscoring the untrustworthiness of women in general as well as their mindless obsession about possessive forms of love.

In many other films, books, and television commercials, the misogyny is not as blatant but lies just under the surface. Audiences are repeatedly shown how well-meaning men are verbally or physically pestered by their wives, lovers, or girlfriends. In a recent McCain's french fries television commercial, a wife (supposedly jokingly) threatens to break her husband's 'other leg' when he is already incapacitated with one broken one. Their preteen daughter repeats her mother's threat, solidifying in the observer's mind the misguided notion of women's propensity for unprovoked violence even in apparently happy families. (After a few months of air time, the ending of this commercial ad was altered – possibly as a response to viewers' complaints.)

Fortunately, the sensationalist nature of media depictions of women's violence is not very prevalent in the social scientific literature. Although rare, there are a few instances when violence against male partners has been paraded as a social problem. Maybe not surprisingly, a well-known proponent of this view is a researcher from the New Hampshire group (see Steinmetz, 1977–8; also see Pagelow's 1985 critique of these assertions).

Where Does the Truth Lie?

It is naive to assume that women are always faultless and that men are always at fault. As sad and as frightening as it is, there are a few Karla Homolkas in this world. (Through 1990–5, Karla Homolka and her husband Paul Bernardo stalked, kidnapped, sexually assaulted, and tortured to death at least two young girls; Karla was also instrumental in the drugging, rape, and death of her own sister, Tammy, on Christmas Eve in the basement of the Homolka home.

Yet the few exceptions do not represent general reality. Women's violence constitutes a small proportion of the violence perpetrated against them. Like men, women are living, breathing, and acting individuals who have good and bad experiences in their lives that shape their current selves. Perhaps the majority of girls and women are basically nonviolent, while a few are violent, just like most men are not violent though a proportion are. If this is the case, how do we apportion responsibility in cases of abuse?

According to the latest national survey, which utilized a revised form of the CTS as well as some open-ended questions, Canadian women report more violence against them than men do. In six of the ten items, including the most serious four categories such as beaten (25% vs 10%), choked (20% vs 4%), threatened or used a gun or a knife (13% vs 7%), and sexual assault (20% vs 3%), women reported much more violence than men did. Men reported more violence in threw something (56% vs 44%), slapped (57% vs 40%), and kicked or bit (51% vs 33%), which implies that the attacks against men may not have been so serious and/or they might have been defensive acts by women (GSS, 2000). The most noteworthy gender differences are seen in the consequences of the violence. When the survey asked about the consequences in the form of injury, 40 per cent of women and only 13 per cent of men reported experiencing some form of physical injury. Similarly, 15 per cent of women and only 3 per cent of men reported requiring medical attention as the result of their injury. Importantly, 38 per cent of women compared with 7 per cent of men claimed that they feared for their lives. When the frequency of violent events was taken into account, 65 per cent of women (54% of men) said they were victimized more than once, and 26 per cent of women (13% of men) said they were victimized more than ten times.

When one looks beyond the aggregated numbers, studies clearly show that men are more violent than women. There is also the possibility that the findings may be underemphasizing the actual gender differences. According to Pence and Paymar (1993; also see Currie, 1998), men systematically underreport the number as well as the severity of their abusive acts. For example, Dobash and Dobash and their colleagues (1995) find that men consistently underreport the type of abuse and injury they inflict on their partners. However, the interesting point their study highlights is that men only underreport their own violence when there are no objective witnesses or facts pointing to the severity of the violence. If there are objective records or witnesses, men's reports of their violence seem to coincide with the facts. What is equally interesting is that women also underreport the severity of men's violence against them (Currie, 1998). Taken together, these findings challenge the validity of findings from the CTS studies. Now, the interesting question is whether men overreport any form of violence perpetrated against them. To my knowledge, this possibility has never been studied.

The strongest index of violence in intimate relationships can be found in homicide data (see the review in Chapter 2). According to the latest Canadian findings, spousal homicides account for 15 per cent of all homicides in the past two decades, and wives (married, common-law, separated, or divorced) are three times more likely to be killed by male partners than husbands (married, common-law, separated, or divorced) by wives. No calculations are available on dating relationships that may have turned fatal (GSS, 2000). In the media reports I analysed, of the 507 reported cases of severe violence and murder, 86 were in dating relationships (Sev'er, 2001). Although the media reports are neither random nor generalizable, the increased vulnerability of women in more transient relationships compared with those in legal or common-law marriages needs to be taken into account. These observations suggest that intimate violence towards women may even be a wider phenomenon than what the official statistics suggest.

In sum, simply counting violent acts is a very misleading way of asserting symmetry between women's and men's violence towards one another. When one also considers the initiation of such acts, their severity, the probability for injury, and the frequency of victimization, it becomes very clear that women are victimized disproportionately. This pattern finds even more clarity in the homicide data where Canadian women are killed by husbands 3.4 times more frequently than husbands are killed by women (GSS, 2000). In the United States, every year, approximately 1,500 women are killed by their male partners (BJS, 1995).

Women's Reported Aggression in the Current Study

I already discussed some examples of my participants' own violence (Chapter 7). In addition, I talked about the negative implications of using aggressive strategies as coping mechanisms. Without repeating the same points, let me expand on part of my interview with Ava. I remember her looking right into my eyes and saying, 'I am not a victim you know. Please don't write about me as a victim. I did my bit. I shouted. I cussed. I threw things around. I threatened to leave. I demanded affection. I tried to withhold sex! I told him I wanted to be loved, not fucked. I told him I masturbated in the bathroom after he finished with me. I did all that ... Well, all I got was a licking and sex every night, and I hated it. I hated him, but that's beside the point! So ... Don't write me up as a victim!'

Indeed, I became a witness to a demonstration of what Ava meant about not being a victim, in the altercation with her 14-year-old son Stan (see Chapter 6). In one sense, Ava was not a victim at all. She was angry. She was verbal, and she was aggressive in the face of her son's challenge about there being nothing in the house to eat. Yet she was also deeply hurt about not being understood, not being appreciated by her son, and by his ability to intimidate her. Ava was deeply frustrated about being misjudged and being challenged as a mother in front of a total stranger (me). And in these dimensions, I think, Ava was indeed a victim despite her own aggressive behaviour.

I think, the same goes for the relations in abusive relationships. Women like Ava may be verbally aggressive, challenging, shouting, crying, and demanding a change. They may even throw things around, or threaten to hit or bite their partners, as in the cases reported by a relatively large proportion of men (GSS, 2000). And, of course, there is absolutely no justification for either women's or men's aggression or violence. Nevertheless, it is women who are more seriously threatened, or beaten up, or sexually assaulted and raped. Women are the ones who disproportionately get killed. Usually, the type, severity, and frequency of violence does indeed make women the victims, whether they like that attribution or not. By her own admission, Ava tried to assert herself by confronting her partner, but she was still forced to have sex every night against her will. It was her body that was penetrated by household objects. Although she never used the term, what she went through was chronic marital rape.

There is also another dimension that needs highlighting. Even Ava, who neither considered herself nor wanted others to consider her a victim, was terrorized. This dimension of living in terror is often omitted in the discussions of equality of violence between men and women. Even when women are aggressive towards men, men rarely report a debilitating, crippling feeling of terror. Women often report such feelings (Dworkin, 1993).

During the exacting interviews to collect these data, I found myself asking whether some of the things that my respondents were telling me they had done were the best things to do in the circumstances. Often, I found my answer to be a 'No.' Whether it was getting pregnant over and over again from partners who were very cruel to them (Amber, Debbie, Laurette, Nancy Ottawa, and Kim are the most obvious examples), or shutting out their family support systems upon the partner's demand (Ann and Laurette are examples), or drinking or using drugs excessively and thus becoming dependent not only on the substance but also on its supplier (Lisa Kingston and Debbie) were not the most reasonable actions to take in the volatile landscape of these women's lives. Cursing, shouting, challenging, and even daring an outraged partner to kill them (like Elly and Debbie have done), or scratching the partner's face deep enough to draw blood (like Nancy Sudbury) were not the best things to do either. Nevertheless, it must be said that these were my thoughts and judgments when I had the luxury of never living in an abusive relationship and the additional luxury of not having been raised in a violent family environment. What appeared to be common sense to me was obviously not an easy or clear choice for women who were caught up in threatening and demeaning life circumstances. The women I interviewed were trying to live and avoid getting hurt in the ways they knew how. They do not want or deserve to be judged and/or labelled for doing that.

During discussions of some of the puzzling observations of my research with my colleagues, one question repeatedly put forth was 'What were they doing, surely they must have done something?' meaning but not verbalized as 'Did they deserve what they got?' Some of my colleagues were more blatant about it. They asked me how these women 'provoked' their partners, not whether they provoked them. In my judgment, some of the women I interviewed may have had many shortcomings, faults, miscalculations, misjudgments, problematic personal habits, or poor hygiene. A few of them may have engaged in what most people would consider to be immoral or illegal activities such as taking drugs or having sex with already married partners. However, I could find no evidence in anything they said to justify a belief that 'they deserved what they got.' They were wary, scared, and at least in their own minds, doing everything necessary to avoid provoking their partners' violence. That what they were doing or not doing may actually have contributed to the escalation of violence by their mates does not make them responsible for the violence. Neither does it justify the violence of their male partners.

A related question is, who starts the violence when both parties engage in violence? In the CTS literature, the claim is that both women and men are equally likely to start violence (Steinmetz, 1977–8; Straus et al., 1980). In the feminist literature, there is a strong assertion that women's aggression is defensive, to protect themselves and/or their children (Dobash et al., 1995; Pence and Peymar, 1993). As far as the participants in this study are concerned, I heard many examples of aggressive and violent acts perpetrated by them. Some like Laurette, Ann, Carrie, Suzan Windsor, Sam, and Sonny had tried to cope with the violence without reciprocating with violence. Debbie, Clara, DeeDee, Kathy, Elly, Monica, Ava, Nancy Sudbury, and Sue did reciprocate at times. As passive aggression, a few openly had wished that the partner was dead (like Elly), and at least two (Amber and Debbie) had celebrated when their partners were killed in traffic accidents. A few admitted that they have been either verbally or physically aggressive towards their children (Carmen, Erika, Debbie, Lisa Algoma, and in earlier years, Elly). In a way, then, some women turned their aggression outward. Others internalized their frustration and turned their anger upon themselves. The following are examples of the external type.

Elly had her own form of aggression. 'I never shut up,' she said. 'I'm stubborn. I'm never tired of complaining about things I don't like. I complain, complain, complain. That's who I am. Stephan used to hit me in the mouth, but he couldn't shut me up.' Elly was never totally silenced. She would complain, shout, and even use threats against Stephan. During the driveway incident when Stephan almost ran her over with the new car she had just purchased, she 'dared' him to complete the task (Chapter 5). I was amazed at her spirited way of trying to have a say in her own life, given the years of abuse she has suffered. However, her feisty challenges may have endangered her safety and even her life at the hands of a ruthless husband.

Kathy would also get aggressive. She would hit back when she was hit. Kathy did not start the fights. She did not start pushing and shoving Ted. But when Ted pushed and shoved her, she tried to do the same to him. More often than not, she was the one who got hurt. She was the one who ended up with bruised ribs and a dislocated jaw on one occasion and a black eye on a few others. But, as she put it, 'I was no missy missy. I tried to hit back. I even tried to hurt the bastard when he hurt me so bad! Couldn't do it though [she laughs]. He was twice my size. I guess, he had a meanness in him that I didn't have.'

Anna broke close to a dozen cups and dishes and the kitchen window:

'We were in the kitchen, you see. I was trying to wash the dishes. Small kitchen, we are all stuffed in there, no room to manoeuvre. He lifts up my skirt, pinches me ... shit like that, right in front of the kids. I tell him to stop ... he does it more. I ask him ... No, he does it again ... Something took over me, I snapped! I started throwing the dishes ... one by one, on the wall, on the floor. I liked the sound they made when they hit the floor. Boom, they explode. I was angry ... humiliated. I whirled one to the kitchen window ... crassshhhh! You should see his face, white as a ghost. Didn't expect it, you know, caught him by surprise. It is a miracle I didn't get blind or something. It's a miracle I didn't hit him on the face and end up in jail. I could've cut up the kids with the shards [of glass] ... You should've seen the mess ... For the rest of the day, he didn't mess with me. I caught him staring at me a few times ... and I stared right back!'

Although Anna's first show of anger had caught John by surprise, a couple of months later, she was severely beaten after she threw a glass of water at him during one of their endless arguments.

Turning Anger Within

The interviews made it clear to me that there were instances where women engaged in violence towards their partners or children. Yet the majority of this anger, frustration, and hatred gets turned back onto themselves. More than two-thirds of the women I interviewed (27) had seriously thought about killing themselves, on at least one occasion. Nine (23%) have actually attempted suicide. At least two additional women overdosed on drugs because they did not really care whether they lived or died.

These are very serious consequences of long-term abuse that are also present in the findings from other studies. Kendall-Tackett and Marshal (1998) report that up to 66 per cent of adults who have been subjected to serious forms of abuse attempt suicide or demonstrate an obsession with killing themselves. Not surprisingly, more than three-quarters of my participants (31) discussed how badly they thought about themselves. Some of them actually used the terms 'low self-esteem' and 'low self-concept,' but most chose the simple word 'hate.' The use of phrases such as 'I can't stand myself' or 'I don't even want to look in the mirror' or 'I wanted to die' were so frequent that I lost count of them. The focus of this self-condemnation was spread among very different personality characteristics. Some hated their weight; others their age, and still others their facial or bodily features. A few hated their skin colour. Many saw themselves as worthless. Regardless of what the focus of self-deprecation was, it seemed to be chronic and exceptionally hurtful. The following are some of the examples of this overwhelming pattern.

Amber
Amber (a light complexioned black woman) complained about her skin colour as something that has excluded her from her own (black) community. Her skin colour has not allowed her easy access to the white community either. On the surface, her tension and attitude could be interpreted as nothing more than a function of the general racism in North American society. Undoubtedly, overt as well as covert incidents of racial prejudice exist and negatively impact people like Amber. Nevertheless, the more she explained her feelings about herself, the more it became clear to me that Amber's discomfort with her skin colour was a product of endless put-downs by her lovers, both white and black. Amber had eventually internalized her partners' put-downs as her own, only in a much more amplified form.

At the time of our interview, Amber was on maternity leave for her seventh child. During part of the interview, she was nursing her baby. Some of her intense dislike of her own skin colour came out as the attributions she made to her little girl in her arms. 'You know, I look at her and my heart sinks! She is going to look in the mirror and see what I see ... not black, not white ... nothing. Men are going to tell her what they told me. The mirror doesn't lie. She'll know she doesn't belong. The mirror is going to tell her she is ugly.'

When I told Amber I thought her little baby was beautiful, she said, 'You say that cause you're not a man! When the night is over and she wakes up beside a guy looking like this, he'll tell her she don't fit! She'll know he's right. You don't understand!'

Angel
Angel called herself a mouse. She said there is nothing about herself that she likes, nothing that she has done that is worthwhile. Angel is happy that she has no children. 'Can you imagine if they turned out like me ... another mouse ... mice?' When I asked her if there was at least one thing she likes about herself, she had to think for a long time, then she said, 'Nothing!'

Debbie
Debbie drank, took drugs, put on extra weight, and hated herself for all of these things. She loved her children, but hated herself as a mother. 'I yell at them, yell and yell and yell. Mark [her 4-year-old son] bangs his head. I could kill myself. I would kill myself if it wasn't for them' (meaning her children).' At one time, Debbie challenged Gary to run her over. 'I really wanted him to take my life then and there. I had no life. Fuck, what am I saying, I have no life! ... Do you know why I came to see you today? It's not for you, you know, it is not for your fancy research or nothing like that. It's for me! I don't have no one to say the things I told you. I can't tell no one how horrible my life is. The baby snatchers [Children's Aid Society] are already hounding me ... They're trying to grab my kids. Well, I'm not blameless. How can I talk to them? How can I say how hopeless I feel without being judged. I'm glad I came today. You listened, you did not judge me. Don't thank me for coming here, I should thank you!'

Elly
Elly has wanted to kill herself on many occasions. She also challenged Stephan to run over her with her brand new car. As she put it, she had nothing to lose. This exceptionally thin, fragile, and emaciated-looking woman also thought about killing Stephan. 'I saw no way out! Beat-

ings, beatings, beatings ... No place to turn to. It just gets to you after a while. I hated him, I hated my parents for taking his side ... No matter what *he* did to me, they told me it was my fault. Many times, I felt so bad, I beat up my chest like this [beating her chest with her fists]. I did it till my lungs hurt, till my chest got bruised ... I guess, I hated myself too!' (Elly's emphasis).

Gwyn

During many years of mostly psychological and economic abuse, Gwyn thought about killing herself. She thought about different ways of accomplishing this. 'The one that appealed to me was filling the tub with hot water, pouring bubble bath, and slashing my wrists. I thought I'll watch the bubbles changing colour before I checked out ... I also thought about pills, but thought that was too cowardly ... even for me. I wanted to make a scene, to be the centre of attention once in my life ... But, when I started dreaming about my body floating in a tub of blood, I really got scared. I thought I was losing it [her mind]. Horrible nightmares. That's when it hit me: I didn't really want to die. I didn't really want to leave Ronny [her son] behind ... I guess, I was just so desperate.'

Kim

Before her extensive therapy, Kim hated herself. Whatever she did, always seemed to be the wrong thing to do. She never trusted her own instincts. She always felt vulnerable. 'I only felt safe when I was with men ... maybe that's why I fell for cops (her second and third husbands were police officers).' When Ken, her second husband, started controlling her whereabouts, where she went, for how long, and with whom, Kim felt at first safe. When Ken flew into jealous tantrums, and when he once broke 'some guy's hand,' Kim felt 'flattered.' Then, the control started suffocating her. Soon came the constant stalking, checking telephone calls, and timing the minutes Kim was allowed for shopping for groceries or to go to and return from work. 'He sent his buddies in cruisers. I would be visiting a friend, a cop car pulls over, stops, his cronies peer into the house. Every 15 to 20 minutes of this! I felt trapped. I lost all my friends. My sisters were no help. I had to explain myself ... minute by minute. Believe you me, it gets to you!'

When Ken's abuse and the control got the better of Kim, she lost her job, the last remaining connection she had to a normal world. She took a handful of pills to end it all. But before she passed out, she called a good friend – Rick, who is her current husband. 'Looking back, my suicide attempt was the best thing for me ... Don't get me wrong, I'm not proud of it. It was pretty desperado. It was good because it made me see I was just trying to find a way out ... When I hit the bottom, "crash and bang!" I discovered I had options ... For one thing, Rick ... He just became a friend, well more than a friend really [winks], I married the guy. Also, I got into therapy ... five years now, I'm still at it. The therapy was the best thing. Without it, *I would* have killed myself' (Kim's emphasis).

Laurette

There were years in Laurette's life when she thought she was the ugliest, stupidest person in the world. Laurette even thought she was fat, although she has never been much over 100 pounds. 'Sam made sure I felt that way. He made sure I always felt like a failure ... and I did.' There were many years when Laurette thought about killing herself, on a daily basis. 'I felt listless. I felt useless. If it wasn't for the kids, I would've done it. But the kids, especially Tommy [her 13 year old] ... I couldn't leave him alone with his father ... I just couldn't.'

Lisa Algoma

I have never met anyone in my life who seemed to loathe herself more than Lisa Algoma. From early in her life, Lisa had been exploited by many men including her stepfather, brother, two husbands, a brother-in-law, and friends (see Chapter 5). Most of the exploitation that she suffered had taken the form of abuse of her body, including numerous rapes. Referring to Randy, her alcoholic husband, she said, 'He saw me as a piece of meat. He treated me as a whore. Why not, everyone else did.' Lisa's disgust with her own body and self was profound. As she put it, she had 'eaten herself' into size 18. Although she was only 33, she had health problems. It was no wonder that she had twice overdosed on drugs. 'Well, I can't say what I was doing was trying to die that day ... I mean when I OD'd [overdosed]. I don't know what I was thinking ... Hell, I don't know if I was thinking at all. What I can say is I liked being high, no hurt when you float up there. I just didn't care whether I lived or died ... That much, I can say.'

Lorie

Lorie felt like an ugly duckling. She felt old even before she reached her early 20s. She felt like a castaway. That Emanuel, her younger husband, always held her age against her did not help her existing insecurities either. On the contrary, it put Lorie's already shaky self-concept into a tailspin. 'Remember, I told you I help out blind people? Well, I like helping them out ... but guess what? I feel good being around them. I feel good because they don't see me, they just know me for who I am. It makes it easier.'

Stacy
Stacy has a lot of problems with her 10-year-old son Leo, who seems to be depressed, bitter, and possibly suicidal. 'You know, my heart bleeds for him! I can't look into his eyes before something right here [showing her throat] starts choking me ... Call it guilt, call it regret, call it whatever you like. I feel guilty cause I was depressed. See, I thought about killing myself when he was a baby ... Who knows, maybe he picked up this black mess from me. I am scared for him. If he does anything, I don't know if I can live with myself.'

Erika
Erika is originally from the Bahamas. She has very troubled relationships with her siblings, parents, and her 22-year-old daughter Abby (see Chapter 6). For years, she has struggled with who she really is. Tony, her alcoholic husband, used to call Erika 'stupid,' 'ugly,' and 'fat.' She saw herself as 'ugly' and 'fat.' But most of all, Erika felt that she was not worthy of love. Erika was one of the women who actually used the term 'low self-esteem' to refer to these feelings. When she started her therapy 'a spew of anger came out.' She was frightened. But she now has a very good job, a renewed spiritual awareness (Born Again Christian), and a much more easy-going approach to life.

Sonny
Sonny was always the 'good girl.' Her mother died when she was young, and she helped raise her siblings like a mother. For a long time, the role Sonny played in her family made her feel important, needed, and wanted. But when her father remarried, troubles started at home. 'I was walking on eggshells, whatever I did was wrong. She took over! My father did whatever she wanted, never once asked me what I want.' Sonny rebelled and ran away from home, and this is when her self-esteem tumbled. 'I tried to help everyone, that's what I knew. I dated men with problems ... You know, like total losers ... trying to relive my mothering role, I guess ... make them better or something. I fell in love with the worst one [Theodore] ... Love is not supposed to

hurt, but it hurt like hell. I lost confidence in myself. I lost my grounding in life. It was like a free fall.'

It took nine months for Sonny to orchestrate her escape from Theodore. Fortunately, she has a good job and good relations with her work mates. However, Sonny knows that it is going to take longer to regain her old sense of self, the one she had before her mother died. She claims that she is a workaholic and that she is too eager to please, making it easy for others to take advantage of her. Sonny was still in therapy at the time of our interview, trying to reconfigure her new life with her son.

Chapter Ten

Prospects and a Model for Post-Violence Adjustment

In this chapter I will try to connect the dots. By combining the information I gathered from my thirty-nine participants, I am now ready to present a conceptual picture about what works in terminating abusive relationships and establishing more functional lives. By now, it should be clear that my insights are limited by the methodological constraint of a small sample size. Indeed, as I have acknowledged several times, each woman's experience is unique in many ways. Even when I see strong similarities among the thirty-nine women, how such patterns reflect other women's suffering at the hands of their partners is anyone's guess. In this regard, the reader must look at the following section with caution, just as I must try to stay aware of the limitations of my small sample.

A Wheel of Adjustment

In the theory chapter of this book (Chapter 3), I reviewed the power and control model of Pence and Paymar (1993). After over 110 hours of interviewing for this project, I am proposing a post-violence wheel of adjustment as an extension of the conceptual work in this area. The conceptual model is not absolute, since some women may be doing a little better in some dimensions than others, while slightly worse in others. There may also be swift changes for better or for worse in any of the dimensions such as finding or losing a job or establishing or terminating a relationship. In that sense, the wheel of adjustment cannot be thought of as a two-dimensional plane, but rather as a multi-dimensional object in motion. The different possibilities in each segment of the wheel may produce either a positive or a negative spin for some or all of the other segments. Before I develop the wheel of adjustment model, however, I will start with my observations about two groups of women who were identifiably different from one another. I will describe the first group as the 'naively caught' (N-C) and the second group as 'caught in a labyrinth' (C-L).

The Naively Caught (N-C)

Women who fall into the N-C category have basically had a happy and carefree upbringing. In general, their early experiences were what can be called 'normal.' Normality, in this case, signifies an absence of major problems or crises, rather than a presence of a specific mental or social condition. During their upbringing, these women may have had frictions, arguments, and social or economic ups and downs like everyone else. Certainly they may have suffered either family or personal losses, sickness, and / or death which may have affected them in serious ways. However, these women do not report major problems such as serious alcohol dependencies or drug abuse or debilitating problems such as incest or other types of violence among family members. Neither had they witnessed physical or sexual violence directed at their mothers and / or siblings. Instead, these women have learned some social skills, developed some positive goals and expectations, and been able to establish some trustworthy relationships in their early life. Basically, they have been able to develop a neutral if not a positive self-concept, rather than falling into the ravaging self-doubt that I saw in the C-L group.

What I would also like to emphasize is that the above description is not simply a social class difference. Although class could be one of the many important factors, it is not the sole determinant of this typology. For example, a few women in this group were brought up in quite modest, working-class families yet had the opportunity to trust others and respect themselves. Some women had the added bonus of being raised in quite affluent households with access to many resources; yet their class position was only one of many positive experiences and connections nested in a more general experience of life.

We must bear in mind that the above generalizations are only meant to formulate a very general typology. I am not trying to denote an unrealistic aura of perfection in these women's early lives, since each life is unique. Moreover, no woman was able to escape the occasional ups and downs of life while on her journey to adulthood. Nevertheless, there are those who were not exposed to ill effects from contact with destructive significant others in their family of origin or with extended family or friends during their early socialization. In my study, the women who fit this conceptual typology were Ann, Carrie, Laurette, Sam, Sonny and Suzan Windsor, and to a lesserer degree, Kim.

In the beginning of my conceptual discussion about violence against intimate partners, I took the stance that such violence can and does cut across class, ethnic or racial boundaries, and culture and religion. Now, I also suggest that violence spills across the background experience typologies that I am developing here, but with different consequences. Women who are not accustomed to violence in their upbringing can still get trapped into a life with a violent partner. My research is not about and cannot answer how women who are raised in basically trouble-free families, who have well-developed social skills, and a workable or positive sense of self fall for domineering, controlling, and violent partners. Perhaps the answer to such a question lies in the manipulative and deceitful ways in which violent men are capable of presenting themselves in the early stages of the relationship (Jacobson and Gottman, 2001). It may also be that the naiveté, love, or infatuation of women hinders their ability to recognize the early signs. For example, I did notice a commonality among the N-C women: their experiences with their partners were relatively trouble-free in the early parts of the relationship. The true exposure to violence often occurred only after a relative permanency in these relationships had set in. I also recognized that some of the abusive partners happened to be particularly witty, charismatic, and manipulative, approximating the 'Cobras' category suggested by Jacobson and Gottman (2001; see Chapter 3). Although I will return to this point in my examples, my work is not about the characteristics of the abusers. My work is about women who manage to escape abuse, regardless of the characteristics of the partner.

First, I will start with my insights into what happens to N-C women when they find themselves in a violent relationship. I will classify these incremental stages of reaction to violence as shock, disbelief, despair, secrecy, and breaking out. As it is going to become clear, their pattern of reaction is significantly different from those who have had prior exposure to violence (C-L).

Shock
During the first few explosions of violence, N-C women are shocked by it. The initial shock is reflective of a lack of expectation and a lack of

preparedness. These women are ill-equipped to deal with violent partners because of their relatively smooth, sheltered personal backgrounds. Because they were spared violence during their childhood, they do not know how to contextualize their partner's outbursts. They may have seen plenty of violence in the mass media and books, but they may have considered those phenomena as something that happens to 'other people,' not to them. These are also women who have exercised some or a lot of discretion in choosing their partners, only to later find out about their partner's violent side. Initially, their partners may have been quite charming and charismatic, thus compounding the shock value of their subsequently abusive behaviour. The readers will recall the eerily charming facades of Rob and Sam (Ann's partner and Laurette's husband, respectively). As Kim repeatedly pointed out, 'He was a cop, for Christ's sake! The knight in shining armour, the knight who was supposed to protect me ... Some protection ... He almost spilled my brains!'

Disbelief
Second, I would like to emphasize the disbelief factor. I heard N-C women repeat time and time again that they could not believe their man could do such a thing. They could not believe such violence could happen in their own homes. They were dumbfounded by it all. Disbelief has a whitewashing effect on women's desperate attempt to find reasons for what happened. For example, whitewashing may involve justifications such as 'he is not really like that, he just snapped' or 'he is under a lot of pressure at work' or 'he is such an important person/ good provider/good father.' The justifications may take the form of endless I-Should-Have's (I-S-H). For example, 'I-S-H put the kids to bed before he arrived, knowing how tired he is' or 'I-S-H cooked a better meal' or 'I-S-H worn a different dress' or 'I-S-H been more understanding' or 'I-S-H come home earlier.' Such justifications can be endless and seem to serve two functions. First, they explain away (albeit erroneously) the incident of violence that happened as an isolated event rather than allowing the victim to see a chronic pattern. The N-C women are not initially prepared to acknowledge a pattern of violence. Second, women internalize some or all of the blame to preserve a measure of mental control over the situation. By shifting the blame onto themselves, they are able to continue caring and loving the partners or husbands who have degraded and abused them. For example, Laurette endlessly tried to do the right thing, striving to be better

in cooking, cleaning, mothering, hostessing, and everything else she could think of. Her eagerness to please never satisfied her abuser, but she was too busy to notice. Ann desperately tried to reduce contact with her own family to avoid arguments, but Rob always found new reasons for abuse. Sonny tried to participate in Theodore's strange sexual games. Kim tried to cut down on her visits to her female friends. She also tried to ignore the police cruisers (loaded with Ken's comrades) that checked up on her wherever she went.

Ferraro and Johnson (1983) report numerous psychological mechanisms or rationalizations women use to help them cope with the violence in their lives. They may overemphasize their nurturing role, deny that their partners are victimizers, deny that they are being injured, deny that they have other options, or appeal to higher loyalties (such as religion). It is my contention that these cognitive strategies reflect the gender-based socialization that is still common in North American society. Through differential socialization, women and men learn to use different cognitive strategies to make sense of the realities that surround them (Sev'er, Ungar, and Tanner, 1991).

Men and women also learn to make differential judgments when confronted with ethical dilemmas (Gilligan, 1982). A conglomeration of thoughts and feelings about trying to understand the other person and putting others' needs and wants first even if this requires personal sacrifices are relational mechanisms women learn from very early on. Gilligan (1982) calls this the 'ethic of care' which is qualitatively different from the more rational, self-preserving, convenience-oriented 'instrumental ethic' of men. Women are taught to think that they are primarily responsible for relationships (Cancian, 1993) which means that they will try their hardest to assure the continuation of a relationship even if it may be a destructive one. The ironic twist is that the more normatively socialized the women are, the higher their tendency to appease will be. Indeed, one unifying aspect of the N-C women in this study was their attempt to justify and explain away their partners' violence for a long time, even if this meant exposing themselves to escalating victimization.

Despair
Eventually, abused women reach the point of despair. Even N-C women come to realize that the violence of their partners is not just an exception, but is repetitive. They realize that no matter what they do, no matter how much they try, the violence of their partners will erupt

again. This recognition may further erode the lowered level of self-efficacy that results from the earlier shock and disbelief stages. It is then that women lose their energy. Some lose all hope and move into a dark, hopeless, apathetic existence. They may retreat from most or all social connections. Some may seriously think about killing themselves. Others may just feel numb and listless. In this research, seven women who fall into this typology (Ann, Carrie, Kim, Laurette, Sam, Sonny, and Suzan Windsor) considered suicide at one time or another. Laurette came very close to killing herself, and Kim actually swallowed pills. This is a unique finding about the N-C women that attests to their unpreparedness to deal with the abuse. It is also a stark departure from their earlier views about their own sense of self-worth. The N-C women are increasingly isolated as an outcome of their partner's constant complaints, cutting remarks, stalking, and put-downs.

Having reached the despair stage, Laurette talked about waking up under a 'thick blanket of cement,' feeling isolated, vulnerable, immobile, and entombed. Ann's escape into a prescription drug world was partially the result of the pain from her physical injuries, but it also was a way of escaping the constant terror, helplessness, and despair that she felt. Carrie felt she was caught up in an 'endless night where there were no stars.' Suzan Windsor felt 'numb' all the time, and Sam mentioned feeling 'frozen, just like deer ... caught in headlights.' Sam also 'felt like part of the furniture.' For Kim, it was like being in a 'straightjacket.'

Secrecy
An additional factor works against N-C women. This factor is their own desperate attempt to keep their situation a secret. I interpret this tendency as another artefact of their unpreparedness to deal with violence and the lack of social comparisons among their family and friends. For example, Gelles's 1976 study clearly indicates that experience with family violence in early childhood was the most reliable predictor of whether women will seek intervention or separate or divorce their abuser. Pagelow (1981) also observes a negative correlation between being a victim of family violence as a child and staying in violent conjugal relationships. In other words, early exposure to violence gave women a perceptual and behavioural readiness to acknowledge it and/or to escape from it. N-C women do not have this readiness, and their sense of entrapment is overwhelming.

The secrecy N-C women weave into their lives almost always works against them. They seem reluctant to reach out to their once-positive social networks such as the members of their family of origin or friends. Isolation reduces the possibility of receiving help before these women are seriously hurt or injured (Ann's case is the most glaring example of this process). Likewise, N-C women are much less likely to call the police or contact women's agencies, shelters, or help lines, unless they or their children are in very serious trouble. They are more likely to think of the abuse as happening only to them. They feel different, alone, and profoundly ashamed. It is also possible that their violence-free families would not know what to do in these situations either, because they would be equally unprepared. Families and former friends may sense some trouble, but may respect the privacy of the woman and not probe. The barriers erected by the abusive partner further hide the suffering and keep the extended family in the dark.

One natural outcome of long-term secrecy is that N-C women suffer for a long time before professionals or family members get involved. Or, it can take a very serious violation to break this code of silence, one either directed at the woman herself (such as the violent rape and torture of Ann; gun threats on Sonny and Kim) or against her children (such as the abuse of Laurette's son Tom).

Breaking Out
We do not know how many women stay in their abusive relationships. From different surveys and shelter statistics, we do know that some leave, and some leave more than once (OAITH, 1998, 1999). Once the violence in their lives becomes known and once they decide to seek help, an advantage for the N-C women is their previously established social links. Through the relative affluence of their families of origin (in Ann's and Laurette's cases) and/or through their warmth, caring, and willingness to help, N-C women do receive a protective shield around them and their children. The type of help can range from being welcomed to their family homes, some or a lot of material help, and of course, love and comfort to their bruised bodies and souls. Family help may also include finding lawyers, counsellors, and/or therapists to advocate on behalf of the abused woman (Weisz, 1999). In the present research, one family (Carrie's) hired a private security guard since they were quite concerned about Carrie's physical safety. Ann's family hired good lawyers and got a conviction against Rob, although his sentence was only one month. Laurette's mother provided grocery money for Laurette and her four children. Unlike the other six women in this cat-

egory, the help Kim received from her family was marginal, although Kim's friend (who later became her third husband) protected her from stalking by Ken's police friends. Kim is absolutely sure the stalking would have continued if she had not married another 'cop.'

None of the stated measures is capable of providing an absolute guarantee of women's safety. As the literature repeatedly shows, and as the Toronto study corroborates, violent men may continue or even increase their abuse when the relationship is broken off (Bergen, 1998; Ellis and DeKeseredy, 1997; GSS, 2000; Sev'er, 1997a, 1998). For example, out of the 347 severe abuse or murder victims reported in the *Toronto Star*, 69 (20%) were wives and female partners who had already separated from their abusive partners (Sev'er, 2001). Moreover, women report more severe forms of violence by a former partner than at the hands of a current partner (GSS, 2000). It is clear that outside help does not insulate abused women and their children from physical or psychological harm. It does mean, however, that the N-C women will not be travelling alone on the difficult road that awaits them. By itself, this may be a positive shift in the power balance in crossing over to a nonabusive life.

Caught in a Labyrinth (C-L)

There are women who are much worse off. Their difficulties stem from being crushed by repeated violence, both as children and as adults, as well as from occupying structurally disadvantaged positions in life. For these women, it is more difficult to initiate a change to break the cycle of violence in their own or in their children's lives (Levendosky and Graham-Bermann, 2001). I will describe this type as being caught in a labyrinth (C-L).

Earlier, I argued that violence can occur among all social classes of people. For example, women who were N-C in a violent relationship could have come from affluent or not so affluent backgrounds. However, when I look at the group of women who are most likely to be represented at the negative spin of the adjustment wheel, their socioeconomic and affective disadvantages seem to intermesh. This does not mean that all or even most interpersonal violence occurs among the socioeconomically disadvantaged. However, it does mean that when violence occurs amongst the lower classes, there are additional complexities to sustain the violence, unlike the situation of the N-C women. For example, women in the C-L group may be less likely to tolerate violence by the same partner for a long time. If Pagelow's (1981) and Gelles's (1979) findings are any indication, they are more likely to call the police, go to shelters, or permanently leave their abuser. On the surface, this tendency may appear to be an advantage. However, when socioeconomically disadvantaged women are subjected to violence, they may have a harder time finding the personal, social, or economic resources to permanently break away from the repetition of violence. Both within a generation and across generations, they may remain more vulnerable (Levendosky and Graham-Bermann, 2001). The probability of these women going back to their abuser or finding other partners who also abuse them is high (OAITH, 1998, 1999; Sev'er, 2002).

In the C-L group, exposure to violence seems to start early. I do not mean to suggest that these women want violence or are accustomed to violence. It would be a gross injustice to each and every woman in this study to ever suggest that they are used to violence or seek violent relationships. On the contrary, each seems to be wary of violence, each wants to live a violence-free life. However, most women in the C-L group have grown up with a sense of social and/or economic deprivation, a lack of privacy, conflicting messages about good and bad, and a confusion about their world and their own location in it. A sizable number may have faced violations and developed a sense of worthlessness. From very early on, these women or girls may have seen their mothers being beaten on a regular basis, may have experienced violence among their siblings, and may have fallen prey to physical or sexualized violence by their father figures, male siblings, other relatives, or friends of their families (Debbie and Lisa Algoma). The boundaries of their own bodies and their sense of self may have been made permeable by the very people who should have protected them. Sadly, most of these transgressions were committed before they could make an adult claim over their own precious selves.

Aside from violence, C-L women may face challenges related to alcohol and hard drugs. In this study, most of their natural fathers or stepfathers, a sizable proportion of their mothers, most brothers, and some sisters have had alcohol and/or drug-related problems. Moreover, the structural constraints surrounding their lives, such as their early family living conditions may have predetermined their circle of friends and the type of mates they eventually chose (or who chose them). In this study, the likelihood that these women paired up with men who were also products of families of deprivation, violence, alcohol, and even hard drug abuse was high. To use Jacobson and Gottman's (2001) classification, they are more likely to pair up with 'Pit-Bulls.' In this subcultural configuration, some women are further victimized by their own addictions.

In this analysis, I am going to use Clara, Debbie, DeeDee, Lisa Algoma, Lisa Kingston, Lorie, Lou, Nancy Sudbury, Sue, and Terry as examples of the C-L group. The reader should immediately notice that there are more examples from the labyrinth group than the N-C group. If I had kept the conceptual boundaries a little more elastic, I could have included numerous others to the above list. This finding is not unique to this study; other researchers also report the disproportional occurrence of interpersonal violence among the structurally disadvantaged (Conway, 1997; DeKeseredy, 1999; Gelles, 1974). Moreover, women who are caught in the labyrinth have very different reactions to violence than their N-C sisters. Their reactions can be subsumed under ritualistic coping and a revolving-door strategy.

Ritualistic Coping and a Revolving-Door Strategy
In my conceptualization of the N-C group of women, I identified shock and disbelief as the first two stages of reaction to partner abuse. I could find no comparable stages in the C-L group. Instead, the feelings expressed were unavoidability and resignation dotted with short-term strategies and reactions. The violence the C-L group experienced from their partner(s) may have been only one of many incidents in a life full of similar experiences. The coping strategies they use may themselves be quite problematic, such as using sex to calm their partners (DeeDee and Lisa Algoma, see Chapter 7). They may challenge their partners (Debbie), or they may shout, swear, run outside, hide, or even kick or bite (Nancy Sudbury). They may have seen their mothers or sisters use similar techniques, or they may have used such techniques with different partners. What I want to emphasize is the ritualized aspects of these techniques despite the history of their ineffectiveness.

The pattern I am identifying here is not a direct result of class, since there are many lower-class women who are not caught in a vicious cycle of violence. There is also violence in some middle-class women's lives. Nevertheless, the class disadvantages of those who are caught in the labyrinth seem to exacerbate their situation. For example, one artefact of the socioeconomic constraints and multiple deprivations (money, education, and good role models), is an easily permeable boundary of the self. In a way, the public and private aspects of these women's lives may be more blurred than their more affluent counterparts. In the short run, this may appear to work for them. As already mentioned, C-L women are more likely to make their situation public by involving their neighbours, parents, and siblings or professionals such as the social workers or police. Studies from shelters also attest that C-L women are more likely to seek institutionalized forms of help (MacLeod, 1980, 1987; OAITH, 1998; Weisz, 1999). In the present study, Clara, Debbie, DeeDee, Lisa Algoma, Lorie, and Nancy Sudbury, and Sue could not even remember the exact number of times they had called the police. Numerous times, the grievousness of their situation required that a third party call the police. Similarly, these women have had countless encounters with health services and hazy memories about the number of hospitalizations. In contrast to the N-C group, this group has a much shallower tendency for secrecy and a much higher propensity to seek help.

Unfortunately, their economic or social resources are not sufficient to help them break or reverse the tide of violence in their lives. After a police contact or a shelter stay, they may return to the same partner, or after leaving an abusive partner, they may quickly end up in another abusive relationship. They may have abusive siblings or parents, and they may live in areas that are not safe (Clara, Lorie, and Sue). In turn, they may become abusive towards their children (Debbie; see Levendosky and Graham-Bermann, 2001).

Women in the Middle

The typologies of the N-C and C-L women are just conceptual tools to understand why some women may be coping better than some others after one or more experiences with intimate violence. It should be clear that my intention is by no means to pigeonhole these women's unique selves but to identify some common threads in their experiences. Again, it will not hurt to mention that post-violence adjustment is more like a wheel in motion, rather than bipolar points in a straight line of social interaction. If the current research provides a valid picture, fewer women are represented in the positive spin of the wheel than at its negative revolution. However, the largest number of women fall somewhere in the middle.

When I discussed the labyrinth category, I highlighted its close interaction with class, although my findings do not indicate class as a singular determining factor. Other factors also come to play. For example, we need to take into account the cultural differences among women (West, 1998). Culture, in its own right, may be an accelerating factor in the negative treatment of women or it may interact with a host of other factors, including the class position. Major cultural shifts made without an opportunity to adjust to the values of the host society may increase the vulnerability of women who are daughters, sisters, and wives of abusive men (West, 1998). People from different cultures may also occupy the lower rungs in the socioeconomic stratification system. It is this complex interaction that has made a number of women in my study particularly vulnerable to their abusive partner(s).

Amber, Ava, and Elly are three interesting examples of the cultural complexity surrounding women in the middle. How perceptions of women's roles intersect with patterns of abuse is clearly visible in their cases. Their cases also provide a glimpse of hope about the possibility of positive change. All three are very bright women, first-generation immigrants (two from Jamaica one from Eastern Europe). The following are snapshots from their stories.

Amber's parents were abusive and alcoholic. Amber had run away from home numerous times and got tangled up with men who were not good companions. At a very early age, she had an unplanned pregnancy and she left her baby in her sister's custody. That she immigrated to Canada on her own, without friends or family did not help either. Cultural differences between her birth country and Canada made her vulnerable to exploitation from both black and white men. Amber felt marginalized by her skin colour.

Ava's parents, especially her father, were also abusive. Ava told me she was stripped down and whipped with a wet towel at least three times a year. Some years, the wet towel punishments were more frequent. Despite these problems, what is interesting in these two cases is that both women managed to develop a relatively coherent sense of self. They attributed their strength to having been brought up by their grandparents. In each case, their grandparents had managed to give them enough love, freedom, and respect to cushion some of the detrimental effects of their biological parents. The positive intervention of the grandparents has acted as a buffer against the hardships of their lives. Despite the fact that their families of origin were enveloped in problems and despite the fact that they made cultural shifts on their own, which made them easy prey for some exploitative men, they have retained some inner confidence to pull them through the worst of times.

Elly is another, albeit quite different example. The majority of her troubles were rooted in the patriarchal norms of her country of origin that treat women as second-class citizens. Her mother was a strict enforcer of these norms. Both her parents and her in-laws repeatedly put down her abilities and individuality, demanding silence, conformity, and compliance to her abusive husband. It is my contention that what kept Elly's inner strength intact was her language and educational skills, which her immigrant parents lacked. Despite the put-downs in her growing years, Elly was nevertheless needed as an income producer, translator, and a general liaison between her parents' old country ways and the complex demands of their host country. Elly was able to broker a difficult existence from a very early age, and thus she was able to nurture a sense of self even her parents could not destroy. Despite the violence of her husband and later, of her older sons, Elly's perception of her own agency has survived.

A General Model of Adjustment

Much can be learned from the intriguing and sometimes triumphant, other times frustrating and disheartening lives of the survivors of abuse. Yet, the complex lives and experiences of the thirty-nine partici-pants in my study lead me to believe that survival does not guarantee a positive post-violence adjustment. Instead, adjustment is contingent upon numerous factors which may work together or in opposition. Although in itself a daunting task, the ability to leave an abusive part-ner is only one of many difficulties these women have to struggle through and master.

The synthesis of the ideas that I have developed up to this point is subsumed in the following post-violence adjustment model (Figure 10.1). Just like the power and control model of Pence and Paymar (1993), the adjustment model is envisioned as a wheel. In the model, the hub of the wheel consists of self-acceptance, self-confidence, and self-respect. As I argued in relation to the N-C group, it may be more difficult for women who have basic self-respect to find themselves in violent relationships. The partners of such women may also be particu-larly vicious in their attacks on this core of self in their attempt to sub-jugate their partners. Therefore, it is not surprising that women's path to a healthier life will be closely related to reclaiming their most basic sense of self.

For women whose sense of self was never fully developed or was damaged from an early age, the route to establishing violence-free lives may be even more difficult, but not impossible, had not this been the case. In the above examples, Lou, Ava, Amber, and Elly are exam-ples of the possibility of success, although it is also clear that their struggle to reclaim their lives has been arduous.

I suspect that some of my readers will quarrel with me for placing

Figure 10.1 Self-acceptance, confidence, and respect model of adjustment after leaving abusive relationships.

the social-psychological dimension of the self at the hub of a model of the social and structural problem of violence against women. I must immediately point out that my aim is not to reduce a complex social problem to the personal realms of the self. My research also amply shows that there are many layers of complexities that sustain abuse, certainly including but not exhausted by the characteristics of the abusive men and the victimized women. However, if women are going to find a way out of their dilemma and stay on a path that will protect them from a revolving door of violence, the most basic requirement is appropriating a sense of self. Starting from this centre, I envision eight spokes of the wheel of adjustment.

Assuring Physical Safety

Abusive partners often continue or even intensify their abuse after a separation (Sev'er, 1997a; Ellis and DeKeseredy, 1997; Dobash et al.,

1995; VAWS, 1993; GSS, 2000). But adjustment is only possible within a safe environment. How women cope with living under a real or imagined threat to their safety varies. Some of them move long distances (e.g., Amber), some repeatedly contact the police and obtain peace bonds (e.g., Sue and Debbie), some hire personal security (e.g., Carrie). Regardless of the strategy, abused women often have legitimate concerns about their safety. Even when their concerns or fears do not seem to be well founded, just the feeling of threat may deprive them of the most basic freedoms that most other people take for granted. As unorthodox as it may seem, Amber's and Debbie's relief and celebratory moods after their abusers were accidentally killed are testaments to the debilitating oppressiveness of living in fear.

Finding a Way to Deal with the Past

As the famous Gestaltist Frederick Perls (1974) would insist, people who carry 'garbage bags' full of unresolved emotions will not have the energy to move forward, seek change, and pursue growth. For Perls, energy is a finite commodity. Those who use it up in worrying about the past will deprive themselves from positively dealing with the 'here and now,' or positively impacting the future. Suffering long-term violence by an intimate partner is an ominous emotional burden to carry around. Some women I interviewed mentioned debilitating flashbacks. Some had developed phobialike fears. Others had lost their trust in people, especially men. Some of my participants had serious sleep or eating disorders, all rooted in their past problems. Some were overburdened with guilt, especially in relation to their children (Glass, 1995). A few were full of hate. It is absolutely necessary for women to find a way of dealing with the crippling experiences of the past to garner the energy to move towards a better future. Most of my respondents talked about having been in some sort of therapy (all of those in the N-C group). A few had been involved in self-help groups, as participants or as volunteers. One woman has found a religious group that has been instrumental in her resolution of some of her past fears and hatred. These efforts seem to be a necessary first step in post-violence adjustment.

Re-establishing Social Networks

One of the outcomes of living with controlling and abusive men is the dilution of existing networks. Among others, in Daisy's, Erika's, Laurette's, and Monica's cases, we saw the intense pressure from partners to limit the social contacts of women. In Ann's, Debbie's, and Lisa Algoma's cases, we even saw the possibility of enlargement of destructive networks. In other cases, women did not have social networks in the first place, either as a result of their immigrant status or the problematic nature of their own families of origin (like Amber, Ava, Debbie, Elly, Lisa Algoma, and Lorie). Yet, one important factor in getting out and staying out of abusive relationships is the establishment of new and positive social links (Erika and Kim). Another way is reclaiming the old ones (Ann and Laurette).

Reassignment of Blame

As the review of the literature shows (Chapter 3) and the stories of the respondents corroborate, abused women use various strategies to cope with their situation (Chapter 7). Some of these strategies deflect blame away from their abusers onto themselves. The way to a more positive life requires that women learn to think and believe that what they have endured by being violated is not their own fault. It is true that what they wore, said, did or did not do, and what they wanted may have been less than helpful. Yet none of these justify what their partners did to them (Jacobson and Gottman, 2001).

Shifting the blame does not suggest that women should stop taking responsibility for their own lives. Instead, it suggests that they should stop feeling responsible for the violence, unless they themselves perpetrated non-defensive violence. Reassignment of blame to the perpetrator is yet another way of reaching a sense of self-acceptance and self-respect – the hub of the wheel – en route to adjustment.

Creating or Reclaiming Opportunities and Establishing Economic Well-being

From the early social scientific studies on abuse of women, what has been clear is that the level of dependency of women on men determines the extent of victimization. For example, either younger or older women, women with young or numerous children, immigrant women, women with little or no education, and women without paid employment may be more vulnerable to abuse and less likely to leave an abusive partner. The challenge for women is to be able to create or reclaim opportunities that will shift the balance of power slightly in their favour. In the present study, three women (Anna, Debbie, and Suzan Toronto) went back to school as adults. A number of others (Elly and Laurette) were taking university courses while engaging in part-time or full-time work. Establishing economic well-being is important for women in general. It is an absolute must for women who have suffered partner abuse. School and/or work is important for developing confidence and increasing self-regard and self-respect (which are linked with the hub of the wheel in the model). With few exceptions, most women in this study were not employed during their abusive relationships or had transient work experiences. At the time of the interviews, however, twenty-eight women (72%) were employed either part-time or full-time. Although most did not like their work environment very much, and a few said that their working conditions were unacceptable, all of them recognized the importance of their economic independence.

Re-establishing Relationships with Children

Strategies to prevent violence must ultimately start with patterns of early socialization, especially in terms of gender relationships. In North American society (and in patriarchal societies all over the world), overt or covert preference for boys and men is a hurdle that must be dismantled if we are to reverse the propensity for gendered violence (Nelson and Robinson, 1999; Chapter 4). This book is not about prevention of violence, but about women who were able to get out of relationships where violence was already present. Nevertheless, the most desirable strategy to combat violence is not escaping from its devastation after the fact. The most desirable strategy is to be able to set the ground for relatively egalitarian, respectful, tolerant, and violence-free relationships in the first place.

One theme that emerged in my interviews was how problematic the self-concept of the majority of the women is. For example, even when they were obviously attractive and smart by societal standards, most women referred to themselves as fat, ugly, rat, stupid, failure, and even as 'meat.' Some of this self-deprecation could have been the result of the years of abuse they had suffered: the handiwork of abusive partners who have crushed these women's self-esteem. However, I also have the strong impression that more than half the women I interviewed had gone into these relationships with already bruised self-perceptions, either because of their maltreatment as children, maltreatment from peers, parental neglect, or missed opportunities. In the worst-case scenario, women's inner selves were dismantled through physical, psychological, and/or sexual abuse, especially those women I classified as C-L.

The above line of thinking gets even more grounded when we look at the problematic backgrounds of their abusers. I have absolutely no intention of either excusing or justifying these men's cruel, controlling, hurtful, demeaning, and often vicious behaviour. Nevertheless, if we are to eradicate violence in intimate relationships, we have to make sure to raise males to be psychologically mature, self-assured but sensitive, strong but also gentle. During my interviews, my participants told me many stories about their abusive partners. The majority have had quite intolerable childhood experiences, ranging from alcoholic or abusive fathers, to either abused or too punitive mothers, and violent peers and/or siblings. Some were severely beaten, most were demeaned and repeatedly made to feel incompetent, and a few were sexually exploited as children. These boys who had intolerable childhoods turned into the exploitative, controlling, and ruthless men who inflicted immeasurable amounts of pain on my participants. Thus, for the vast majority of people, the most important agent of socialization is certainly the parents and immediate family. Although there is never a one-to-one correspondence between a relatively good family life and turning out to be a well-adjusted man or a woman, there is a more than coincidental likelihood that violent families do create serious problems in children's lives. In the statistical findings, this connection is clearly demonstrated (VAWS, 1993; GSS, 2000). In this study, the connection was clear in the additional difficulties we saw in some children's behaviour (Chapter 6) and the women's agony in relation to these problems.

In Chapters 3 and 6, I discussed the effects that witnessing parental violence have on children. One possibility was general adjustment problems. Two other possibilities were either turning the hurt onto themselves (self-directed problems) or unleashing on other people (other-directed problems). A number of children had developed either cold and elusive (Terry's daughter Teddy, Stacy's son Leo) or strained and even aggressive and exploitative relationships with their mothers (Elly's abusive sons Jimmy and Andy and Ava's and Gwyn's aggressive sons Stan and Ronny). Yet, these women still love their children. They feel guilty and hurt about their own role in what happened to their children (Glass, 1995). Perhaps, re-establishing good relations with their children is one of the greatest challenges these women face, but a challenge that needs to be pursued for two reasons. On the one hand, this connection seems to be crucial for the mothers' own lives and mental health (Cory and McAndless, 2000). On the other hand, it is even more important for the children if they are to remedy the caustic effects of witnessing or experiencing violence in their formative years. A significant victory in post-violence adjustment is the ability to nurture those of the new generation to prevent them from replicating the past. Yet, for a large proportion of the abused women in my study, this repairing of wounds and reconnecting with their children seem to have a bleak potential for success (see Chapter 6).

Setting Roots

Women who come from disadvantaged segments of society may have problems with establishing roots since they often move, change jobs, schools, and partners. For immigrant women, these problems may be compounded if they leave their families of origin, kin, friends, and neighbours behind (Dasgupta, 1998; West, 1998). We saw some examples of these shifts, especially in the lives of the C-L women. Nevertheless, women who are N-C in violence are not immune to some of these uprooting experiences either. Their partners may insist on many moves to disconnect them from their former family and friends (e.g., Ann and Laurette). Thus, survivors of violence have a long way to go towards but much to gain from setting some community roots, engaging in community activities, volunteering, forming work connections, or establishing some new hobbies and pursuits. Increased stability may also improve relationships with children (sixth spoke on the wheel).

In this study, very few women felt that their lives had stabilized, although they had been away from their abusive partners for at least six months (condition of participation). The C-L group in particular had more limited access to acceptable housing, good schools, and desirable neighbourhoods (the reader will recall my own uneasiness in the elevator of an apartment building, see Chapter 4). It is perhaps not surprising that there seems to be a void of leisurely or hobbylike activities in these women's lives as well as a general feeling of unconnectedness with their social surroundings (Chapter 7). It was as if their time and energy were being depleted by their past and current problems to such a degree that they had little time for anything else. For example, a few expressed a wish to win a lottery but very few talked about a positive, enjoyable, relaxed mental space or a satisfaction derived from belonging to a group (Kim, Erika, and Laurette being possible exceptions).

Reformulating Gender Expectations

Abusive men never treat their partners as equals (DeKeseredy and Kelly, 1993; Dobash and Dobash, 1998; Kelly and Radford, 1998). After countless put-downs and other forms of degradation, women often internalize the faults, shortcomings, and even lack of morality that are attributed to them (e.g., Laurette, Lisa Algoma, Lorie, and Sue). Another strategy abusive men employ is to make women believe that their survival depends on the men. For example, Rob was meticulous in supplying Ann's painkillers, and Ann rarely questioned the fact that the only reason she needed painkillers was because of Rob's violence. Ralph, Gary, and Gerard respectively provided Lou, Debbie, and Lisa Algoma with alcohol and drugs. Once formed, these vicious cycles of dependence on men were difficult to break. Even women who claimed to have become very cautious in their dealings with men expressed a deep yearning to find a new partner as a condition of their own happiness. In their haste to find a partner and in their eagerness to be loved by a man, some women rushed into a series of very damaging relationships (e.g., Debbie, Lisa Algoma, Lisa Kingston, and Lorie). The challenge for many is to learn to respect themselves as women and to begin to feel confidence in their own judgment, with or without a man in their lives. The wait for someone who respects them and treats them as an equal may indeed be a long one. Rather than having enough confidence in themselves and being patient enough to let themselves heal, some women are settling for new and potentially problematic partners.

Long-Term Prospects for Women Caught in a Labyrinth Group

What works against women who are caught in a negative spin of the adjustment wheel? I propose that their dilemma is better understood in terms of at least one core dimension and numerous interrelated dimensions. The core dimension relates to themselves (the hub of the adjustment model). Even before finding themselves in one (often more than one) abusive relationship, these women's opportunities to develop a strong sense of self were compromised early in life. The setbacks they faced either personally (the most blatant example would be Lisa Algoma's subjection to repeated incestuous and marital rapes) or through their proximity to other troubled or victimized people (abused mothers, alcoholic and/or abusive fathers, and violent siblings) were not conducive to the development of a positive self-concept, self-confidence, or self-respect. In short, even before the partner abuse starts, and certainly after being subjected to repeated forms of abuse, these women have little strength left to reverse the tide. Even when they find the strength to leave an abusive relationship, their victory is rarely an assurance of the continuation of a violence-free life. For example, Clara's family was full of violence. So was her marriage. Her current relationship is less than supportive for Clara's bruised self. Debbie's husband as well as partner (Ron and Gary) were extremely abusive. So were her parents. DeeDee's husband Stuart was an alcoholic; he was also very abusive. DeeDee is not sure where she stands in relation to her new partner. The reader will recall the horrendous cycle of violence in Lisa Algoma's life, starting from her early childhood and including both partners (Randy and Gerard). Lisa Kingston's partners abused alcohol, drugs, and of course, Lisa. Lorie's husband Emanuel was extremely violent and oppressive. However, Lorie's second marriage and current partner are not much better. Lorie's tattered self-concept was first damaged by being called the 'ugly duckling' of her family. This association never seems to release her from an inferiority complex that abusive men exploit. Sue's husband Ed was exceptionally abusive to her. Sue did not mention physical violence from her current partner, but she did mention repeated put-downs in her new relationship. Terry's marriage and two other relationships were problematic. Her troubles with her daughter Teddy are perhaps reflective of the inter-generational cycle of violence in her life. Nancy Sudbury's relationship with her two children is continuing to be problematic.

From this group of women, perhaps the only one who may indeed break free from violence for good is Lou. Indeed, by going to school, by doing everything in her power to stay away from abusive men, Lou may be moving towards a much better future for herself (her daughter is now an adult). However, even in Lou's case, some of the effects of her previous alcohol and drug abuse linger on. She has been in therapy for her nightmares. Debbie has also gone back to school, and is eager to better herself and resolve the difficulties with the Children's Aid Society in relation to her children. However, her substance abuse problems seem to hover just below the surface, and Debbie also has difficulty controlling her severe mood swings.

Another aspect that works against women in the labyrinth category is the inefficacy or the sheer destructive nature of their social networks. Even though they may be more open to seeking help, and even when they are less secretive about their personal dilemmas, this group is less likely to get help in comparison with the N-C women. Their parents, siblings, and neighbours may be too inundated with their own (sometimes just as serious) problems to be effective help providers or role models. In acute cases such as the incestual attacks against Lisa Algoma, the family members may be the worst offenders.

The efficacy and empathy of the professionals these women contact is also crucial (Weisz, 1999). Stereotypes and prejudices held by the people from whom they seek help will likely determine the outcome. If the contact is negative, women may continue along the treacherous and violent route of their relationship. If the contact is positive, they may find the courage to explore new alternatives. The direction of the outcome is not discernible from class constraints, but class is nevertheless intermingled with the outcome in complex ways. Police, social workers, medical personnel, and lawyers and judges these women encounter may be riddled with stereotypes about lower-class women and women associated with violent subcultures. Police, as the frontline help providers to disadvantaged groups, must have non-judgmental attitudes and behaviour to adequately respond to physical and sexual abuse. Whether the police will protect the victim, whether they will lay charges against the perpetrator, whether they will initiate a peace bond or arrest all depend on how much legitimacy they attribute to the women's narrative of the violent event. Similar cognitive processes that lead to attributions may also colour how women are treated at hospitals, emergency centres, shelters, or in the courts. Recognizing the very problematic backgrounds some of these women may indeed lead to conclusions such as 'she must be lying' or 'she must have asked for it' or 'she must be violent herself' or she is just 'a nagging ...' As an example of this kind of intolerance, Sue's encounter with the judge needs to be recalled. After numerous violent events including the kidnapping of her son, constant stalking, and as many as thirty threatening phone messages a day, Sue had to frequently use the court system. Yet, the judge's response was 'Is that you again?' rather than showing any real understanding of her dire situation.

Positive examples were rare. One was Lisa Kingston's absolute surprise to find a kind constable after the violent Niagara Falls incident. She just could not believe that police would treat her 'like a nice girl.' This says a lot about the kind, gentle, and humane constable. At the same time, Lisa Kingston's surprise also speaks volumes about all the other professionals (including other police) who had earlier treated her as less than human.

Another serious hurdle to overcoming violence may be the particularly problematic background of the partners and the male-dominated nature of the subcultures they are a part of (Bowker, 1998; DeKeseredy and MacLeod, 1997; Hatty, 2000). For example, abusive men see women as mere possessions. How women perceive themselves is also a key factor in this complex puzzle. I will call upon Lisa Algoma's extreme case to make this point clear, although slightly more tame examples from other women were plentiful. The reader will recall that Randy actually invited his buddies to rape his young wife on a number of occasions. He sometimes participated; at other times he just watched. This example says a lot about Randy, but it also speaks volumes about his buddies who were willing to partake in such an unwholesome and criminal act. Unfortunately, Lisa Algoma also saw herself as a 'piece of meat.' Ann's partner engaged in similar rituals of public humiliation (asking Ann to squirt herself with a water bottle in the presence of his drinking buddies), without transforming them into physical assaults. Unlike Lisa Algoma, however, Ann did not see herself as a 'piece of meat.' Ann's core values about herself protected her from internalizing the symbolic assault despite the fact that she could not stop the degrading acts. Although the damage caused in each case may have varied, one must still acknowledge the similarity in treating women as sexualized possessions in these androcentric rituals and violent male-centred gatherings.

Women who fit the C-L category seem to have a better understanding of their partner's violent nature. They live in a state of fear and terror, expecting the very worst. They do not go through the disbelief stage that the N-C group experiences. Instead, they understand what is happening to them and what the consequences may involve. Within this context, the availability of help lines, safe homes, shelters, legal advocacy, and affordable housing is crucial if the cycle of violence is to be broken (OAITH, 1998; Weisz, 1999). Women who do not have previously established social support systems and women whose social networks have been decimated through many years of abuse are at grave risk. Women who are socioeconomically destitute are at an even greater risk of being locked into violent relationships. Even when they make attempts to break away, they may be more likely to go back to their abusers. The lack of economic independence and lack of availability of housing, coupled with the presence of small children, severely delimit the potential for success in establishing a violence-free life (OAITH, 1998, 1999). Within this context, the community networks and state-sponsored social safety systems are vitally important in changing the status quo (Sev'er, 2002).

What are the prospects for these women? If the above examples of the C-L women have any generalizability at all, positive outcomes are difficult. Among the ten women, I counted twenty-six marriage or common-law relationships which averages to 2.6 long-term relationship per woman. More than 60 per cent of these relationships (16) were violent. In Debbie's, DeeDee's, and Lisa Algoma's cases, all their partners have emotionally, physically, and sexually abused the women. Moreover, numerous short-term relationships these women have had (which are not recorded in Appendix G) were also infested with degradations and some explosive episodes. Violence seems to be a revolving door through which these women pass repeatedly.

A discussion I had with Debbie was very insightful for me. I am almost certain that Debbie also gained an insight through this discussion, although I am not at all sure that she will act on this insight. The conversation was about Mark (her 4-year-old son) who was born prematurely and has various behavioural problems and is a slow learner (see Chapter 6). Debbie was blaming the biological father of Mark who had kicked her in the stomach when she was pregnant. Mark also had witnessed a lot of shouting, things being thrown around, and severe beatings of his mother from infancy on. Debbie's position was that all these troubles and the effect they had on her (she frequently yells at Mark) were the cause of Mark's problems. Debbie said she would never allow anyone to do this to Mark again. What is interesting about this declaration is that just a few minutes before, she had told me that her new partner was also abusing her, throwing things around, and shouting and threatening both her and her children. Although the players had changed, the dynamics of Debbie's and Mark's situation were really not that different from when Mark's biological father was around. Debbie also caught this irony and said, 'I'm letting someone else to do it to him, ain't I?' Debbie's children are under CAS watch, and Debbie is scared of losing them.

The revolving door of exposure to abuse has also taken its toll on children of some other women. For example, Sue's now adult sons Billy and Trevor have serious drinking problems and are abusing their partners. Terry's daughter Teddy is on the verge of developing substance dependencies and engages in promiscuous behaviour with men who may not be good companions. Lisa Algoma's children are already under CAS care. Although she is working very hard to get them back, the likelihood of her being able to control her own drinking and drug problems is not very high. Lisa Kingston is still struggling with her drinking problem. After her very scary experiences with Emanuel, Lorie is still establishing relationships with illegal immigrants under the auspices of helping them get Canadian landed immigrant status. In at least three cases, these transient men have treated Lorie very badly, although Lorie was adamant about saying she had learned her lesson. Lou is undergoing therapy for recurring nightmares. After the water bed incident, she developed a phobia for most activities that involve water which includes avoiding taking a bath. Lou says she feels 'weird' even after taking a shower. She tries taking showers when she is not alone in the house.

Even under so many adverse conditions, there are glimmers of hope and demonstrations of the struggle for a better future. Lisa Algoma is trying very hard to overcome her addictions. Sue is volunteering with shelters, and Lorie is helping a blind relative. Although Debbie is still shouting at her children, at least she is trying to be the best mother she can be by analysing her own behaviour. Terry is trying to help her daughter, although their relationship is difficult. In short, after living through experiences, which would have made many people give up long ago, these women are still courageously trying to better their lives and are achieving some success.

Long-Term Prospects for Women in the Middle

From our long interviews, I cannot conclude that either Amber, Ava, or Elly is clearly triumphant. They have survived their violent marriages, but they may still have a long and winding road ahead of them. Amber has seven children, only three of whom are living with her. Two of her children are living in Vancouver with their biological father. The very first daughter was brought up by her sister (in Jamaica), and Amber has very little knowledge of how she is doing. One of the middle boys is living with another former partner. Amber has had two marriages and two long-term relationships which were problematic to varying degrees. During the time of our interview, she was getting out of yet another relationship, although she was still on maternity leave for her last child (2-month-old daughter). Amber had unresolved feelings about her skin colour and how both black and white men treated her. She was living in a row-house complex which was not in a very good neighbourhood. Despite all this, Amber was employed, loved her job (see Chapter 7), and felt that she could provide for her children. During our interview, I met her 12-year-old son, and he offered me fresh sugar cookies that he had baked by himself. In short, despite her past and continuing problems, Amber seems to have retained a sense of agency and confidence and has established a place to call home for three of her children.

Ava feels she is pretty and basically a good person. In her own words, her former husband Greg abused her body, but was not able to harness her soul. As her insightful poem shows (Chapter 1), she has hope for her own future. She has hope in finding some other man who would love her and treat her with respect. Conversely, she seems to have quite a tense relationship with her son Stan (see Chapter 6). If the shouting match I witnessed is any indication, she has the potential to lose her cool and get locked in a spiral of aggression (see Chapter 9). As a first-generation immigrant, Ava does not have an established social support system in Canada. The few friends she mentioned appear to have their own serious problems, and at least two of her female friends may also be in abusive relationships. Ava recommended that I talk to them, but her friends did not contact me. In sum, Ava has certain things going for her, but there are other factors that seem less favourable for a long-term growth process. The lack of an established support system remains a problem.

Elly is in school and also in therapy. Eventually she wants to be in an occupation that will allow her to help other women. One of her ways of coping is through her appearance and grooming which seem to boost her self-esteem. She has managed to combat some of the humiliation she was made to feel by her parents, in-laws, and husband. Unfortunately, her relationship with her children, especially her two oldest sons is very problematic. Because of his violence towards her (including hitting Elly with wooden sticks, plastic baseball bats, and chasing her with a knife), one of her sons was placed in a reformatory school. The second oldest has been in and out of foster care. Elly has her own psychological and social ghosts to deal with for years to come. Almost miraculously, Elly seems hopeful about her future. As she put it, 'Whatever happens now is much better than what happened in the past.'

Long-Term Prospects for the Naively Caught

There are few fairy tale endings for women who suffer long-term abuse. Therefore, I should immediately caution against drawing any conclusion that the seven women I based my N-C typology on are now totally okay. As I emphasized in earlier chapters of this book, living through violent relationships exacts a toll regardless of who the woman is. Even at this positive spin of the wheel, Laurette still has to deal with her son's behavioural problems, has flashbacks of the beatings, and is afraid to form a new relationship with any man. Even the four women who have new relationships are not entirely comfortable within them and are trying to be very cautious. Their previous life experiences have made them shun deep intimacies. Sonny's son is quite hyperactive and she considers herself a workaholic. Sonny admits that she may be using (over)work as a psychological escape. Moreover, Sonny has a very serious problem with excessive spending, which has made things very difficult for her and her 6-year-old son. Carrie and Suzan Windsor have severe sleeping problems, and Carrie is afraid she may be taking too many sleeping pills. Sam has a lot of difficulty in trusting her new partner. She knows that this lack of trust is putting pressure on her new relationship, but she cannot help but question everything her partner says or does. Kim is trying to rediscover her old self and is benefiting from her therapy. Yet her relationship with her family, especially with her mother remains strained.

Through the long interviews, I felt a sense of relief and peace after talking to women whom I have ended up characterizing as the N-C. All seven had received some therapy and three were continuing to do so (Ann, Kim, and Laurette). All had developed a few new friendships and were in the process of re-establishing bonds with their families. Some were starting to envision a better future for themselves and for their children (Ann, Carrie, and Suzan Windsor had no children). Six of the seven women had jobs. Two of them were back at school on a part-time basis (Laurette and Carrie). Five of the seven had a more fulfilling relationship than the ones they had experienced before, although they were all more cautious in the new relationship. Even Ann, who was on a disability pension, was learning to get her confidence back and was in the process of reconnecting with her family (particularly with her sister). In short, these women already had a positive core of self because of their early socialization. Their challenge was how soon and how completely they could reclaim this positive core. From their revelations, I have the feeling that these women are on their way to establishing a better future for themselves and are the least likely to become caught in yet another violent relationship. Let us hope that the society we all live in will cherish their strength and provide opportunities for them and for their children to reach their potentials.

I would like to end my analysis with a personal ode to all survivors of abuse, and especially the thirty-nine participants in this book.

An Ode to Survivors of Abuse

Some women fear the dark,
Some feel pain right in their homes,
Not because of the arrows of Cupid,
But because of marital blows.

How many women are hit?
How many children get slapped?
Not because of what they said or did,
But because they were trapped.

A handful of women get maimed,
A handful die painful deaths,
Not because they reach a ripe-old age,
But in a war that masquerades as romance.

Hundreds of women seek shelter,
Thousands yearn for the extended hand of a friend,
Countless cry themselves to sleep at night,
When every door gets slammed on their face.

Yet a few escape the mayhem, flee the quagmire,
A few triumph against all odds,
A little tattered, wary and disoriented,
They pick up the pieces of their lives, and try to rise.

They are the Nancys, Ellys, Debbies and Sues,
They are the mothers we pass by at the subways and malls,
They are the ones who cuddle their children, who need to be cuddled,
They are those who've survived partner abuse.

Aysan Sev'er
30 December 2001

An Afterthought

The emotional path of my research with the thirty-nine women often forced me to think of hundreds, thousands, perhaps million of others who are also caught up in violence, not only here in Canada, but in all parts of the world. I hope that this book gives some voice to their silent suffering as well as acknowledges their own struggles, wherever they may be. Moreover, during the final revisions of this book, the world experienced a different layer of violence: a terrorist attack on the economic and political nerve-centres of America. Men's violence against men, women, and children has been rampant across the world and throughout the ages. (The Holocaust, Ukrainian man-made [sic] famine, ethnic cleansing in Bosnia, Kosova, Rwanda, and Brundi, as well as Kashmir, Chechnya, and Tibet are just a few examples.) Yet the gruesome attacks on 11 September 2001 made it clear that not even the most powerful nation in the world is immune to such violence.

Regrettably, the response to the terrorist violence has been more violence, albeit the fierce response is sanctioned by the military and political powers of the western world and legitimized as an unavoidable self-defence. At the expense of going way beyond the modest goals of this research, I nevertheless feel an obligation to point out the almost universal suffering of women and children in a continuum of violence (Eisler, 1997). Be it at the hands of their husbands or fathers, or under the inhumane rule of brotherhoods like the Taliban, or the assault of invading armies, ruthless warlords, or because of the relentless bombing or raid of their homelands by superpowers, it is women and children who fall through the cracks (Albenese, 2001; MacKinnon, 1993a, 1993b). Within the wars of gender, power, and an unquenchable thirst for ideological, political, religious or military might, women of the world are repeatedly reduced to 'collateral damage.' I am afraid that North American women also have a lot to lose because of the heightened militarism and blinding patriotism spreading like wild fire across the west.

Somehow, the political and economic priorities of the democratic states have been reconfigured to fuel militaristic protectionism. We have already seen suspensions of individual and civil rights, censure of the media, and attempts to snuff criticisms of the war efforts. We have seen the polarization of the world as black versus white, as wrong versus right, as evil verus moral, with almost total disregard to the wider spectrum of the moral shades of grey. We have heard extreme forms of reductionism such as 'you are either with us or with the enemy' from men who occupy the highest ranks of global power. Given the hyper-sensitized milieu of male camaraderie, I fear that women's silent suffering in their homes, at the hands of their male partners may become a grossly marginalized aspect of life. Moreover, social safety networks that can help their flight may become very low in political priorities. It is my contention that the search for justice and peace within one's own political boundaries must never be at the cost of circumvention of social obligations and responsibilities. Even when driven by fear and feelings of retribution, advanced societies such as ours must never sacrifice the disadvantaged, needy, weak, and disenfranchised, and we must never fail to protect women and children in their homes in our haste to destroy elusive enemies of a different kind. The stories of the thirty-nine women in this book remind us about the urgency of this social mission.

APPENDICES

APPENDIX A: INTERVIEWING SCHEDULE

STRICTLY CONFIDENTIAL

Interview Schedule

Researcher: Professor Aysan Sev'er
University of Toronto, Scarborough College
1265 Military Trail, Scarborough, M1C 1A4
Date of Interview: ....
Time of Interview: Start...
End..
Participant Code (Pseudonym)..

AFTER COVER LETTER IS READ AND THE CONSENT FORM IS SIGNED
DEMOGRAPHIC CHARACTERISTICS QUESTIONS

1 How old were you on your last birthday? ....
2 What is your current marital status?
   ☐ Married
   ☐ Common law
   ☐ Separated
   ☐ Divorced
   ☐ Single
   ☐ Other, please explain...
3 If married
   Altogether, how many times have you been married? ....
   How old were you when you got married?
   1st ....
   2nd...
   3rd ....
   4th...
   Nearest to a full year, for how long were you married?
   1st ....
   2nd...
   3rd ....
   4th...
4 If common law
   Altogether, how many common-law partners did you have? ....

How old were you when you started to live common-law?

1st ....

2nd ....

3rd ....

4th ....

Nearest to a full year, how long did you live together?

1st ....

2nd ....

3rd ....

4th ....

Did you marry any of your common-law partners?

Yes ☐   No ☐

If yes, which one(s)? (in the order of Question 4)

5 Are you currently living with or married to someone?

Yes ☐   No ☐

If yes, for how long? ....

6 What is the highest formal education you completed?

☐ Elementary

☐ High school

☐ College or trade school

☐ University undergraduate

☐ University graduate

☐ Other ....

Please elaborate...

If program not completed, what is the highest year attained? ....

7 What is the highest formal education your mother completed?

(if biological mother)	(other than natural mother)
☐ Elementary	☐ Elementary
☐ High school	☐ High school
☐ College or trade school	☐ College or trade school
☐ University undergraduate	☐ University undergraduate
☐ University graduate	☐ University graduate
☐ Other	☐ Other
Please elaborate	Please elaborate

If program not completed, what is the highest year attained? ....

8 What is the highest formal education your father completed?

(If biological father)	(Other than natural father)
☐ Elementary	☐ Elementary
☐ High school	☐ High school
☐ College or trade school	☐ College or trade school

☐ University undergraduate   ☐ University undergraduate
☐ University graduate   ☐ University graduate
☐ Other   ☐ Other
Please elaborate   Please elaborate
If program not completed, what is the highest year attained? ....

TURN ON THE TAPE RECORDER AT THIS POINT.

9 Are you currently employed outside of home?   ☐ Yes   ☐ No
   If employed, for how long (nearest to a full year) ....
   What is your occupation? ....
   Do you work full-time or part time?...
   Tell me a little about what you actually do at your job.
10 Did you work before?   ☐ Yes   ☐ No
    If yes:
    For how long (nearest to a full year)...
    What was your occupation?...
    Did you work full-time or part-time?..
    Can you tell me a little about what you did?...
11 Altogether, how many children do you have? ....
    How many of them are your own? ....
    How many are adopted? ....
    How many are your stepchildren?...
    Are there any that I missed?...
    Starting from the oldest child, can you tell me their age and sex? You do not
    have to use their names, just make sure that you start from the oldest one.
    How many of these children are currently living with you?

Age	Sex	Living with mother
.....	.....	.....
.....	.....	.....
.....	.....	.....
.....	.....	.....
.....	.....	.....

12 Currently, are there other children or adults living with you? If so, what is
    their age, sex, and relationship to you?

Age	Sex	Relationship
.....	.....	....
.....	.....	....
.....	.....	....

    Are there others that we missed? ....

Now, I am going to ask you some questions about the type of relationship you had with your parents as well as your siblings. Please keep in mind that any information you provide will be treated in the strictest of confidence. If you do not want to talk about a specific issue, we will just go to the next question. Take all the time you want in answering these questions.

RELATIONSHIP WITH FATHER/MOTHER/SIBLINGS

A1 Can you tell me a little about your parents?
   Probe – Who raised the respondent (ie., biological parent(s), stepparent(s), others?
A2 Looking back on it now, do you think you had a generally happy or sad childhood? How so? Do you want to tell me a little about it?
A3 Again, looking back on it, do you think your parents (or parent figures) generally got along alright or did not get along? How so? Do you want to tell me a little about their relationship?
   If negative:
   Do you remember what types of problems your parents had?
   Can you tell me a little about these experiences?
   Probe – Who was the most likely initiator of the unhappy episodes?
   Probe – Verbal abuse, psychological abuse, physical abuse possibilities among the parents / parent figures?
   How did your mother react on these occasions?
   How did your father react on these occasions?
   Did they stay together?
   Probe – Feelings, emotions
   If separated/divorced:
   Who decided to leave? How? Were there problems with the separation arrangements? What happened to the children?
   Probe – Possible violence after separation?
A4 Did you have any brothers or sisters? How many? Older or younger than you?
   Can you tell me a little about your relationship with them in your growing years?
   What is your relationship like now? Tell me about it.
A5 Can you tell me a little about your relationship with your mother in your growing years?
   If negative:
   What did you do?
   Probe – Verbal, psychological, physical, sexual abuse possibilities?

Probe – Feelings, emotions, coping strategies?
What is your relationship like now? Tell me about it.

A6   Can you tell me a little about your relationship with your father in your growing years?
If negative:
What did you do?
Probe – Verbal, psychological, physical, sexual abuse possibilities?
Probe – Feelings, emotions, coping strategies?
What is your relationship like now? Tell me about it.

RELATIONSHIP WITH PARTNER(S)

B1   Can you tell me a little about how you get along with your current partner? (If no current, go to previous.) How so?
If negative:
Can you tell me about what types of problems you have?
Can you tell me how you deal with these experiences?
Probe – Who was the most likely initiator of these episodes?
Probe – Verbal abuse, psychological abuse, physical abuse, sexual abuse possibilities?
Probe – Feelings, emotions, coping strategies?

B2   When you were having these problems with your partner were your child(ren) involved in any way? How so? Tell me a little about it.

REPEAT AS MANY TIMES AS THE NUMBER OF PARTNERS.

Now that you have provided me with some background information, I am going to ask you about how you got out of your relationship.

START FROM THE MOST CURRENT, REPEAT AS MANY TIMES AS PARTNERS.

C1   Let us start with the most recent relationship that is ended. That will be your marriage/relationship with (recent partner).
Can you tell me a little about how your relationship to (recent partner) ended? What happened? Whose idea was it?

C2   Was there an event/occasion that precipitated the split-up? Tell me about what happened.
Probe – Verbal, psychological, physical, sexual abuse possibilities?
Were your child(ren) involved in these events? How so?

Probe – Feelings, emotions?
What did you do? How did they react?

ASK FOR OTHER PARTNERS.

C3 In the process of getting out of this relationship, did you have someone who helped you? If so, can you tell me a little about him/her/them and how he/she/they helped?

ASK FOR OTHER PARTNERS.

C4 Can you tell me about the role your family played (parents / parent figures, siblings, others)?
Did you feel supported or did you feel a lack of support?
Probe – Significant events, feelings, emotions, satisfaction?

ASK FOR OTHER PARTNERS.

C5 Can you tell me about the reactions of your child(ren)?

ASK FOR OTHER PARTNERS.

C6 Were you employed at the time? If employed, what kind of a role did your work mates play? Can you tell me a little about this?

ASK FOR OTHER PARTNERS.

C7 Did you seek help from any social service agencies? If so, which agency? Can you tell me a little about these experiences?
Did you feel supported or did you feel a lack of support?
Probe – significant events, feelings, emotions, satisfaction?

ASK FOR OTHER PARTNERS.

C8 In case of precipitating violence:
Did you contact police? If so, can you tell me a little about these experiences?
Did you go to a shelter? If so, how was that for you?
Probe – Significant events, feelings, emotions, satisfaction?

ASK FOR OTHER PARTNERS.

C9   Did you contact lawyers, or other legal professionals? Did you go to
      court? If so, can you tell me a little about these experiences?
      Probe – significant events, feelings, emotions, satisfaction?

ASK FOR OTHER PARTNERS.

C10   In all of these events, is there any one person who comes to your mind as
      playing the most crucial role? If so, can you tell me about this person and
      his or her relationship with you? What made his or her role so impor-
      tant?

ASK FOR OTHER PARTNERS.

C11   In the process of getting out, how did you feel about yourself? Why?
      Probe – Perceived weaknesses, perceived strengths, roles?
C12   How do you feel about yourself now? In your judgment, what changed?
      What did not change?
      Probe – Perceived weaknesses, perceived strengths, roles?
C13   If you were to re-do it all, what would you do differently? Why?
C14   For women who are experiencing the difficulties you have gone through,
      what advice would you give?
C15   For children whose parents are experiencing difficulties such as those
      you have experienced, what advice would you give?
C16   Do you have anything to ask about any part of this interview? Do you
      want to add anything to what I have already asked, or add anything that
      I have not asked?

*Thank the respondent for her help, reassure her of the confidentiality of the responses,
ask whether she wants a post-study report. If so, record her name and address and store
separately from the interview material.*

APPENDIX B: NEWSPAPER ADVERTISEMENT

Professor A. Sev'er from the University of
Toronto is interviewing survivors of abuse
for an SSHRC funded (federal) study. All
information will be kept strictly confidential,
and every measure will be taken to protect
your anonymity. If you want to participate,
or if you require more information, please
call Professor Sev'er at 416-267-4800.

APPENDIX C: RECRUITMENT LETTER

URGENTLY NEEDED

In our society, many women experience abuse in their intimate relationships. There is growing knowledge about the incidence and consequences, as well as the factors that relate to abuse. Nevertheless, we know very little about what contributes to getting out of abusive relationships successfully.

I am an Associate Professor of Sociology at the University of Toronto. I am conducting a study on the process of ending abusive relationships and would like to interview women who have left their male partners on their own or with the help of others, and have not returned to the same partner for at least six consecutive months. Interviews with volunteers will be conducted at the time and place most convenient for them. To participate in the study you must be able to understand and speak English. If you choose to participate, all efforts will be made to keep the information you provide confidential, and every measure will be taken to protect your anonymity. You are totally free to withdraw from the study at any time should you change your mind about participating. A summary of the findings of this study will be available to the participants upon their request.

If you would like more information or would like to participate, please call the number below or write to the address provided.

APPENDIX D: CONSENT FORM

RESEARCH ON BREAKING THE CYCLE: GETTING OUT OF ABUSIVE
RELATIONSHIPS

Name of the investigator: Professor Aysan Sev'er
Name of the participant:...

I, Aysan Sev'er, Professor of Sociology, University of Toronto, agree to be
responsible for ensuring that (1) the content of all interviews will be kept
strictly confidential; (2) all interview tapes will be kept under lock after they
are transcribed; (3) all measures will be taken to protect the identities of the
participants, including measures to code names; (4) all results will be used for
either academic teaching and dialogue or for professional publication purposes.

I,.................................. (participant) voluntarily agree to participate in this
research study entitled 'Breaking the Cycle: Getting Out of Abusive Relationships.'
   I have been fully informed about the nature of the study, and the interviewing procedure to be followed. I understand that, if I require, the purpose, procedures and/or the results will be further explained to me after the completion
of the study.
   I understand that I am free to withdraw from the study at any time I choose.
I am also free to refuse to answer any particular question or questions. I am
also free to use pseudonyms for myself and other people that I mention.
   It has been explained to me that the promise of confidentiality in this type of
research cannot be absolute in possible cases of future legal action. I understand that I can reduce this risk by not making my participation in this study
common knowledge.
   It is my understanding that there is no reason to expect adverse effects from
the procedures involved in this study, and there is no reason to suppose that
there will be any permanent physical or psychological adverse effects.

Signature of the Investigator   Date
....
Signature of the Participant   Date
....

APPENDIX E: COVER LETTER

Professor Aysan Sev'er
Department of Sociology
University of Toronto
1265 Military Trail
Scarborough, ON. M1C 1A4
Tel. 416-287-7296

Dear survivor,

I am conducting a study about the process of getting out of abusive relationships. Although there is growing knowledge about the incidence of intimate abuse, and the circumstances linked to staying in abusive relationships, we know very little about how women find the strength and courage to end such relationships. My study will attempt to give voice to women who have suffered abuse but left it behind. There is much to be learned from the struggles and experiences of women who have transcended abusive relationships and are in the process of rebuilding their lives.

I am asking you to participate in an interview, which will take approximately two hours of your time. I will ask several questions about you for information purposes (e.g., age, number of years in relationships). I will also ask about the relationship with your parents, spouse(s), and children. How much you tell me will be totally up to you. The interview will be tape-recorded, and later transcribed. The content of the interviews will be held in the <u>strictest confidence,</u> and the tapes will be kept under lock at my university office. You can use pseudonyms if you like, since I will not require your real name, nor any other real names of the people you may mention. Even if you choose to use real names, I will take all necessary measures to protect your anonymity and the anonymity of those you mention. The information you provide will only be used for academic teaching and dialogue and professional publication purposes, and will only be directly accessible to myself and my very carefully chosen research staff for this project. However, it may not be possible to preserve confidentiality if the information you give me is thought to be relevant to a legal action in any way related to your relationship with your ex-partner. In the latter case, the information could be subpoenaed and would have to be revealed in court. You can reduce the risk of this happening simply by not telling anyone of your participation in this study.

Your participation is voluntary. If there is any part of the interview that makes you uncomfortable, you are free to move to another topic. You are free to decline answering as many questions as you want, and are free to withdraw from the study at any time you choose.

I will provide a short summary of my research findings for you upon request. If you decide to give me your name and address for this purpose, I will keep this information totally separate from your interview to avoid identification. If you do not want a report, there is no need for you to state your name or your address.

I really appreciate your time, your consideration, and your help.

Sincerely,

Aysan Sev'er, Associate Professor

APPENDIX F: THANK YOU LETTER TO PARTICIPANTS

Dear Friend,

It may have been a relatively long time since I had the opportunity and the privilege to talk to you about some of your interpersonal experiences. Or, it is possible that I had a chance to talk to you more recently. Whatever the case may be, I would like to take this opportunity to thank you, one more time, for your courage in sharing your experiences with me.

The study I have started a year-and-a-half ago is still going on. I am still talking to women and trying to learn from their experiences and survival strategies. I am still trying to give these experiences a voice so that other women can learn from what you may have gone through. I have published a number of academic papers, exploring the different dimensions of this very crucial issue. I am enclosing a sample of my work which incorporates extracts from my *early* interviews. Please note that although I included segments from what some of you may have shared with me, I did so with a lot of care and sensitivity to protect each identity. Often, I combined experiences under themes. Of course, you may be able to recognize a few of your own words (and the study intended to give your experiences a voice). However, it is almost impossible that anyone else will recognize the woman behind these isolated excerpts.

I also edited a book, which is to appear later on this year (1998). All royalties (every penny) from this book are donated to a Women's Shelter in Scarborough. Thus, many women will benefit from our combined efforts.

I thank you and wish you well. Each one of you deserves my deepest respect and gratitude. If you have questions or comments, please do not hesitate to contact me.

With warm regards,

Aysan Sev'er
Associate Professor of Sociology

APPENDIX G: PRE-TEST DATA

OBS	MONTH	YR	NAME	RACE	DURINT	AGEINT																							
1	3	97	Amber	N	2.5	36	18	2	4	1	.	5	27	5	.	3	3	2	3	Y	3	7	22	20	17	14	12	4	0
2	2	96	Ann	W	2.0	24	2	0	.	.	.	2	22	2	.	3	2	2	3	N	2	0	.	.	.	.	.	4	.
3	1	97	Camilla	W	2.0	48	1	24	1	.	.	.	.	.	.	3	2	2	2	Y	2	1	20	.	.	.	.	.	.
4	5	97	Carmen	N	2.5	47	2	14	1	.	2	20	.	.	2	2	2	4	Y	2	3	17	15	4	.	.	.	.	18
5	4	96	Deedee	N	2.0	27	3	23	1	3	1	17	1	1	1	2	2	N	1	2	4	2	.	.	.	.	.	.	.
6	2	96	Iris	W	2.5	54	4	17	1	12	9	45	.	5	2	5	5	Y	1	1	27	.	.	.	.	.	.	.	.
7	6	97	Laurette	W	4.0	45	3	21	2	1	15	5	22	.	4	1	1	1	Y	4	4	18	15	13	11	.	.	.	.
8	1	97	Olga	W	1.5	51	2	18	1	11	1	17	6	2	2	4	4	Y	2	1	33	.	.	.	.	.	.	.	.
9	4	97	Rose	W	2.0	47	1	20	1	17	4	40	.	3	3	2	3	Y	2	1	18	.	.	.	.	.	.	.	.
10	6	97	Sue	W	2.5	55	4	27	1	5	5	32	.	4	3	3	2	Y	3	3	30	26	21	.	.	26	20	.	.
11	4	97	Terry	W	2.5	32	4	18	1	5	4	17	1	1	1	1	1	N	3	3	14	9	8	.	.	.	14	.	.

Variable Names:

OBS:	Observation number
MONTH:	Month of the interview
YR:	Year of the interview
NAME:	Pseudonym of the participant
RACE:	Race of the participant (W=White), (N=Non-white)
AGEINT:	Age at interview

MARSTAT:	Marital status (1=married, 2=com-law, 3=separated, 4=divorced, 5=single, 6=other)
AGEMARR:	Age at marriage
DURM1:	Duration of first marriage (years)
DURM2:	Duration of second marriage (years)
DURM3:	Duration of third Marriage (years)
DURC1:	Duration of first com-law (years)
AGECOM:	Age at com-law
DURC2:	Duration of second com-law (years)
DURC3:	Duration of third com-law (years)
EDSELF:	Highest completed education (self)
EDMOM:	Highest completed education (mother)
EDDAD:	Highest completed education (father)
EMPLOY:	Employment (Y=employed, N=Not-employed, S=full-time student)
OCCUP:	Occupation (1=professional, 2=skilled, 3=semi=skilled, 4=manual)
CHILD:	Number of biological children
AGEBIO1–AGEBIO7:	Ages of each child (descending order)
AGE1–AGE2:	Ages of each non-biological child (descending order)

APPENDIX H: TEST DATA

OBS	MONTH	YEAR	NAME	RACE	DURATCATET	AGEINTTRO	MARGESTARTTRO	AGEMARNMRO	DDURRMM1	DDURRMM23	DURMARUM	AGUERRCO1M	DDUURRCC2	DDUURRCC3	EDSUREUCLO3F	EDEUSDDMO	EDEUSDDAQD	EMEMOPCLOYP	EMOCPCLOULP	EOCHILLOLD	AGEEB-IO-O1	AGEEB-IO-O2	AGEEB-IO-O3	AGEEB-IO-O4	AGEEB-IO-O5	AGEEB-IO-O6	AGEEB-IO-O7	AGGEEB1	AGGEEB2
1	10	97	Angel	N	2.0	44	2		0		14.0	17	2		3	2	3	Y	3	0	2	16	12						
2	6	98	Anna	W	3.0	38	2	17	1		14.0	0	2		3	2	2	Y	3	2	2	16	12						
3	3	98	Ava	N	2.0	38	3	19	1		7.0	1	3		6	1	1	S	3	1	1	14							
4	10	97	Carrie	N	2.0	29	4	18	1		5.0	28	3		3	3	3	Y	3	0	3	11	10						
5	6	98	Clara	N	4.0	35	4	20	1		3.0	26	7		1	1	1	Y	3	3	2	11	10	3					
6	10	97	Daisy	W	2.0	24	2	18	1		4.0	23	1		1	1	1	N	1	0	2	11	4						
7	4	98	Debbie	N	2.5	33	6	25	1		12.0	8	17	1	1	1	1	N	1	2	3	14	11	7					
8	12	98	Elly	W	2.5	37	4	18	1		5.0	6	17		2	1	1	S	3	3	1	22							
9	3	98	Erika	N	2.5	39	4	19	1	7	8.0				2	2	1	Y	1	3	14	11	7						
10	9	97	Gwyn	W	2.0	30	2	21	1	5	5.0	6	30		2	2	2	Y	3	1	1	22							
11	7	98	Kathy	W	2.5	41	3	19	2	7	1.5	1	29		2	2	2	Y	3	1	2	11							
12	4	98	Kim	W	2.0	49	1	21	3	5	3.0	2	39		3	2	3	Y	3	2	20	14	24	23	22	19			
13	3	98	Lisa A.	N	1.5	34	4	21	1		3.0	8	44		2	2	2	Y	3	2	6	2						12	
14	7	98	Lisa K.	N	2.0	33	4	17	1		3.0	6	25		2	2	2	Y	2	2	6	4						11	
15	9	98	Lisa L.	N	2.0	43	1	20	2	15	1.0	3	22		4	4	4	Y	2	2	18	11							
16	5	98	Liz	N	2.5	32	1	22	1		3.0	1	18		2	1	2	Y	3	0									
17	2	98	Lorie	W	2.0	50	1	20	2	4	12.0	2	48		5	4	4	Y	1	2	17	14						20	14
18	5	98	Lou	N	1.5	51	4	23	2	4	12.0	1			3	3	4	Y	1	1	20								
19	7	98	Monica	N	2.0	41	1	17	1	10	5.0	1	28	10	1	1	3	N	3	3	12	10	7						
20	8	98	Nancy N.	W	2.0	40	2	24	2	5	2.0	2	20		1	1	2	Y	3	2	7	4	16						
21	5	98	Nancy O.	W	2.0	41	1	25	3	1	1.0	2	37		3	1	3	Y	3	4	17	16						8	5

```
22  1 98  Nancy S.  N 2.5 33 2 17 1 3.0  .  . 2 19 2 1 1 1 Y 5 2 15 14 . . . .    19 16
23  9 97  Sam       W 2.0 51 4 19 2 4.0 14  . 3 17 . 4 3 3 Y 2 3 20 16 15 . . . .   .  .
24  5 98  Sonny     W 1.5 30 4 22 1 1.0  .  . 2 18 1 . 2 3 4 Y 2 1  6  .  . . . .   .  .
25  2 98  Stacy     W 2.0 40 2 17 3 4.0  1  1 . .  1 1 2 N . 3 18 10  7  . . . .   .  .
26 11 98  Suzan T.  W 3.0 33 4 20 1 1.0  .  . 1 22 2 2 1 1 S . 2 11  4  .  . . . .  .  .
27  7 98  Suzan W.  N 2.0 30 2  . 0  .   .  . 2 24 4 3 2 6 Y 3 0  .  .  . . . .   .  .
28 12 97  Vicky     W 2.5 21 3  . 0  .   .  . 3 16 1 1 1 3 N . 1  3  .  . . . .   .  8
```

Variable Names:

Variable	Description
OBS:	Observation number
MONTH:	Month of the interview
YR:	Year of the interview
NAME:	Pseudonym of the participant
RACE:	Race of the participant (W=White), (N=Non-white)
AGEINT:	Age at interview
MARSTAT:	Marital status (1=married, 2=com-law, 3=separated, 4=divorced, 5=single, 6=other)
AGEMARR:	Age at marriage
DURM1:	Duration of first marriage (years)
DURM2:	Duration of second marriage (years)
DURM3:	Duration of third Marriage (years)
DURC1:	Duration of first com-law (years)
AGECOM:	Age at com-law
DURC2:	Duration of second com-law (years)
DURC3:	Duration of third com-law (years)
EDSELF:	Highest completed education (self)
EDMOM:	Highest completed education (mother)
EDDAD:	Highest completed education (father)
EMPLOY:	Employment (Y=employed, N=Not-employed, S=full-time student)
OCCUP:	Occupation (1=professional, 2=skilled, 3=semi=skilled, 4=manual)
CHILD:	Number of biological children
AGEBIO1–AGEBIO7:	Ages of each child (descending order)
AGE1–AGE2:	Ages of each non-biological child (descending order)

APPENDIX I: TOTAL STUDY DATA

OBS	MONTHS	YR	NAME	TRT	DUR	AGE	C8	C9	C10	DURMAR	C12	C13	C14	C15	C16	C17	C18	C19	C20	C21	C22	OCC	C24	C25	NCH	O1	O2	O3	O4	O5	O6	O7	X1	X2
1	3	97	Amber	N	2.5	36	3	18	2	4.0	1	·	·	5	27	5	·	3	3	2	3	Y	3	3	7	22	20	17	14	12	4	0	·	·
2	10	97	Angel	N	2.0	44	2	17	0	·	·	·	·	2	17	2	·	2	3	3	2	Y	3	0	0	20	12	·	·	4	·	·	·	·
3	2	96	Ann	W	2.0	24	2	·	0	·	·	·	·	2	22	2	·	3	2	2	2	N	·	·	0	14	15	4	·	·	·	·	·	·
4	6	98	Anna	W	3.0	38	3	17	1	14.0	1	·	·	0	·	·	·	3	2	2	2	S	·	3	2	16	10	·	·	·	·	·	12	·
5	3	98	Ava	N	2.0	38	3	19	1	14.0	1	·	·	·	·	·	·	6	2	1	3	Y	3	1	1	14	·	·	·	·	·	·	·	·
6	1	97	Camilla	W	2.0	48	1	24	2	14.0	1	·	·	2	20	2	·	3	2	2	2	Y	2	1	3	20	17	15	·	·	·	·	·	18
7	5	97	Carmen	N	2.5	47	4	18	0	7.0	·	·	·	7	28	·	·	3	4	1	2	Y	3	3	0	18	17	4	·	·	·	·	·	·
8	10	97	Carrie	N	2.0	29	4	20	1	5.0	·	·	·	1	26	·	·	3	3	3	3	Y	3	3	3	11	10	3	·	·	·	·	·	·
9	6	98	Clara	N	4.0	35	4	18	1	3.0	·	·	·	7	23	·	·	3	3	1	3	Y	3	3	3	11	10	·	·	·	·	·	·	·
10	10	97	Daisy	W	2.0	24	2	18	1	4.0	·	·	·	8	17	1	1	1	1	1	3	N	1	0	0	·	·	·	·	·	·	·	·	·
11	4	98	Debbie	W	2.5	33	6	25	1	3.0	·	·	·	8	17	1	·	1	1	1	2	N	1	2	2	11	4	·	·	·	·	·	·	·
12	4	96	Deedee	N	2.0	27	3	23	1	3.0	·	·	·	1	17	1	1	1	1	1	2	S	1	2	3	4	2	·	·	·	·	·	·	·
13	12	98	Elly	W	2.5	37	4	18	1	12.0	1	·	·	·	·	·	·	2	1	2	4	N	2	3	1	14	11	7	·	·	·	·	·	·
14	3	98	Erika	N	2.5	39	4	19	1	8.0	·	·	·	6	30	·	·	2	2	2	2	Y	2	1	1	22	·	·	·	·	·	·	·	·
15	9	97	Gwyn	W	2.0	30	1	21	1	5.0	·	·	·	1	29	·	·	2	2	2	2	Y	2	1	1	11	·	·	·	·	·	·	·	·
16	2	96	Iris	W	2.5	54	4	17	1	12.0	·	·	·	9	45	·	·	5	2	2	5	Y	3	1	1	27	·	·	·	·	·	·	·	·
17	7	98	Kathy	W	2.5	41	3	19	2	5.0	7	·	5	9	45	5	·	2	2	2	3	Y	3	2	2	20	14	·	·	·	·	·	·	·
18	4	98	Kim	W	2.0	49	3	21	3	1.5	5	·	5	1	39	2	·	3	2	2	3	Y	3	3	4	24	23	22	·	·	·	·	·	·
19	6	97	Laurette	W	4.0	45	3	21	2	1.0	15	7	5	2	44	5	·	4	1	3	1	Y	1	4	4	18	15	13	11	·	·	·	·	·
20	3	98	Lisa A.	N	1.5	34	4	21	1	3.0	·	·	·	8	25	2	·	2	2	2	3	Y	3	2	2	6	2	·	·	·	·	·	12	·
21	7	98	Lisa K.	N	2.0	33	4	17	1	3.0	·	·	·	6	22	·	·	2	2	2	2	Y	2	2	2	6	4	·	·	·	·	·	·	11
22	9	98	Lisa L.	N	2.0	43	1	20	2	1.0	15	·	3	3	18	·	·	4	4	4	4	Y	2	2	2	18	11	·	·	·	·	·	·	·

```
OBS MONTH YR NAME      RACE
23   5  98 Liz       N 2.5 32 1 22 1  3.0  4  .  .  .  2  .  .  .  1  . 3 0 Y 2 2 1 .
24   2  98 Lorie     W 2.0 50 1 20 2 12.0  4  .  2 48 10  5  .  .  1  Y 4 3 5 1 . 2 17 14 . .  20 14
25   5  98 Lou       N 1.5 51 4 23 2 12.0 10  .  .  .  .  4  .  .  1  Y 1 4 1 1 . 1 20
26   7  98 Monica    N 2.0 41 2 17 1  5.0  .  .  .  1 28 10  3  3  3  4 N 3 3 1 . 3 12 10 7
27   8  98 Nancy N.  W 2.0 40 1 24 2  2.0  5  .  2 20  2  1  2  1  1  Y 3 2 1 . 2 7 4
28   5  98 Nancy O.  W 2.0 41 1 25 3  1.0  1  9  2 37  .  2  1  .  3  Y 3 1 1 . 4 17 16 8 5
29   1  98 Nancy S.  N 2.5 33 2 17 1  3.0  .  .  2 19  2  1  1  1  1  Y 5 2 1 . 2 15 14 . .  19 16
30   1  97 Olga      W 1.5 51 2 18 1 11.0  .  .  1 17  6  2  2  2  4  Y 2 1 1 . 1 33 . . .  26 20
31   4  97 Rose      W 2.0 47 1 20 1 17.0  .  .  4 40  .  3  3  2  4  Y 2 2 3 . 1 18 . . .  14
32   9  97 Sam       W 2.0 51 4 19 2  4.0 14  .  3 17  .  4  4  3  3  Y 3 3 2 . 3 20 16 15
33   5  98 Sonny     W 1.5 30 4 22 1  1.0  .  .  2 18  1  2  1  1  4  N 4 3 2 . 1 6
34   2  98 Stacy     W 2.0 40 3 17 3  4.0  1  1  1  .  .  1  1  1  2  N 3 3 1 . 3 18 10 7
35   6  97 Sue       W 2.5 55 4 27 1  5.0  .  .  4 32  .  4  3  3  3  Y 2 1 2 . 3 30 26 21
36  11  98 Suzan T.  W 3.0 33 4 20 1  1.0  .  2  1 22  2  3  2  1  1  S 2 1 1 . 2 11 4
37   7  98 Suzan W.  N 2.0 30 2  .  .  0   .  .  2 24  4  3  2  2  6  Y 3 3 .  . 3 0
38   4  97 Terry     W 2.5 32 4 18 1  5.0  .  .  4 17  1  3  1  1  1  N 3 1 1 . 3 14 9 8
39  12  97 Vicky     W 2.5 21 3 18 1  0    .  .  3 16  1  4  1  1  3  N 1 1 1 . 3 . . . . 8
```

Variable Names:

OBS:	Observation number
MONTH:	Month of the interview
YR:	Year of the interview
NAME:	Pseudonym of the participant
RACE:	Race of the participant (W=White), (N=Non-white)
AGEINT:	Age at interview
MARSTAT:	Marital status (1=married, 2=com-law, 3=separated, 4=divorced, 5=single, 6=other)
AGEMARR:	Age at marriage
DURM1:	Duration of first marriage (years)
DURM2:	Duration of second marriage (years)
DURM3:	Duration of third Marriage (years)
DURC1:	Duration of first com-law (years)
AGECOM:	Age at com-law
DURC2:	Duration of second com-law (years)
DURC3:	Duration of third com-law (years)
EDSELF:	Highest completed education (self)
EDMOM:	Highest completed education (mother)
EDDAD:	Highest completed education (father)
EMPLOY:	Employment (Y=employed, N=Not-employed, S=full-time student)
OCCUP:	Occupation (1=professional, 2=skilled, 3=semi-skilled, 4=manual)
CHILD:	Number of biological children
AGEBIO1–AGEBIO7:	Ages of each child (descending order)
AGE1–AGE2:	Ages of each non-biological child (descending order)

APPENDIX J: KEY WORDS USED IN TORONTO STUDY OF NEWSPAPER COVERAGE OF INTIMATE VIOLENCE

Husband/murder
Husband/assault

Wife/murder
Wife/assault

Wife/attack
Husband/attack

Husband/batter
Wife/batter

Husband/violence
Wife/violence

Husband/abuse
Wife/abuse

Spouse/abuse
Spouse/assault

Murder/suicide
Rape

Abused
Sexual abuse

Sex crime
Domestic violence

References

Albanese, Patricia. 2001. Nationalism, war and archaization of gender relations in the Balkans. *Violence against Women* 7(9): 999–1023.

Arias, Ileana. 1984. A social learning theory explanation of intergenerational transmission of physical aggression in intimate heterosexual relationships. Unpublished doctoral dissertation. State University of New York.

Bagley, Christopher, and Kathleen King. 1991. *Child Sexual Abuse: The Search for Healing*. London: Tavistock.

Bain, Joan. 1991. *Reports on Wife Assault*. Toronto: Ontario Medical Association.

Baldwin, W., and V.S. Cain. 1980. Social class and help-seeking behaviour. *Family Planning Perspectives* 12: 34–43.

Bandura, Albert. 1973. *Aggression: A Social Learning Analysis*. Englewood Cliffs, NJ: Prentice-Hall.

Bart, Pauline B. 1971. Sexism and social science: From the gilded cage to the iron cage. *Journal of Marriage and the Family* 33: 32–7.

Bart, Pauline B., and Eileen G. Moran. 1993. *Violence against Women: The Bloody Footprints*. Newbury Park, Calif.: Sage.

Bean, Constance. 1992. *Women Murdered by the Men They Loved*. New York: Harrington Park Press.

Bergen, Raquel K. 1996. *Wife Rape: Understanding the Response of Survivors and Service Providers*. Thousand Oaks, Calif.: Sage.

– 1998. The reality of wife rape: Women's experiences of sexual violence in marriage. Pp. 237–50 in R.K. Bergen (ed.), *Issues in Intimate Violence*. Thousand Oaks, Calif.: Sage.

Berk, Richard A., Sarah Berk, Donileen R. Loseke, and D. Rauma. 1983. Mutual combat and other family myths. Pp. 197–212 in D. Finkelhor, R.J. Gelles, G.T. Hotaling, and M.A. Straus (eds.), *The Dark Side of Families: Current Family Violence Research*. Beverly Hills, Calif.: Sage.

BJS (Bureau of Justice Statistics). 1995. (http://www.famvi.com.deptjust.htm).

Block, C.R. and A. Christakos. 1995. Intimate partner homicide in Chicago over 29 years. *Crime and Delinquency* 41: 496–526.

Bograd, Michelle. 1988. Feminist perspectives on wife abuse: An introduction. Pp. 11–27 in K. Ylló and M. Bograd (eds.), *Feminist Perspectives on Wife Abuse*. Beverly Hills, Calif.: Sage.

Bowker, Lee H. 1983. *Beating Wife-beating*. Lexington, Mass.: Lexington Books.

– (Ed.). 1998. *Masculinities and Violence*. Thousand Oaks, Calif.: Sage.

Breines, W., and L. Gordon. 1983. The new scholarship on family violence. *Signs* 8: 490–531.

Brinkerhoff, Merlin, and Eugen Lupri. 1988. Interpersonal violence. *Canadian Journal of Sociology* 13: 407–34.

Browne, Angela. 1987. *When Battered Women Kill*. New York: Free Press.

Brownmiller, Susan. 1975. *Against Our Will: Men, Women and Rape*. New York: Simon and Schuster.

Brush, Lisa D. 1993. Violent acts and injurious outcomes in married couples. Pp. 240–51 in P.B. Bart and E.G. Moran (eds.), *Violence against Women: The Bloody Footprints*. Newbury Park, Calif.: Sage.

Bunch, Charlotte. 1975. Lesbians in revolt. Pp. 29–37 in N. Myron and C. Bunch (eds.), *Lesbianism and the Women's Movement*. Baltimore, Md.: Diana Press.

Burris, C.A., and Peter Jaffe. 1983. Wife abuse as a crime: The impact of police laying charges. *Canadian Journal of Criminology* 25: 309–18.

Campbell, Jacqueline C. 1992. If I can't have you, no one can: Power and control in homicide of female partners. Pp. 99–113 in J. Radford and D.E.H. Russell (eds.), *Femicide*. Toronto: Maxwell Macmillan.

Campbell, Jacqueline C., M.J. Harris, and R.K. Lee. 1995. Violence research: An overview. *Scholarly Inquiry for Nursing Practice* 9(2): 105–26.

Campbell, J., M. Poland, J. Walder, and J. Ager. 1992. Correlates of battering during pregnancy. *Research in Nursing and Health* 15(3): 219–26.

Canadian Panel on Violence against Women. 1993. *Changing the Landscape: Ending Violence, Achieving Equality*. 1993. M.P. Freeman and M.A. Vaillancourt (eds.). Ottawa: Minister of Supply and Services.

Cancian, Francesca M. 1993. Gender politics: Love and power in the private and public spheres. Pp. 204–12 in *Family Patterns and Gender Relations*. New York: Prentice-Hall.

Caputi, Jane. 1987. *The Age of Sex Crime*. Ohio: Bowling Green State University.

Cardarelli, Albert P. 1997. Confronting intimate violence: Looking toward the twenty-first century. Pp. 178–85 in A.P. Cardarelli (ed.), *Violence between Intimate Partners: Patterns, Causes and Effects*. Boston: Allyn and Bacon.

Chalmers, L., and P. Smith. 1987. Wife battering: Psychological, social and physical isolation and counterbalancing strategies. Pp. 15–38 in K. Storrie (ed.), *Women: Isolation and Bonding: The Ecology of Gender.* Toronto: Methuen.

Chatzifotiou, Sevaste. 2000. Conducting qualitative research on wife abuse: Dealing with the issue of anxiety. *Sociological Research on Line* 5: 2. http://www.socresonline.org.uk

Chimbos, David P. 1978a. *Marital Violence: A Study of Interpersonal Homicide.* San Francisco: R&E Research.

– 1978b. Marital violence: A study of husband-wife homicide. Pp. 580–99 in K. Ishwaran (ed.), *The Canadian Family.* Toronto: Holt, Rinehart and Winston.

Collins, Patricia H. 1993. The sexual politics of black womanhood. Pp. 85–104 in P.B. Bart and E.G. Moran (eds.), *Violence against Women: The Bloody Footprints.* Newbury Park, Calif.: Sage.

Conway, John F. 1997. *The Canadian Family in Crisis* (3rd ed). Toronto: Lorimer.

Cory, Jill, and Karen McAndless-Davis. 2000. *When Love Hurts: A Women's Guide to Understanding Abuse in Relationships.* Surrey, BC: Womankind Press.

Counts, Dorothy A., Judith K. Brown, and Jacqueline C. Campbell. (Eds.). 1992. *Sanctions and Sanctuary: Cultural Perspectives on the Beating of Wives.* Boulder: Westview.

Crawford, Maria, and Rosemary Gartner. 1992. *Women Killing: Intimate Femicide in Ontario, 1974–1990.* Toronto: Women We Honour Action Committee.

Curran, Mary. 1996. Rebuilding a wall of silence around 'family matters.' *Toronto Star,* 1 May: A21.

Currie, Dawn H. 1998. Violent men or violent women: Whose definition counts? Pp. 97–111 in R.K. Bergen (ed), *Issues in Intimate Violence.* Thousand Oaks, Calif.: Sage.

Daly, Mary. 1992. Till death us do part. Pp. 83–98 in J. Radford and D.E.H. Russell (eds.), *Femicide.* Toronto: Maxwell Macmillan.

Dasgupta, Shamita D. 1998. Defining violence against women by immigration, race and class. Pp. 208–19 in R.K. Bergen (eds.), *Issues in Intimate Violence.* Thousand Oaks, Calif.: Sage.

Dasgupta, Shamita D. and Sujata Warrier. 1996. In the footsteps of 'Arundhati': Asian Indian women's experiences of domestic violence in the United States. *Violence against Women* 2(3): 238–59.

Davidson, T. 1977. Wifebeating: A recurring phenomenon throughout history. Pp. 2–23 in M. Roy (ed.), *Battered Women: A Psychological Study of Domestic Violence.* New York: Van Nostrand Reinhold.

DeKeseredy, Walter S. 1988. *Woman Abuse in Dating Relationships: The Role of Male Peer Support.* Toronto: Canadian Scholars Press.

– 1989. Woman abuse in dating relationships: An exploratory study. *Atlantis* 14: 55–62.

– 1990. Male peer support and woman abuse: The current state of knowledge. *Sociological Focus* 23: 129–39.

– 1999. Tactics of the antifeminist backlash against Canadian national woman abuse surveys. *Violence against Women* 5(11): 1258–76.

DeKeseredy, Walter S., and Ronald Hinch. 1991. *Woman Abuse: Sociological Perspectives.* Toronto: Thompson Educational Publishing.

DeKeseredy, Walter S., and Katharine Kelly. 1993. The incidence and prevalence of women abuse in Canadian university and college dating relationships. *Canadian Journal of Sociology* 18: 137-59.

DeKeseredy, Walter S., and B.D. MacLean. 1990a. Exploring the gender, race, class dimensions of victimization: A leftist critique of the Canadian Urban Victimization survey. *International Journal of Offender Therapy and Comparative Criminology* 35(2): 143–61.

– 1990b. Researching woman abuse in Canada: A left realist critique of the Conflict Tactics Scale. *Canadian Review of Social Policy* 25: 19–27.

DeKeseredy, Walter S., and Linda MacLeod. 1997. *Woman Abuse: A Sociological Story.* Toronto: Harcourt-Brace.

DeKeseredy, Walter S., and Martin D. Schwartz. 1997. *Sexual Assault on the College Campus: The Role of Male Peer Support.* Thousand Oaks, Calif.: Sage.

DeKeseredy, Walter S., Martin D. Schwartz, and Shahid Alvi. 2000. The role of pro-feminist men in dealing with woman abuse on the Canadian campus. *Violence against Women* 6(9): 918–35.

Dobash, Emerson R., and Russell P. Dobash. 1979. *Violence against Wives: A Case against Patriarchy.* New York: Free Press.

– 1988. Research as social action. Pp. 57–74 in K. Yllö and M. Bograd (eds.), *Feminist Perspectives on Wife Abuse.* Beverly Hills, Calif.: Sage.

– 1992. *Women, Violence and Social Change.* New York: Routledge.

– (eds.). 1998. *Rethinking Violence against Women.* Thousand Oaks, Calif.: Sage.

Dobash, Russell P, Emerson R. Dobash, Kate Cavanagh, and Ruth Lewis. 1995. *Research Evaluation of Programmes for Violent Men.* Manchester: Violence Research Unit.

Dobash, Russel P., Emerson R. Dobash, Margo Wilson, and Martin Daly. 1992. The myth of sexual symmetry in marital violence. *Social Problems* 39(1): 71–91.

Dugan, Meg K., and Roger R. Hock. 2000. *It's My Life Now: Starting Over after an Abusive Relationship.* New York: Routledge.

Dutton, Donald G., and Cynthia Van Ginkel. 1997. The interaction of cultural and personality factors in the etiology of wife assault. Pp. 101–22 in A. Sev'er (ed.), *A Cross-Cultural Exploration of Wife Abuse.* New Jersey: Edwin Mellen.

Dworkin, Andrea. 1974. *Women Hating.* New York: Dutton.

- 1989. Gynocide: Chinese Footbinding. Pp. 15–24 in L. Richardson and V. Taylor (eds.), *Feminist Frontiers II: Rethinking Sex, Gender and Society*. New York: McGraw.
- 1993. Living in terror, pain: Being a battered wife. Pp. 237–40 in P.B. Bart and E.G. Moran (eds.), *Violence against Women: The Bloody Footprints*. Newbury Park, Calif.: Sage.

Egeland, Byron. 1993. A history of abuse is a major risk factor for abusing the next generation. Pp. 197–208 in R.J. Gelles and D.R. Loseke (eds.), *Current Controversies on Family Violence*. Newbury Park, Calif.: Sage.

Eichler, Margrit. 1997. *Family Shifts: Families, Policies and Gender Equality*. Toronto: Oxford.

Eichler, Margrit, and Jeanne Lapointe. 1985. *On the Treatment of the Sexes in Research*. Ottawa: Social Sciences and Humanities Research Council of Canada.

Eisler, Riane. 1997. Human rights and violence: Integrating the private and public spheres. Pp. 161–85 in J. Turpin and L.R. Kurtz (eds.), *The Web of Violence: From Interpersonal to Global*. Urbana, Ill.: University of Illinois Press.

Ellis, Desmond, and Walter S. DeKeseredy. 1997. Rethinking estrangement, interventions and intimate femicide. *Violence against Women* 3(6): 590–609.

Engels, Frederick. 1993. *The Origin of the Family, Private Property and the State* (original publication, 1942). New York: International Publishers.

Estrich, Susan. 1987. *Real Rape*. Cambridge, Mass.: Harvard University Press.

Eth, S., and R.S. Pynoos. 1994. Children who witness the homicide of a parent. *Psychiatry* 57(4): 287–306.

Fantuzzo, John W., and Wanda K. Mohr. 1999. Prevalence and effects of child exposure to domestic violence. *Future of Children* 9(3): 21–32.

Fantuzzo, John W., L.M. Depaola, L. Lambert, T. Martino, G. Anderson, and S. Sutton. 1991. Effects of interpersonal violence on the psychological adjustment and competencies of young children. *Journal of Counselling and Clinical Psychology* 59(2): 258–65.

Faulk, M. 1977. Men who assault their wives. Pp. 21–35 in M. Roy (ed.), *Battered Women: A Psychosociological Study of Domestic Violence*. New York: Van Nostrand.

Ferraro, Kathleen J. 1989. Policing woman battering. *Social Problems* 36(1): 325–39.

Ferraro, Kathleen J., and J.M. Johnson. 1983. How women experience battering: The process of victimization. *Social Problems* 30: 325–38.

Fine, Michelle. 1993. The politics of research and activism. Pp. 278–88 in P.B. Bart and E.G. Moran (eds.), *Violence against Women: The Bloody Footprints*. Newbury Park, Calif.: Sage.

Finkelhor, David. 1993. The main problem is still underreporting, not overreporting. Pp. 273–87 in R.J. Gelles and D.R. Loseke (eds.), *Current Controversies on Family Violence*. Newbury Park, Calif.: Sage.

Finkelhor, David, and Yllö, Kersti. 1985. *License to Rape: Sexual Abuse of Wives*. New York: Holt, Rinehart and Winston.

Firestone, Shulamith. 1970. *The Dialectic of Sex: The Case for Feminist Revolution*. New York: Bantam Books.

Flanzer, Jerry P. 1993. Alcohol and drugs are key causal agents of violence. Pp. 171–81 in R.J. Gelles and D.R. Loseke (eds.), *Current Controversies in Family Violence*. Newbury Park, Calif.: Sage.

Flax, Jane. 1976. Do feminists need Marxism? *Quest* 3 (Summer): 46–58.

Fleury, Ruth E., Criss M. Sullivan, and Deborah I. Bybee. 2000. When ending the relationship does not end the violence. *Violence against Women* 6(12): 1363–83.

Fox, Bonnie. 1988. Conceptualizing 'patriarchy.' *Review of Canadian Sociology and Anthropology* 25(2): 163–80.

Freud, Sigmund. 1959. The woman who felt persecuted. Pp. 25–38 in H. Greenwald (ed.), *Great Cases in Psychoanalysis*. New York: Balantine.

– 1974. *Introductory Lectures on Psychoanalysis* (vol. 1). London: Penguin.

Gartner, Rosemary, and MacMillan, Ross. 1995. The effect of victim-offender relationship on reporting crimes of violence against women. *Canadian Journal of Criminology* 37(3): 393–429.

Gartner, Rosemary, Myrna Dawson, and Maria Crawford. 2001. Confronting violence in women's lives. Pp. 473–90 in B.J. Fox (ed.), *Family Patterns, Gender Relations* (2nd ed.). Toronto: Oxford.

Gayford, John J. 1975. Wife battering: A preliminary survey of 100 cases. *British Medical Journal* 1: 194–97.

Gelles, Richard J. 1974. *The Violent Home: A Study of Physical Aggression between Husbands and Wives*. Beverly Hills, Calif.: Sage.

– 1976. Abused wives: Why do they stay? *Journal of Marriage and the Family* 38(4): 659–68.

– 1979. *Family Violence*. Beverly Hills, Calif.: Sage.

– 1985. Family violence. *Annual Review of Sociology* 11: 347–67.

– 1987. *The Violent Home* (updated ed.). Newbury Park, Calif.: Sage.

– 1993. Alcohol and other drugs are associated with violence – They are not its cause. Pp. 182–96 in R.J. Gelles and D.R. Loseke (eds.), *Current Controversies on Family Violence*. Newbury Park, Calif.: Sage.

– 1994. Introduction: Special issue on family violence. *Journal of Comparative Family Studies* 25(1): 1–6.

Gelles, Richard J., and C.P. Cornell. 1983. *International Perspectives on Family Violence*. Toronto: Lexington.

Gelles, Richard J., and Donileen, R. Loseke. 1993. *Current Controversies on Family Violence*. Newbury Park, Calif.: Sage.

Gelles, Richard J., and Murray A. Straus. 1979. Determinants of violence in the family: Toward a theoretical integration. Pp. 549–82 in W.R. Burr, R. Hill, F.I. Nye, and I.R. Reiss (eds.), *Contemporary Theories about the Family*. New York: Free Press.

– 1988. *Intimate Violence: The Causes and consequences of Abuse in the American Family*. New York: Touchstone Books.

Gilligan, Carole. 1982. *In a Different Voice*. Dambridge, Mass.: Harvard University Press.

Glass, Dee Dee. 1995. *All My Fault: Why Women Don't Leave Abusive Men*. London: Virago Press.

Godenzi, Alberto, Walter S. DeKeseredy, and Martin D. Schwartz. 2000. Toward an integrated social bond / male peer support theory of woman abuse in North American College Dating (unpublished paper).

Gogia, Nupur. 1992–3. Beyond the 'Culturally Sensitive': Violence prevention by education on wife assault. *Women's Education des Femmes* 10(1): 22–4.

Gordon, Linda. 1989. The politics and history of family violence. Pp. 68–86 in A.S. Skolnick and J.H. Skolnick (eds.). *Family in Transition* (6th ed.). Boston: Little Brown.

Graham-Berman, Sandra A., and Alytia A. Levendosky. 1998. Traumatic stress symptoms in children of battered women. *Journal of Interpersonal Violence* 13(1): 111–28.

Grant, J.M. 1992. Who is killing us? Pp. 145–60 in J. Radford and D.E.H. Russell (eds.), *Femicide*. Toronto: Maxwell Macmillan.

Gravenhorst, Lerke. 1988. A feminist look at family developmental theory. Pp. 79–101 in D. Klein and J. Aldous (eds.), *Social Stress and Family Development*. New York: Guildford.

GSS (General Social Survey). 2000. Family Violence. *The Daily*. Ottawa: Statistics Canada.

Hatty, Suzanne E. 2000. *Masculinities, Violence and Culture*. Thousand Oaks, Calif.: Sage.

Health Canada. 1995. *Wife Abuse*. Ottawa: National Clearinghouse on Family Violence.

– 1996. *Wife Abuse: The impact on Children*. Ottawa: National Clearinghouse on Family Violence.

Hillock, David. 1990. The Social Adjustment of Female Lone-Parents: A Social Relations Model. Unpublished doctoral Dissertation for the Faculty of Social Work, University of Toronto.

Hoff, Lee Ann. 1990. *Battered Women as Survivors*. London: Routledge.

Huisman, Kimberly A. 1996. Wife battering in Asian American communities. *Violence against Women* 2(3): 260–83.

Jacobson, Neil S., and John M. Gottman. 2001. Anatomy of a violent relationship. Pp. 475–87 in A.S. Skolnick and J.H. Skolnick (eds.), *Family in Transition* (11th ed.). Boston: Allyn and Bacon.

Jaffee, Peter G., David A. Wolfe, and Susan K. Wilson. 1990. *Children of Battered Women*: Newbury Park, Calif.: Sage.

Jaggar, Alison M. 1983. *Feminist Politics and Human Nature*. Totowa: NJ: Roman and Allanheld.

Jaggar, Alison M., and Paula S. Rothenberg. 1984. *Feminist Fremeworks* (2nd ed). New York: McGraw.

Jasinski, Jana L., and Linda M. Williams. (Eds.). 1998. *Partner Violence: A Comprehensive Review of 20 Years of Research*. Thousand Oaks, Calif.: Sage.

Johnson, Holly. 1988. Wife abuse. *Canadian Social Trends*. Ottawa: Statistics Canada. Cat 11-008.

– 1995. Risk factors associated with non-lethal violence against women by marital partners. Pp. 151–68 in C.R. Block and R. Block (eds). *Trends, Risks and Interventions in Lethal Violence* (vol. 3). Washington, DC: National Institute of Justice.

– 1996. *Dangerous Domains: Violence against Women in Canada*. Toronto: Nelson.

Johnson, Holly, and P. Chisolm. 1990. Family homicide. Pp. 168–9 in C. McKie and K. Thompson (eds.), *Canadian Social Trends*. Toronto: Thompson Educational Publishing.

Johnson, Holly, and Vincent Sacco. 1995. Researching violence against women: Statistics Canada's national survey. *Canadian Journal of Criminology* 37: 281–304.

Juristat. 1999. Canada's Shelters for Abused Women. Canadian Centre for Justice Statistics. Cat. 85-002-XPE. Vol. 19(6).

Kaufman, John, and Edward Zigler. 1993. The intergenerational transmission of abuse is overstated. Pp. 209–21 in R.J. Gelles and D.R. Loseke (eds.), *Current Controversies on Family Violence*. Newbury Park, Calif.: Sage.

Kaufman Kantor, Glenda, and Jana L. Jasinski. 1998. Dynamics and risk factors in partner violence. Pp. 1–43 in J.L. Jasinski and L.M. Williams (eds.). *Partner Violence: A Comprehensive Review of 20 Years of Research*. Thousand Oaks, Calif.: Sage

Kaufman Kantor, Glenda, and Murray A. Straus. 1989. Substance abuse as a precipitant of wife abuse victimization. *American Journal of Drug and Alcohol Abuse* 15: 173–89.

Kelly, Katharine D. 1997. The family violence and woman abuse debate:

Reviewing the literature, posing alternatives. Pp. 27–50 in A. Sev'er (ed.), *Cross-Cultural Exploration of Wife Abuse.* Lewiston, NJ: Edwin Mellen.

Kelly, Liz, and Jill Radford. 1998. Sexual violence against women and girls: An approach to an international overview. Pp. 53–73 in R.E. Dobash and R.P. Dobash (eds.), *Rethinking Violence against Women.* Thousand Oaks, Calif.: Sage.

Kendall-Tackett, Kathleen, and Roberta Marshall. 1998. Sexualized victimization of children: Incest and child sexual abuse. Pp. 47–64 in R.K. Bergen (ed.), *Issues in Intimate Violence.* Thousand Oaks, Calif.: Sage.

Kennedy, Leslie, and Donald G. Dutton. 1989. The incidence of wife assault in Alberta. *Canadian Journal of Behavioural Science* 21: 40–54.

Kirkwood, Catherine. 1993. *Leaving Abusive Partners: From the Scars of Survival to the Wisdom of Change.* London: Sage.

Koss, Mary P., and Sarah L. Cook. 1993. Facing the facts: Date and acquaintance rape are significant problems. Pp. 104–19 in R.J. Gelles and D.R. Loseke (eds.), *Current Controversies on Family Violence.* Newbury Park, Calif.: Sage.

Koss, Mary P., Christine A. Gidycz, and Nadine Wisniewski. 1987. The scope of rape: Incidence and prevalence of sexual aggression and victimization in a national sample of higher education students. *Journal of Consulting and Clinical Psychology* 55(2): 162–70.

Kurz, Demie. 1993. Social science perspectives on wife abuse: Current debates and future directions. Pp. 252–69 in P.B. Bart and E.G. Moran (eds.), *Violence against Women: The Bloody Footprints.* Newbury Park, Calif.: Sage.

– 1995. *For Richer, For Poorer: Mothers Confront Divorce.* New York: Routledge.

– 1996. Separation, divorce and woman abuse. *Violence against Women* 2(1): 63–81.

– 1998. Old problems and new directions in the study of violence against women. Pp. 197–208 in R.K. Bergen (ed.), *Issues in Intimate Violence.* Thousand Oaks, Calif.: Sage.

Lehmann, Peter. 1997. The development of posttraumatic stress disorder (PTSD) in a sample of child witnesses to mother assault. *Journal of Family Violence* 12(3): 241–57.

Levendosky, Alytia A., and Sandra A. Graham-Berman. 2001. Parenting in battered women: The effects of domestic violence on women and their children. *Journal of Family Violence* 16(2): 171–92.

Levinson, David. 1989. *Family Violence in Cross-cultural Perspective.* Newbury Park, Calif.: Sage.

Lombroso, Cesare. 1911. *Criminal Man, According to the Classification of Cesare Lombroso.* Summarized by Gina Lombroso-Ferrero. New York: Putnam.

Lupri, Eugen, Elaine Grandin, and Merlin B. Brinkerhoff. 1994. Socioeconomic status and male violence in the Canadian home: A re-examination. *Canadian Journal of Sociology* 19(1): 47–73.

MacKinnon, Catharine A. 1982. Feminism, Marxism, method and the state: An agenda for theory. *Signs* 7(Spring): 515–44.

– 1993a. Feminism, Marxism, method and the state. Pp. 201–28 in P.B. Bart and E.G. Moran (eds.), *Violence against Women: The Bloody Footprints*. Newbury Park, Calif.: Sage.

– 1993b. Rape, genocide and women's human rights. Pp. 183–96 in A. Stiglmayer (ed.), *The War against Women in Bosnia-Herzegovina*. Nebraska: University of Nebraska Press.

MacLeod, Linda. 1980. *Wife Battering in Canada: The Vicious Circle*. Canadian Advisory Council on the Status of Women. Ottawa: Ministry of Supply and Services.

– 1987. *Battered but Not Beaten: Preventing Wife Battering in Canada*. Ottawa: Canadian Advisory Council on the Status of Women. Cat LW31-27/1987E.

– 1995. Policy decisions and prosecutorial dilemmas: The unanticipated consequences of good intentions. In M. Valverde, L. MacLeod, and K. Johnson (eds.), *Wife Assault and the Canadian Criminal Justice System*. Toronto: University of Toronto Press.

MacLeod, Linda, and Michael D. Smith. 1990. *Isolated and Forgotten: The Service Delivery Needs and Realities of Immigrant and Refugee Women Who Are Battered*. Ottawa: National Clearinghouse on Family Violence.

Mahoney, Janis, and Linda M. Williams. 1998. Sexual assault in marriage: Prevalence, consequences and treatment of wife rape. Pp. 113–62 in J.J. Jasinski and L.M. Williams, *Partner Violence: A Comprehensive Review of 20 Years of Research*. Thousand Oaks, Calif.: Sage.

Mannle, Henry W., and David J. Hirschel. 1988. *Fundamentals of Criminology* (2nd ed.). Englewood Cliffs, NJ: Prentice-Hall.

Maslow, Abraham H. 1954. *Motivation and Personality*. New York: Harper and Row.

Matthews, Nancy A. 1993. Surmounting a legacy: The expansion of racial diversity in a local anti-rape movement. Pp. 177–92 in P.B. Bart and E.G. Moran (eds.), *Violence against Women: The Bloody Footprints*. Newbury Park, Calif.: Sage

McCue, Margi L. 1995. *Domestic Violence: A Reference Handbook*. Santa Barbara, Calif.: ABC-CLIO.

McFarlane, J. 1992. Battering in pregnancy. Pp. 205–25 in C.M. Sampselle (ed.), *Violence Against Women: Nursing Research, Education and Practice Issues*. New York: Hemisphere Publications.

Mercy, James A., and Linda L. Saltzman. 1989. Fatal violence among spouses in the United States, 1976–1985. *American Journal of Public Health* 79: 595–9.

Merrill, Gregory S. 1998. Understanding domestic violence among gay and bisexual men. Pp. 129–40 in R.K. Bergen (ed.), *Issues in Intimate Violence*. Thousand Oaks, Calif.: Sage.

Messner, M. 1989. When bodies are weapons: Masculinity and violence in sport. *International Review of Sociology of Sport* 25(3): 203–20.

Mitchell, Julie J. 1973. *Women's Estate*. Toronto: Random House.

Nelson, E.D., and Barrie W. Robinson. 1999. *Gender in Canada*. Toronto: Prentice-Hall.

Ney, Philip G. 1992. Transgenerational triangles of abuse: A model of family violence. Pp. 15–26 in E.C. Viano (ed.), *Intimate Violence: Interdisciplinary Perspectives*. Bristol: Taylor and Francis.

Nicarthy, Ginny. 1986. *Getting Free: A Handbook of Women in Abusive relationships*. Seattle, Wash.: Seal.

Nielsen, Joyce M., Russell K. Endo, and Barbara L. Ellington. 1992. Social isolation and wife abuse: A research report. Pp. 73–81 in E.C. Viano (ed.), *Intimate Violence: Interdisciplinary Perspectives*. Bristol: Taylor and Francis.

OAITH. 1996. *Locked in–Left out: Impacts of the Progressive Conservative Budget Cuts and Policy Initiatives on Abused Women and Their Children in Ontario*. Toronto: Ontario Association of Interval and Transition Houses.

– 1998. *Falling through the Gender Gap: How Ontario Government Policy Continues to Fail Abused Women and Their Children*. Toronto: Ontario Association of Interval and Transition Houses.

– 1999. *Ten Years for Montreal: Still Working for Change*. Toronto: Ontario Association of Interval and Transition Houses.

O'Brien, Mary. 1981. *The Politics of Reproduction*. Boston: Routledge.

Ofei-Aboagye, Rosemary A.O. 1997. Tradition or tribulation: Thoughts on women's oppression and wife abuse in Ghana. Pp. 123–44 in A. Sev'er (ed.), *A Cross-Cultural Exploration of Wife Abuse: Problems and Prospects*. New Jersey: Edwin Mellen.

Okun, Lewis. 1986. *Woman Abuse: Facts Replacing Myths*. New York: State University of New York.

O'Leary, Daniel K. 1988. Physical aggression between spouses: A social learning theory perspective. Pp. 11–55 in V.B. Van Hasselt, R.L. Morrison, A.S. Bellack, and M. Hersen (eds.), *Handbook of Family Violence*. New York: Plenum.

Pagelow, Mildred D. 1981. *Women Battering: Victims and Their Experiences*. Beverly Hills, Calif.: Sage.

– 1985. The battered husband syndrome: Social problem or much ado about little? In N. Johnson (ed.), *Marital Violence*. London: Routledge and Kegan.

Pence, Ellen. 1983. The Duluth Domestic Abuse Intervention Project. *Hamline Law Review* 6(2): 247–75.

Pence, Ellen, and Michael Paymar. 1993. *Education groups for men who batter: The Duluth Model.* New York: Springer Publishing.

Perls, Frederick S. 1974. *Gestalt Therapy Verbatim* (8th printing). New York: Bantam.

Petersen, Ruth, Julie Gazmararian, and Kathryn A. Clark. 2001. Partner violence: Implications for health and community settings. *Women's Health Issues* 11(2): 116–25.

Pleck, Elizabeth. 1987. *Domestic Tyranny.* New York: Oxford University Press.

Pleck, Elizabeth, J.H. Pleck, M. Grossman, and Pauline Bart. 1977–8. The battered data syndrome: A comment on Steinmetz's article. *Victimology* 3(4): 680–3.

Pottie, Bunge V., and A. Levett. 1998. *Family Violence in Canada: A Statistical Profile.* Ottawa: Canadian Centre for Justice Statistics.

Propper, Alice. 1997. Measuring wife assault by surveys: Some conceptual and methodological problems. Pp. 51–78 in A. Sev'er (ed.), *Cross-Cultural Exploration of Wife Abuse.* New Jersey: Edwin Mellen.

Radford, Jill. 1992a. Womanslaughter: A license to kill? The killing of Jane Asher. Pp. 253–66 in J. Radford and D.E.H. Russell (eds.), *Femicide.* Toronto: Maxwell Macmillan.

– 1992b. Where do we go from here? Pp. 351–7 in J. Radford and D.E.H. Russell (eds.), *Femicide.* Toronto: Maxwell MacMillan.

Renzetti, Claire M. 1992. *Violent Betrayal: Partner Abuses in Lesbian Relationships.* Newbury Park, Calif.: Sage.

– 1997. Confessions of a reformed positivist: Feminist participatory research as good science. Pp. 131–43 in Martin D. Schwartz (ed.), *Researching Sexual Violence against Women.* Thousand Oaks, Calif.: Sage.

– 1998. Violence and abuse in lesbian relationships: Theoretical and empirical issues. Pp. 117–28 in R.K. Bergen (ed.), *Issues in Intimate Violence.* Thousand Oaks, Calif.: Sage.

Reppucci, N. Dickon, and J. Jeffrey Haugaard. 1993. Problems with child sexual abuse: Prevention programs. Pp. 306–22 in R.J. Gelles and D.R. Loseke. *Current Controversies in Family Violence.* Newbury Park, Calif.: Sage.

Richie, Beth E., and Valli Kanuha. 2000. Battered women of colour in health care system: Racism, sexism and violence. In A. Minas (ed.), *Gender Basics* (2nd ed.). Belmont, Calif.: Wadsworth.

Roberts, H. 1981. *Doing Feminist Research.* London: Routledge and Kegan.

Rodgers, Karen. 1994. *Wife Assault in Canada: The Findings of a National Survey.* Juristat 14(9). Ottawa: Canadian Centre for Justice Statistics.

– 2000. Wife assault in Canada. Pp. 237–42 in *Canadian Social Trends*, vol. 3. Toronto: Thompson Educational Publishing.

Rubin, Gayle. 1975. The traffic in women. In. R. Reiter (ed.). *Toward an Anthropology of Women*. New York: Monthly Review Press.

Russell, Diana E.H. 1989. Sexism, violence and the nuclear mentality. Pp. 63–74 in *Exposing Nuclear Fallacies*. New York: Pergamon.

Russell, Diana E.H., and Rebecca M. Bolen. 2000. *The Epidemic of Rape and Child Sexual Abuse in the United States*. Thousand Oaks, Calif.: Sage.

Rubin, Lillian B. 1976. *Worlds of Pain: Life in the Working Class*. New York: Basic Books.

– 1983. *Intimate Strangers: Men and Women Together*. New York: Harper and Row.

Schwartz, Martin D. 1988. Ain't got no class: Universal risk theories of battering. *Contemporary Crises* 12: 373–92.

– (Ed.). 1997. *Researching Sexual Violence against Women: Methodological and Personal Perspectives*. Thousand Oaks, Calif.: Sage.

Schwartz, Martin D., and Walter S. DeKeseredy. 1997. *Sexual Assault on the College Campus: The Role of Male Peer Support*. Thousand Oaks, Calif.: Sage.

Scully, Diana. 1990. *Understanding Sexual Violence*. Boston: Unwin.

Sears, Robert R. 1961. Relation of early socialization experiences to aggression in middle childhood. *Journal of Abnormal and Social Psychology* 63: 466–92.

Seccombe, Wallace. 1980. Domestic labour and the working-class household. Pp. 25–99 in. B. Fox (ed.), *Hidden in the Household*. Toronto: Women's Press.

Sev'er, Aysan. 1992. *Women and Divorce in Canada: A Sociological Analysis*. Toronto: Canadian Scholars Press.

– 1996. Current feminist debates on wife abuse: Some policy implications. Pp. 121–37 in *Sonderbulletin*. Berlin: Humboldt University Press.

– 1997a. Recent or imminent separation and intimate violence against women: A conceptual overview and some Canadian examples. *Violence against Women* 3(6): 566–89.

– 1999. Exploring the continuum: Sexualized violence by men and male youth against women and girls. *Atlantis* 24(1): 92–104.

– 2001. Media coverage of lethal and non-lethal violence against women during 1995–1999 (analysis in progress).

– 2002. Flight of abused women, plight of Canadian shelters: Another path to homelessness. *Journal of Social Distress and the Homeless*. Forthcoming.

– (Ed.). 1997b. *A Cross-Cultural Exploration of Wife Abuse: Problems and Prospects*. Lewiston, NJ: Edwin Mellen.

– 1998. *Frontiers in Women's Studies: Canadian and German Perspectives*. Toronto: Canadian Scholars Press.

Sev'er, Aysan, and Marion Pirie. 1991a. Factors that enhance or curtail the social functioning of female single parents: A path analysis. *Family Conciliation Courts Review* 29(3): 318–37.

– 1991b. More than making it: An analysis of factors that enhance the social functioning of female single-parents. *Family Perspective* 25(2): 83–96.

Sev'er, Aysan, Sheldon Ungar, and Julian Tanner. 1991. Gender-based attributions and morality: A sports event application. *Journal of Social Psychology* 131(3): 439–41.

Shecter, Susan. 1982. *Women and Male Violence: The Visions and Struggles of the Battered Women's Movement*. Boston: South End.

Smith, Michael D. 1987. The incidence and prevalence of woman abuse in Toronto. *Violence and Victims* 2: 173–87.

– 1989. Woman abuse: The case for surveys by telephone. *Journal of Interpersonal Violence* 4(3): 308–24.

– 1990. Socioeconomic risk factors in wife abuse: Results from a survey of Toronto women. *Canadian Journal of Sociology* 15: 39–58.

Snell, John, Richard Rosenwald, and James Robey. 1964. The wife-beater's wife. *Archives of General Psychiatry* 11: 107–12.

Spender, Dale. 1981. Doing feminist research: A feminist critique of academic publishing. Pp. 186–202 in H. Roberts (ed.), *Doing Feminist Research*. Boston: Routledge.

– 1982. *Invisible Women: Writers and Readers*. London: Routledge.

Stanko, A. Elizabeth. 1997. I second that emotion. Pp. 74–85 in M.D. Schwartz (ed.), *Researching Sexual Violence against Women: Methodological and Personal Perspectives*. Thousand Oaks, Calif.: Sage.

Stanley, Liz, and Susan Wise. 1983. *Breaking Out: Feminist Consciousness and Feminist Research*. London: Routledge and Kegan.

Stark, Evan, and Anne Flitcraft. 1996. *Women at Risk: Domestic Violence and Women's Health*. London: Sage.

Statistics Canada. 1994. *Processing of Sexual Assault Cases*. Ottawa: Canadian Centre for Justice. Cat. 85–538E.

Steed, Judy. 1994. *Our Little Secret: Confronting Child Sexual Abuse in Canada*. Toronto: Random House.

Steinmetz, Suzanne K. 1977–8. The battered husband syndrome. *Victimology: An International Journal* 2: 499–509.

Stefan, Susan. 1994. The protection racket: Rape trauma syndrome, psychiatric labelling and law. *Northwestern University Law Review* 88(4): 1271–1329.

Stout, Karen D. 1992. Intimate femicide: Effect of legislation and social services. Pp. 133–40 in J. Radford and D.E.H. Russell (eds.), *Femicide*. Toronto: Maxwell Macmillan.

Straus, Murray. 1989. *The Social Causes of Husband-Wife Violence*. Minneapolis: University of Minnesota Press.

Straus, Murray, and Richard J. Gelles. 1990. *Physical Violence in American Families: Risk Factors and Adaptations to Violence in 8145 Families*. New Brunswick, NJ: Transaction.

Straus, Murray A., Richard J. Gelles, and Suzanne K. Steinmetz. 1980. *Behind Closed Doors: Violence in the American Family*. New York: Doubleday.

– 1986. The marriage license as a hitting license. Pp. 290–303 in A.S. Skolnick and J.H. Skolnick (eds.), *Family in Transition* (5th ed.). Boston: Little Brown.

SWAN. 1996. Scarborough Women's Action Network. *Breaking the Cycle: A Feasibility Study*. Toronto.

Terr, L. 1990. *Too Scared to Cry*. New York: Harper Collins.

Tifft, Larry L. 1993. *Battering of Women: The Failure of Intervention and the Case for Prevention*. Boulder, Col.: Westview.

Tucker, Robert C. 1978. The Marx-Engels Reader (2nd ed.). New York: W.W. Norton. Two Struggles: Challenging Male Violence and the Police. 1992. Southall Black Sisters. Pp. 312–16 in J. Radford and D.E.H. Russell (eds.), *Femicide*. Toronto: Maxwell Macmillan.

VAWS. 1993. Violence Against Women Survey. *Daily Statistics*. Canada. 18 November 1993. Ottawa: Statistics Canada. Cat 11-001.

Viano, Emilio C. (Ed). 1992. Violence among intimates: Major issues and approaches. Pp. 3–12 in E.C. Viano (ed.), *Intimate Violence: Interdisciplinary Perspectives*. Bristol: Taylor and Francis.

WAC Stats. *The Facts about Women*. 1993. New York: Women's Action Coalition.

Walker, Gillian A. 1990. *Family Violence and the Women's Movement: The Conceptual Politics of Struggle*. Toronto: University of Toronto Press.

Walker, Lenore E.A. 1979a. Battered women and learned helplessness. *Victimology* 2(3–4): 525–34.

– 1979b. *The Battered Woman*. New York: Harper and Row.

– 1984. *The Battered Woman Syndrome*. New York: Springer.

– 1993. The battered woman syndrome is a psychological consequence of abuse. Pp. 133–53 in R.J. Gelles and D.R Loseke (eds.), *Current Controversies on Family Violence*. Newbury Park, Calif.: Sage.

Warshaw, Carole. 1993. Limitations of the medical model in the care of battered women. Pp. 134–46 in P.B. Bart and E.G. Moran (eds.), *Violence against Women: The Bloody Footprints*. Newbury Park, Calif.: Sage.

Weisz, Arlene N. 1999. Legal advocacy for domestic violence survivors: The power of an informative relationship. *Families in Society: The Journal of Contemporary Human Services* 80(2): 138–47.

West, Carolyn M. 1998. Lifting the 'political gag order': Breaking the silence around partner violence in ethnic minority families. Pp. 184–209 in J.L. Jasinski and L.M. Williams, *Partner Violence: A Comprehensive Review of 20 Years of Research*. Thousand Oaks, Calif.: Sage.

Wilson, Margo I., and Martin Daly. 1992. Who kills whom in spousal killings? *Criminology* 30(2): 189-215.

– 1993. Spousal homicide risk and estrangement. *Violence and Victims* 8: 3-16.

– 1994. *Spousal Homicide*. Ottawa: Canadian Centre for Justice Statistics.

Without Fear: A Video About Violence Against Women. 1994. Canadian Panel on Violence Against Women. ISBN 0-662-20682-7.

Wolak, Janis, and David Finkelhor. 1998. Children exposed to partner violence. Pp. 73–111 in J.L. Jasinski and L.M. Williams (eds.), *Partner Violence: A Comprehensive Review of 20 Years of Research*. Thousand Oaks, Calif.: Sage.

Wolfe, David A. 1999. *Child Abuse: Implications for Child Development and Psychopathology* (2nd ed.). Thousand Oaks, Calif.: Sage.

Wolfe, David, L. Zak, and D. Wilson. 1986. Child witness to violence between parents: Critical issues in behaviour and social adjustment. *Journal of Abnormal Child Psychology* 14(1): 95–102.

Yllö, Kersti A. 1993. Through a feminist lens: Gender, power and violence. Pp. 47–62 in R.J. Gelles and D.R. Loseke (eds.), *Current Controversies on Family Violence*. Newbury Park, Calif.: Sage.

Yllö, Kersti A., and Michelle Bograd, (Eds.). 1988. *Feminist Perspectives on Wife Abuse*. Newbury Park, Calif.: Sage.

Zima, Bonnie T., Regina Bussing, and Maria Bystritsky. 1999. Psychological stressors among sheltered homeless children: Relationship to behavioural problems and depressive symptoms. *American Journal of Orthopsychiatry* 69(1): 127–33.

Index